The Shaking of the Foundations

THE SHAKING OF THE FOUNDATIONS

FAMILY AND SOCIETY

Ronald Fletcher

ROUTLEDGE
London and New York

First published in 1988 by
Routledge
a division of Routledge, Chapman and Hall
11 New Fetter Lane, London EC4P 4EE

Published in the USA by
Routledge
in association with Routledge, Chapman and Hall, Inc.
29 West 35th Street, New York, NY 10001

Set in 10/11½ point Times & Optima
by Witwell Ltd, Southport
and printed in Great Britain
by Billings Ltd, Worcester

© Ronald Fletcher 1988

British Library Cataloguing in Publication Data
Fletcher, Ronald
   The shaking of the foundations
   Family and society.
   1. Family
   I. Title
   306.8'5   HQ728

Library of Congress Cataloging in Publication Data also available

ISBN 0–415–008735 c
ISBN 0–415–008743 p

The ancient trinity of father, mother, and child has survived more vicissitudes than any other human relationship. It is the bedrock underlying all other family structures. Although more elaborate family patterns can be broken from within or may even collapse of their own weight, the rock remains. In the Götterdämmerung which over-wise science and over-foolish statesmanship are preparing for us, the last man will spend his last hours searching for his wife and child.

Ralph Linton, 'The Natural History of the Family', in *The Family: Its Function and Destiny*, ed. Ruth Nanda Anshen, 1949

Contents

Contents

Contents

Diagrams, Tables and Graphs

Acknowledgments

Grateful acknowledgments are especially due to all those (the Registrar General, the Central Statistical Office, the Office of Population Censuses and Surveys, and other government departments) responsible for the wide range of official publications (*Social Trends* the General Housing Survey, etc., etc.) which are nowadays available and on which social scientists so much rely. I am indebted to these for the many tables, diagrams, graphs and 'official comments' which I have used and critically considered in my ongoing argument, and all of them are fully documented in the text and notes. Similarly, I am indebted to the authors of the specially written papers which nowadays supplement the official reports: especially to Mark Abrams, Roger Jowell and Colin Airey, Kathleen Tiernan, John Haskey, Richard Leete, and Michael Anderson. These, too, are fully documented as they appear in the text.

Grateful thanks are due, too, to other authors and publishers for the use of quotations as follows: C. H. Cooley and Schocken Books (from *Human Nature and the Social Order* and *Social Organization*); G. H. Mead and University of Chicago Press (from *George Herbert Mead on Social Psychology*); Frederick Engels and Charles H. Kerr & Co. (from *The Origin of the Family*); Griselda Rowntree, Norman Carrier, and John Haskay (from issues of *Population Studies*); David Lockwood *et al.* and Cambridge University Press (from *The Affluent Worker: Industrial Attitudes and Behaviour*); M. P. M. Richard and the National Marriage Guidance Council (from *Relating to Marriage*); Axel Munthe and John Murray (from *The Story of San Michele*); A. N. Whitehead and Cambridge University Press (from *Symbolism: Its Meaning and Effect*); Ernest Crawley and Methuen (from *The Mystic Rose*); Henrik Ibsen (from *The Lady from the Sea* and *The Doll's House*) in *A Doll's House and other Plays*, Penguin, 1965, translated by Peter Watts; the Executors of the Estate of C. Day Lewis, the Hogarth Press and Jonathan Cape Ltd (for 'Where are the War Poets?' by C. Day Lewis, from *Collected Poems*, 1954); Faber and Faber Ltd (for lines from 'Choruses from The Rock' and 'Whispers of Immortality' by T. S. Eliot, from *Collected Poems 1909–1962*); A. P. Watt Ltd, on behalf of Michael B. Yeats and Macmillan London Ltd (for lines from 'The Second Coming' from *The Collected Poems of W. B. Yeats*).

Preface

May I ask the reader to consider this book in close conjunction with
The Abolitionists: The Family and Marriage Under Attack. The two
were written together, and are, therefore, in the fullest sense,
companion books.

R.F.

Introduction

This book has two objectives: first, to examine the facts relating to the family and marriage since the coming into force (in 1971) of the 1969 Divorce Reform Act – a crucial point in the development of the family in Britain – and second, to go beyond the immediacy of these recent statistics and probe more deeply into longer-term changes in the nature of society to seek a satisfactory explanation of them.

In *The Family and Marriage in Britain: An Analysis and Moral Assessment*[1] I took issue with the critics of the 1950s and early 1960s whose almost universally shared position was that of blaming the *decline* of the family (its weakness, decay, and diminishing social importance as its functions were 'stripped away from it' by the State; the moral deterioration of its relationships and the sentiments and qualities of life experienced within it, etc.) for the declining standards of society at large. In *The Abolitionists: The Family and Marriage Under Attack*.[2] I took issue, similarly, with the critics of the later 1960s, the 1970s, and the 1980s (still influential among many) who also, and with equal passion and forcefulness, blamed the family as 'the source of all our discontents', but this time from *exactly the opposite point of view*: attacking it, now, because of its *strength*, its tenacity, its essentially conservative nature in preserving the exploitative nature of capitalist society – destroying our individual nature to make us fit into the social system, and standing in the way of progress. The arguments against these critics – old and new – are there for those who wish to consider them, and need not be repeated here. Their upshot, however, can be very briefly summarized.

It was possible to demonstrate that the many changes attendant upon the process of industrialization (from a pre-industrial condition of abject poverty for the great majority of the population) and the century of reforms since early Victorian times, had resulted in a clear contemporary form of the British family which, for the very first time in our history, was common to all social classes with qualities which were a decided improvement on anything known in Britain before.This modern form of the family can be clearly characterized. It is:

(1) founded at a relatively early age of both husband and wife, and – with increasing longevity – is therefore of long duration;

(2) consciously planned (by means of the various methods of birth control) to limit the number of children to that desired;

(3) therefore usually small in size: most typically consisting of husband, wife, and two children;

(4) separately housed (satisfying a universal desire for independence and privacy), and, usually, in a material and neighbourhood environment much improved upon those of earlier periods;

(5) economically self-responsible, self-providing, and therefore (a) relatively independent of wider kindred, and (b) living at a 'distance' from them – frequently geographically, but also in terms of a diminished degree of intimately shared social life;

(6) founded and maintained on a completely voluntary basis by partners of equal status; entailing, therefore, a marital relationship based upon mutuality of consideration and a sharing of tasks: seeking (as Geoffrey Gorer put it in his book *Sex and Marriage in England Today*) to be 'a marriage of true friends';

(7) democratically managed in that husband and wife (and frequently children) discuss family affairs together during the taking of decisions;

(8) so centrally concerned with the care and upbringing of children as to be frequently called 'child-centred'; and

(9) widely recognized by government and the whole range of social services as being crucially important for the life of individuals and society alike, and helped in its efforts to achieve health, security, and stability by a wide-ranging network of public provisions.

A study of the evidence showed that on every count – material, moral, with reference to the quality of relationships within the family and to the relationship of the family with the wider social institutions lying beyond it – this was a decided improvement on anything that had existed in Britain at any earlier time. The family, most certainly, had *not* deteriorated. It was *not* 'in decline' or 'on its way out'. Also, it was by no means true that, in contemporary society, its functions had been in any sense diminished. The basic functions of the family, without any doubt, remained, and these, too, can be very clearly stated. The family:

(1) regulates sexual behaviour in relation to the satisfaction of both sexual needs and the achievement and maintenance of other desired qualities and relationships;

(2) secures a legitimate basis for procreation and the responsible care and upbringing of children;

(3) provides for the protection, sustenance, and care of all its dependent members – whether children, the aged, or those dependent for other reasons (illness, accident, disabled, or other kinds of misfortune);

(4) provides (of necessity – by the very nature of family life) in a continuing and detailed fashion the earliest education of the young during their most impressionable years, and in so doing introduces the child to those values and modes of behaviour appropriate to all kinds of social activity both within and beyond the family, and so serves as one of the most important agencies for the preservation and perpetuation of approved sentiments, customs, and social traditions;

(5) and (since the many 'titles' of the members of the family – 'husband', 'wife', 'father', 'mother', 'eldest son', 'brother', 'sister', 'next-of-kin', etc. – bear specific and different social connotations) invests its members with all those rights, duties, customary and legal demands which are recognized, required, and insisted upon in the local community and the wider society in which they live.

These functions, certainly, were in no way diminished. But, in addition, they have been progressively *increased* by all the ongoing reforms. Each new piece of legislation (the many economic regulations – of employment, taxation, social insurance, social benefits, welfare services, etc.; the regulations of public health; the extended regulations of education, etc., etc.) actually *added* to the responsibilities of parents – extending and raising to a higher level the standards of care expected from them. The family, in short, had come to have *more* – not *fewer* – functions as the State (in the service of the people) had extended its demands.

This was the gist of the judgment arrived at, and – strange though it was to find support among the large number of moralists, who were almost entirely deprecating – it was in keeping with the considered judgment of the Church of England Moral Welfare Council. The conclusion of their report on *The Family in Contemporary Society*[3] was that 'the modern family is in some ways in a stronger position than it has been at any period in our history of which we have knowledge' – a very decided and far-reaching statement.

It might have been thought, however, that objections of at least some weight would have emerged from the varied attacks of the 'Abolitionist-type' critics who came into prominence from the late 1960s onwards. An examination of their many positions proved, however, that this was far from being so. Sometimes resting on no evidence at all (like the assertions of Edmund Leach in his third Reith Lecture in 1967), sometimes resting on simple but quite fundamental misunderstandings (e.g. the modern exponents of 'Marxism' misunderstood and misrepresented the teachings of Marx and Engels; most contributors to 'the New Feminism' did *not* call for the abolition of the family, or try to justify such a position; the 'communes' – reputedly proposing alternatives to the family – were, in fact, actually trying to create community conditions within which the life of the family could be improved), these positions proved to be not so much criticisms of the nature of the family and its place in society as *ideological attacks* upon both the family and society alike, and all proved superficial.

The character of the modern family, then, as we have outlined it, stood firm, needing no amendment. Much, however, has happened since 1971, and, in a variety of ways, the sequences and complicated nature of the changes since that time have been such that the two kinds of criticism have persisted. The two questions underlying my two objectives therefore arise.

First: what have the facts and trends of the situation actually *been* since the coming into force of the 1969 Act? – and what are the most correct interpretations of them? Are they such as to substantiate, and perhaps even further support, extend, and elaborate the conclusion we have stated? Or are they such as to challenge and perhaps even refute it? – making some other appraisal of the nature of the family and its place in society necessary?

Second: going beyond these immediate statistics and interpretations (about which there is continual comment in the press – certainly with each annual volume of *Social Trends*), are there deeper facts and longer-term tendencies in our society which – placing these very recent facts within the context of changes which have been taking place throughout our century – can be identified, enabling us to understand and explain them? These deeper questions are rarely asked; have certainly not been answered; and even the posing of them encounters difficulties. The questions and answers alike are far from simple.

In order to set the problems out as clearly as possible – so that our answers, too, can be as clear as possible – at least three sets of preparatory considerations seem necessary. At the outset, at first glance, these may well seem rather arbitrary, an ill-assorted set of bedfellows with no immediately clear connection, but each is introduced as a necessary foundation for arguments I want to advance later (and kinds of analysis I want to explore), each is important in its own right, and the close relationship between them all will be seen when they are drawn together in the later discussions and final conclusions. Here, I want only to state them, but in such a way as, at least, to *indicate* their significance for my later reasoning.

PREPARATORY CONSIDERATIONS

The significance of the 1960s: Prelude to the Divorce Reform Act

True though it is – and in many ways which we shall consider – that the 1969 Divorce Reform Act was a highly significant landmark (a distinctive point of arrival and departure) in the public conception of the nature of marriage and the family in Britain – improving the conception we have outlined still further – it must not be forgotten that it came at the end of an entire *decade* which was remarkable for the range, scale, and detail of its legislative changes: many of them very radical indeed. In a sense, therefore, it was a *culmination* of a long period of public debate. The decade was remarkable, too, for the continual awareness displayed, the continual questioning and consideration of these changes as they were made, and for the undertaking and reporting of much related social research. All of these had direct relevance to the judgment concerning the modern family as we have outlined it.

(i) A distinguished record of legislation

The 1960s had, in fact, been distinguished by a wide and effective range of legislation on many of the most fundamental matters of behaviour relating to marriage and the family. With the Church of England's publication *The Family in Contemporary Society* in the background (1958), the decade began with the Legal Aid Act of 1960. From then on, it was filled with intense and important public debate on divorce law reform, on the just provision of financial and property arrangements for all parties following divorce, on legal questions relating to homosexuality, on the rights and wrongs of legalizing abortion, and on many aspects of the status of children and young people, including the illegitimate. Not every Act was followed by approval (the Abortion Act, for example, raised grave doubts as to possible abuse, and has subsequently given rise to much further ethical reconsideration), but the success of serious and searching public debate, and of effective legislation on issues as fundamental as these was, from any point of view, a matter for public and political congratulation. Indeed, the 1960s might well come to be seen as a decade of considerable historical distinction in these important changes in the law, especially when it is borne in mind that these difficult and deliberate pieces of legislation and subsequent administration were achieved during a period when so many other large-scale problems – in the more immediately pressing fields of economic, political, educational affairs, etc. – were afoot. The list of the more important Acts, all of which carried earlier legislation much further, and on the basis of much prolonged debate, is itself impressive:

The Family Provisions Act (1966)
The Matrimonial Homes Act (1967)
The National Health Service (Family Planning) Act (1967)
The Abortion Act (1967)
The Sexual Offences Act (1967)
The Maintenance Orders Act (1968)
The Family Law Reform Act (1969)
The Divorce Reform Act (1969)
The Children and Young Persons Act (1969)

Each of these did much to improve the status of women both within and beyond marriage; to improve the status of children including reducing the age (to 18) at which they attained responsible adulthood and citizenship; to eradicate many of the most distasteful encumbrances of the previous legal procedures for divorce; to give effect to a more knowledgeable and humane judgment concerning sexual differences; and many other quite specific matters. The Divorce Reform Act, it can be seen, was one well-considered Act among many.

(ii) Related developments, questions, considerations, judgments

This was accompanied, moreover, by other more general developments of considerable significance. Judgments over divorce, custody of children, etc. were transferred from the former 'Probate, Divorce and Admiralty Division' to a new 'Family Division'; and 1965 saw the establishment of the Law Commission to undertake a thoroughgoing revision of family law. These legal developments, taking place as the 1960s advanced, substantiated very forcibly the fact that both in changing legal procedures and in the provision for systematic deliberations to consider the need for law reform, there was a very evident *concern* for the qualities of marriage and the family in society, and a concentration on providing the best legal, administrative and social framework for them. This picture of the law in relation to the family was excellently summarized by Dr Olive Stone in 'The Family and the Law in 1970'. Her conclusion was quite definite, though by no means final:

> An indication that the law does not contemplate any drastic change in the role of the family in the near future may be found in the many compromises and reformulations that took place before the publication of the Children and Young Persons Act, 1969 ... No substitute for the family in the upbringing of children seems in sight.

None of the far-reaching changes in the law, therefore, had at all questioned the importance of the family in society. On the contrary, all had been the outcome of a concern for its health and stability, for the welfare of its members and the achievement of justice in family relationships. At the same time, the facts of divorce during the 1960s had revealed a marked trend which gave rise to new considerations.

The most conspicuous (though not necessarily the most significant) development which became apparent as the records of the 1960s became clearly known was the continuous increase in the number of divorces. This increase was one of the most marked facts that had to be taken into account for several reasons. Naturally enough, it is the facts relating to the evident breakdowns of marriages which are taken to indicate the quality of marriage and family life in society generally. As soon as one stops to reflect on it, it is clear that this may well be a basically mistaken assumption; but it is commonly held and understandable. Closely related to this, the continual increase during the 1960s was, on the face of it, a reversal of the tendencies which had been in evidence between the end of the Second World War and the end of the 1950s. Then – after the post-war peak – the annual number of divorces was consistently decreasing. There was even speculation as to whether the lower pre-war rate of the 1930s might be reached. The subsequent increase therefore seemed a turnabout, needing close scrutiny.

I say that it was a reversal on the face of it, however, because, in fact, the interpretation of the statistics was far from easy. One important consideration was that the incidence of divorce seems always sensitive to new legislation (such as new terms of legal aid, the enactment of new grounds for divorce, etc.) and such new legislation had, in fact, occurred in 1960 (the Legal Aid Act), and the *immediate* increase seemed, at least, explicable in these terms. A second fact was that of the very large accompanying increase in the number of marriages. The marriage rate had increased as consistently as had that of divorce; and the gross number of marriages each year had increased very substantially indeed. Far larger numbers were therefore 'at risk'. A third fact is that this larger number of marriages had been predominantly among men and women in the younger age-groups, in relation to which there is always a larger rate of divorce; and there is no doubt that a predominant proportion of the increased number of divorces came from these age-groups. This tendency to early marriage, however, was related to a great many other facts – educational, economic, the political change made in the age of maturity, and perhaps even to an earlier physiological maturation. And a fourth fact is that the increase in divorce following any particular piece of legislation can often be no more than evidence of an overdue *legal recognition* of a *social actuality* that has long existed. For example, it was already known that a large increase in divorce would follow the new Divorce Reform Act of 1969, but that this would be, in large part, only a legal termination of marriages long ago broken in fact (which, indeed, would not have been in existence for a long time), and would then be followed by a legal regularization (by marriage) of the many other stable alternative families which had also, in fact, long existed. The increase resting on these grounds would therefore not indicate a new tendency at all (excepting that for which the Act was created); it would merely be a legal recognition of an old fact. (For a discussion of the full significance of this point, see pp. 48–51.)

There is also, however a final and quite basic point which perhaps few of us have considered and accepted fully. When faced by high divorce rates, our impulse, still, is immediately to look for some kind of legal or statistical 'excuse' for them – as though, in itself, a higher divorce rate is necessarily a bad thing. Now, no one can – in general – advocate divorce. A divorce, after all, is an acknowledgment of failure, frequently a tragic one. Even so, we must consider the possibility that if the conceptions, status and expectations of marriage and family life in our society are of a high standard (and if our law is made increasingly accessible, to provide for the least harmful termination of those relationships which are found to be 'irretrievably' unworkable and unhappy) then it may be that *we must expect* a greater degree of resort to divorce. May it not be that high standards and expectations of marriage and family life actually *entail* a high rate of resort to divorce? This is something which, at present, we are reluctant to concede, and we may be right to be reluctant, but it is at least possible that a higher rate of divorce might well be indicative of a higher conception, a healthier condition, of marriage in society, rather than of a worsening of it. These are difficult problems, but it is an initial thought deserving much consideration: that the face of social facts may be stranger than we think.

The most central concern about the trends of the 1960s, however, was, perhaps, that of the very high divorce rate of young people during the early years of their marriage, but – and despite the over-all increase in the number of divorces – there seemed to be no grounds for changing the earlier judgment about the family as we have outlined it. These figures did not indicate a growing instability, or qualitative worsening of the nature of marriage and the family in Britain, and it is worthwhile to note that this is by no means a purely personal judgment. It was also, at that time, the view of some leading members of the legal profession who might be expected to see the facts and procedures of divorce more clearly and in more detail than the rest of us. The legal correspondent of *The Times*, for example, reporting a 54 per cent increase in the number of divorce petitions lodged in Britain during 1971, as compared with 1970 (resting on the new provisions of the Divorce Reform Act which became operative on 1 January 1971) said that this 'was not considered alarming'. He believed that it was one of the new grounds for divorce provided by the Act (the five-year separation provision) which was responsible for the sharp increase. (It was the legal recognition of marriages broken in fact a long time ago, mentioned earlier.) Commenting on the same figures in a correspondence in *The Times* during January 1971, Sir George Baker, President of the Family Division, claimed that, with the new Act, 'some of the bitterness and public degradation have been taken out of divorce', and it was interesting, indeed, to see that press reports of divorce no longer carried the salacious and 'adversarial' character that many of them once did. Perhaps the most heartening estimation of the new situation, however, came from a source that could hardly be more reputable and responsible. Addressing the twenty-fifth anniversary of the Marriage Guidance Council (of which he was the National President) Lord Denning, Master of the Rolls, said that the new divorce law was 'entirely beneficial'. Its most impressive result, he claimed, was that *contested* divorce cases had almost disappeared. He did not feel

13

that its changes would be so disastrous to the institution of marriage as some had foretold, and emphasized that marriage was still recognized by the great majority as a lifelong union not lightly to be dissolved.

Those, therefore, who had been most involved in the continuing legal debates, and who most understood the detailed grounds for all the legal changes, did seem firmly agreed that the removal of the unjust and distasteful obstacles to the termination of marriage was, indirectly, improving the conditions and quality of it. The evident trend in the increase in the number of divorces did not therefore, in itself, indicate any flight from the family or any weakening in the public concern for it. Even so, it did seem to call for a deeper scrutiny and a more detailed and satisfactory explanation than was then available.

(iii) Continuing social investigation: direct and indirect evidence

Coinciding with the sequence of legislation, the new Act, and this continual awareness of the trends of marriage and divorce throughout the 1960s, there was also one other development of considerable significance: the growth and publication of a body of new research. This was very variable, but one interesting distinction was noticeable. Some books and articles were the outcome of *direct* investigations of the family, marriage, and divorce; but others – perhaps more interestingly – were the *indirect* findings on enquiries into quite different subjects (changes in occupations and social class, for example.) Both, however, provided new knowledge about the family in contemporary Britain, and threw new light on the family in periods of the past – providing an improved perspective (a more reliable basis) for historical judgment.

The Family and Social Change by Rosser and Harris (1965), had repeated, rather more extensively, in Swansea, the kind of study undertaken by Young and Willmott in Bethnal Green, and produced similar findings. The 'extended family', resting chiefly on the relationship between a wife and her mother, was found to be still important – as a basic unit of social identification and social support – despite industrial and urban change; and the 'standardization' of this family-type was found among all social classes. But later reports were of greater interest, both in their actual findings and in their indication of a breaking of new ground (and new depths) in research. *Separated*

14

Spouses, an investigation by the Bedford College Legal Research Unit (O. R. McGregor, Louis Blom-Cooper and Colin Gibson), threw light on the 'submerged' proportion of broken families reflected in separation and maintenance orders rather than in the more conspicuous statistics of divorce. A related (though not similar, and by no means so extensive) development was represented by a few small articles in *New Society*[2] and the *British Journal of Sociology*.[3] These probed *beyond* the formal statistics (which only record the *legal* termination of marriages, for example) to a better knowledge of the *actual* duration of marriages, and the actual factors involved in family disruptions.

A third, highly significant piece of research was Geoffrey Gorer's *Sex and Marriage in England Today*. When first writing *The Family and Marriage in Britain*, I had been able to draw on Gorer's earlier study, *Exploring English Character*, published in the mid 1950s. Now, his new study compared his findings at the end of the 1960s with those of some fifteen to twenty years earlier. This was especially relevant, therefore, to the question of confirmation or required reappraisal. Also, Rhona and Robert Rapoport piloted and published several studies relating to what they regarded as the creation of a new family pattern attendant upon the improved status of women and the problems of managing a stable family life whilst both husbands and wives followed careers of their own choosing, and to the extent they desired. This was best presented, despite the fact that it covered only a small number of middle-class families, in their book *Dual Career Families*.

What was also impressive, however, was the cumulative force and support of research *other* than that mentioned above: that is to say, research which had *not* been specifically directed to the study of the family, but which had, none the less, produced striking evidence of its continuing importance – for individuals and society alike. It fully substantiated the picture of the historical improvement in the conditions and qualities of the British family, and showed, without any doubt, the growing priority given to the family in terms of current political and administrative concern. A few examples will make clear what I mean.

Books such as Peter Laslett's *The World We Have Lost* (drawing upon original historical sources) and Ronald Blythe's *Akenfield* (drawing upon first-hand accounts of present-day villagers) showed graphically how unfounded was the widespread myth of the 'closely-knit community' of pre-industrial times, within which the family has been thought by some to have had its golden age, with all its 'functions' richly intact. The impoverished actuality of such communities and of most of the families in them was laid bare in these books. In another direction, all researches devoted to the study of education and educational opportunity in modern society pointed indubitably and inescapably to the central importance of the family – not only as a 'mechanism' for transmitting social values, and even class inequalities, but also as the essential ground for individual growth, advancement, and fulfilment through education, when a child has the sensitive understanding, support and encouragement of its parents. Similarly, researches on the attitudes and patterns of life of industrial workers, on industrial relations, and on the 'social class' orientations and motivations involved in them, revealed one quite clear and conspicuous finding: that, for middle-class professional and modern worker alike, it was the concern for the family's welfare, security, happiness, and advancement, which was the strongest and continuing nucleus of economic motivation. The best example of this was the study of *The Affluent Worker* by Lockwood, Goldthorpe and others though I shall also mention later Mark Abrams' systematic study of social attitudes (pp. 107–11). In yet another direction, the inquiry of the Seebohm Committee, and its proposals (then just beginning to come into administrative effect) concluded that the whole organization of the social services could be most effective if focused upon the family as the most basic social unit of shared experience and need.

So ... when *all* the social researches of the 1960s were considered – not only those on the family as such – the impression given was overwhelmingly one of the great and continuing strength of the family in our society. The judgment we have outlined was substantially confirmed and supported.

It is worthwhile next, however, to reflect a little further on the *two-fold* nature of the *criticisms* of the family – the opposition between those who believed the family was *in decline*, and those who believed it to be so *deeply entrenched and powerful an obstacle* to the changes they desired as to want to see it abolished – because, strange though it may seem, the very *polarity* of these criticisms, when fully considered, revealed certain shared concerns and continuing anxieties.

Continuing anxieties and common concerns

Despite the inadequacies of both these sets of criticisms (those of the 1950s emphasizing the family's decline; those of the late 1960s and 1970s emphasising its reactionary strength), the detailed criticism of them conducted earlier did have the advantage of making two things perfectly clear. First: the two opposed judgments could not possibly be true of *the actual nature of the family itself.* The family itself could not possibly be – at one and the same time, or over so short a period as that of a few years or so – *both* in decline *and* the strongest and most resistant obstacle to 'progressive' change. But second: it demonstrated more clearly than anything else could have done, the wide range of disagreement and great ambiguity of public opinion about the changes which had taken place in the family since the Second World War. And this enables us to arrive at a clear and useful formulation. In the continual debate of the past thirty to forty years, three major points of view have emerged.

The first, represented by the earlier critics (and in the minds of many still holding good today) is that the old conventional values involved in a well considered and complete commitment to life-long marriage – to the maintenance of family stability, a secure and affectionate context of home life and the careful upbringing of children with reciprocal feelings of love and care – *have* been lost in that explosion of new libertarian values (within which freedom quickly became licence) which followed the war. Family life, these people feel, *has* deteriorated. It *is* this which is the root cause of our gravest social ills. And this view (say those who hold it), has surely been proved true beyond all doubt by the rapidly worsening social behaviour and all the social and personal problems which have greatly *increased*, not diminished, since that time. The increase in the number of broken marriages and broken homes *has* continued far beyond any 'back-log' which could have been expected at the time of the 1969 Divorce Reform Act (these critics say); the increased incidence of separation and divorce *has* led to an ever-growing number of single-parent families living in poverty, of unsatisfactory 'step-families', of children abandoned or taken into care; there *has*, in fact, been a continuing increase in abortion, illegitimacy, baby-battering, wife-beating, rape, incest, the abduction, sexual abuse and murder of small children. All these *have* become more evident in society – making plain a condition which no one before the war would ever have believed possible. The family *has* deteriorated! Society *has* deteriorated! The earlier critics were *right*! This . . . is the one point of view.

The diametrically opposed view – represented by the newer 'radical' critics – is that, on the contrary, these very problems are, in fact, *caused* by the *strength* of the socially isolated, over-privatized nuclear family itself, and the resistant obstinacy and obduracy of its hold in a rapidly changing world. The family is the source of the trouble. It is the very intensity of life within the small modern family which causes mental stress, mental illness, conflict and violence, sexual repression, disorder, abnormality, and outbreaks of violent rebellion against the conventional order of society. Even murder (says the present-day cliché) 'is a family crime'. All this (they might well agree), may also have been enhanced by the continual increase in the number of relatively deprived families: those who, through the continual barrage of advertisements and titillations on the television screen, see all that an affluent society has to offer but which they themselves (generation after generation – caught in the trap of 'the cycle of deprivation') can never, and will never, have. Those in situations of progressive employment and steadily increasing wealth (who are succeeding in 'the affluent society') go their own way within their own private family worlds. Those who have fallen into failure are lost – and are increasingly without hope. But for the gravest of our social and personal problems, it is *the very tyranny of the family itself which is to blame.*

These are the two extremes: the two opposed positions.

But a third view rests between them, and is even sympathetic to some elements within each of them. This position finds it impossible not to recognize that – both before and since the Second World War – a great many improvements, building upon the achievements of earlier reforms, have been brought about in the nature and quality of the family in Britain. The improved status and opportunities of children and women (let alone the improved conditions of work and life of men) have improved family relationships themselves. Qualities of housing and equipment within the home have improved conditions of life *within* the family. The material and social improvement of neighbourhood facilities have improved the family's wider social context. The provisions of the many social services since the Second World War – relating to conditions of cleanliness, sanitation, health, education, etc., etc. – have all improved beyond doubt, and in themselves reflect the serious concern of government for the family and its deliberate action to help it. Recently, it is true, there have been some areas of growing deprivation, of worsening conditions (inner cities, areas of large-scale unemployment, etc.) but that is another story. This view cannot help but believe, too, that many of the changes that have been brought about in the area of sexual behaviour and the liberation of women (the more open knowledge and understanding of sexuality, the improved opportunities for women which extend their own degree of independence and choice) have been improvements; just as the wider availability of separation and divorce among all social classes for those whose marriages have become intolerable and have, in fact, broken down, have been changes we have *wanted*. Yet, at the same time, those holding this view feel, none the less, that in some way or other, and certainly for some people, these very improvements have themselves given rise to new problems. Has there been some *abuse* of these improvements and freedoms? – which has brought about more casual and irresponsible attitudes towards sex, pregnancy, abortion, marriage, divorce, the care or lack of care for children? Or have the improvements themselves – in ways quite unforeseen and which we do not understand – undermined the nature of the family? Might the new freedoms and the new collective conditions have had the unintended and unexpected effect of *diminishing* conjugal sentiments, parental sentiments, sentiments of mutual care, affection, and respect between parents and children? This third viewpoint is therefore one of perplexity? It acknowledges the improvements made as being improvements, but feels that, somehow, unforeseen problems have arisen from them. *Progress* ... and *retrogression; gain* ... and *loss*; the two, strangely, seem to have gone hand in hand.

Two decided and opposed points of view, and one troubled area of part-knowledge and part-perplexity occupying the middle ground in a considered but genuinely unsure way: this seems to be the present state of public opinion. As always, it is the two extremes which make the most noise and (as the newspapers reveal) keep the same headlines rolling year after year. But I believe that most of us, in fact, hold the midway position of considered knowledge and positive judgment in some things and genuine doubt, uncertainty, and even misgiving, in others. The upshot is clear. To have demonstrated the errors and insufficiencies of the critics of the family – whether old or new – is far from being in itself enough. When all these arguments are over, the truth remains that there is, in some deeply felt sense, a widespread and continuing *malaise* in our society – about its condition in general, and, in particular, about the nature, place and influence of the family within it. Somehow, everyone feels, something, somewhere, has gone wrong. The old anxieties, though now perhaps in a more complicated form, continue; but new concerns also arise in that – whatever we do to reform matters – the problems seem to remain, and even worsen. Obviously, it is necessary to probe further – to try to discover what the root causes of our troubles might be. And for this, strangely enough, the 'Abolitionist-type' criticisms of the family turn out to have a certain advantage: providing us with a starting-point. Widely different though some of these criticisms have been (from the Neo-Marxists, the New Left, the New Feminism, the Commune Movement, etc.), it is clear that they share, and perhaps even stem from, a few common persuasions and concerns. At least three are clearly identifiable.

(i) The strength of the family: for better, for worse

First, as though, in their own way, reinforcing our own conclusion about the family as against the earlier critics, they all, without exception, demonstrate *the great strength of the family* within the entire post-war scene of political, economic, and social change. Indeed, had it not been for their conviction about the strength of the family, their diagnoses and attacks would not have been made. Leach attacked the strong hold and influences of the intense privacy of the family's too-restricted world. The Marxists attacked it as the last bastion of capitalism and the chief obstacle to socialism. Laing, Cooper and Esterson (in their several books *The Politics of the Family*, *The Leaves of Spring*, *The Death of the Family*, etc.) blamed its strength for the shaping and breaking of individual personalities. The extremists among the New Feminists attacked it as the most powerful upholder of the 'patriarchal society' and

20

the strongest obstacle to the realization of womens' freedom and equality. The communes were either so constructed as to preserve, uphold and enrich the family (convinced of its importance) or, if extremely challenging conventions, proved its resilience by revealing its capacity to reassert itself and survive against even the most deliberate attempts to remove it. A conviction of the *strength* of the family, for good or ill, lies at the heart of these criticisms; indeed, this conviction is the very ground from which they start. Concerning the continuing strength of the family, then – though, for different critics, it is 'for better' or 'for worse' – there seems general agreement and little doubt.

(ii) Sexuality and the changed position of women: great uncertainties

Second, however, and demonstrated in various ways, there is clearly much uncertainty, if not bewilderment, about the ways in which changes in matters concerning sexuality and the position of women have affected, and might be expected to affect, marriage and the family. Have the new knowledge of sexuality itself and of contraceptive techniques, the wide availability of both to people of all ages (even to children below the age of consent), the new degree of freedom to choose to have sexual experience and relationships both before and after (and outside) marriage, and, particularly, the new degree of equality and independence achieved by women in these and other respects, had any marked effect on *marriage* itself (as an institution) and – as a connected but different thing – on the nature of *the family* (as the most desired domestic group)? For some extremists, all these changes are synonymous with an outright rejection of *both* marriage *and* the family. For some (less extreme) they entail the view that it is only *marriage*, as such, which is no longer necessary. It has become 'only a piece of paper' ('what difference does a piece of paper make?'), and living together (cohabitation) can be a relationship every bit as responsible. But for them, none the less, the family as a domestic group remains desirable, as does the security and stability of the family's home. It is only marriage as an 'institutionalized procedure' which has lost its importance. Among others (how many – who knows?) there has been the spread of what can only be called 'half-baked' conceptions of the entire area of private relationships and public responsibility, and of the most casual attitudes towards sex itself, cohabitation, and the having or not having of children. ('If you can't be good – be careful!' 'Well ... if you get caught –

you can easily get rid of it.' 'It's *my* body, isn't it? I can do what I like with it, can't I?' 'Who I sleep with, or live with, and what I do is *my* business – nobody else's!') For others – given many factors such as the increased longevity of life itself, the long extension of marriage within this, the new breadth of social intercourse in work and leisure, the new liberty to experience other relationships (not necessarily sexual) – seriously considered questions and problems arise: about the desirability or otherwise, for example, of pre-marital and extra-marital experience. The new sexuality, the new position of women ... these have very considerably *disturbed* the scene of marriage and the family, and crowded our horizon with questions (whether responsibly or irresponsibly approached) to which we do not know the answer. The literature of 'the New Feminism' offers a wide spectrum of views. The communes, too, have varying views about sex within the family and within the wider community. Even the much-quoted (and often misunderstood) Engels offered no prescription – leaving it to free men and women to work out their own solution for themselves. But free men and women have not yet come to any conclusion. We do not know!

(iii) Social isolation: a many-dimensioned actuality

But a third area of concern has become conspicuously clear, and is especially interesting: so much may lie within it. It is a deeply sensed persuasion – though still far from being well-defined or well-articulated – that, somewhere at the heart of our troubles, there lies a problem of *social isolation*. Some believe that the intensified privacy of the 'nuclear' family, which they consider ruinous, exists because the family is now shut off from the wider kinds of social intercourse which other (more 'primitive') societies enjoy. Some believe that it is the inwardly directed intensity of the relationships within this self-contained world which shapes the individual's 'psyche' for good or ill – and often for ill. Some regard the 'nuclear' family as a prison, and advocate wider and freer kinship and community relationships – which, they believe, will bring a liberation and relaxation of feeling with the broadening and sharing of activities with others. The communes are clearly based on this very conviction: that the family, for the richest fulfilment of the lives of its members, *needs* the supportive conditions of a wider but closer community. The ubiquitous emphasis on the evils of the *nuclear* family presses this same point home. To use the terms Germaine Greer uses in her book *Sex and Destiny* (chapter 9) it is in the isolation of *the cell* of familial relationships from the wider context in which it should have its full being that the fault chiefly lies. In some sense or other, then, *social isolation* emerges as a common concern. From all directions, all approaches, the persuasion is encountered: that much of the malaise from which our society suffers has *this* at its root; that *this* is the source from which a great deal of our personal dissatisfaction and lack of satisfying personal identity stems. A personal emptiness is felt in a world of social emptiness; a lack of personal entity in a lack of social entity. It is, however, by no means presented (by all writers) as one simple thing only, but seems to possess several dimensions. Perhaps more than one factor has to be looked for and taken into account in any satisfactory explanation.

First, and most simply, it suggests *the absence of community in modern society*, and the underlying suspicion that the collective conditions of our modern urban *society* may well have come to be such as to make the experience of *community* impossible. Second, it suggests that the family, though tied in a hundred and one administrative ways into *the organization of society* is not related in any living way (finding no basis for inter-personal life) with the community. The complexity of *society* has overwhelmed and destroyed *community*. A vast girdered framework of societal regulations is there, with an intricate timetable for all the particular journeys and purposes of those who have to move about within it – like some over-arching station for particular comings and goings – but it is *empty* of any settled body of living relationships. And third, as one corollary of this vast House of Administration, it implies some basically flawed nature of *communications*. Something is *missing* in this whole complex network of communications. Something of *human* communication has gone out of it; is lacking within it. In a thousand regulatory ways – wages or unemployment benefits, rents, rates and mortgages, national insurance contributions and social security claims, taxation, social services, parental contributions to education, etc., etc. – families are most certainly formal parts of society's network of organization, part of 'the social system', but, in terms of inter-personal social *life* they have come to be separated and isolated cells within it, lacking any *primary* communications with other *primary groups* in the community. Perhaps even the sense of being a *person* of any significance to others has been lost. The *secondary group communications* of *society* have somehow come to dominate, usurp, drive out of existence, the *primary group communications* of smaller groups, including the *family*, within the *community*, so that when people feel real need (sometimes in situations of dire extremity and ultimate desperation) they require counsellors, Samaritans, advice bureaux. They have to resort, in secrecy, to the telephone. Hence, too, perhaps, the 'living rough', the lonely drug-taking, the suicides. For many, the intimate tissue of confident, confidential, taken-for-granted communications between persons who know each other well – has gone. Long ago, Aristotle emphasized the importance of *friendship* for the quality of personal life and of society, and perhaps it is this which has been lost.

These, at least, are some of the dimensions of this one persuasion. Clearly, a complex actuality is indicated here which calls for more detailed analysis; but, equally clearly, almost all writers *do possess* this underlying persuasion that some such actuality does, in fact, *exist*, deep within the nature of our society, and that it is in *this* that some of our difficulties may well lie. Our social and personal malaise may, at root, be a *spiritual malaise*, lying in the fact that those primary influences and values which are essential in the growth of any individual for the recognition, realization, and fulfilment of our distinctive human nature *as persons*, are being eroded, rendered increasingly impossible, by the nature of our society today.

These, at any rate, are three key concerns which can be seen to be embedded in the thinking of all the critics and all the criticisms alike. Whatever particular position of critical appraisal we ourselves hold, clearly we all believe – each with our different diagnosis – that something, somehow, somewhere, is *wrong*. What can the cause (or causes) of this malaise be?

One thing is clear. To move towards any satisfactory answer we must first of all face the facts themselves: to see what they are, to consider the varying interpretations of them, to form the most careful judgments about them of which we are capable, and see, among all the possible explanations, which of them seems most plausible. Following this, we may be better placed to consider possibilities as to how – if at all – the problems may be resolved.

For this, however, a third and perhaps even more fundamental set of considerations must be introduced.

Because I want to go *beyond* the very recent changes and statistical records themselves into deeper questions of social causation, and because, in doing this, I want to bear these continuing concerns, anxieties, and perplexities centrally in mind, it is necessary to consider in sufficient detail some of the essential characteristics of the family as the universal basic domestic group in society. Despite the wide variations in the forms it has come to assume in societies throughout history, and which it still assumes in societies throughout the world, the family *is*

24

(with exceptions of negligible importance) *universal*, lying, indeed, at the heart of the most deeply established values in terms of which we describe and characterise our 'human nature'. Of all groups in society, without exception, it is the primary group of the family which is most responsible for the creation of our 'human nature'. The central and very evident concern felt by all critics for the conditions and qualities of *the family* on the one hand, and those of *society* on the other, are therefore well founded. The relation between them *is*, indeed, of this most fundamental and intimate nature. Later, I want to consider very carefully the ways in which the collective conditions of our modern society (including its changed communications) may have come to invade, disturb, and perhaps even destroy some aspects of the family, and to prepare the ground for this it is essential to reflect on what the basic nature of the family, as a distinctive group, *is*. The best way of doing this, I believe, is to consider what has been said about the family and its context of kinship relationships as the *origin of society*.

3

The family as the basic domestic group in society: some essential characteristics

(i) The origin of society – and the continuity of social values

It is, in fact, not too much to say that the family, within its wider context of kinship, lay at the very *origins* of human society, and that, in every society, from the earliest times, it has remained one of the most basic groups for preserving *social continuity*.

All our knowledge shows that the earliest tie which bound groups of people together (and which has continued from 'prehistoric' into modern times) was the bond of rootedness in and attachment to their *kindred* – the bond which underlay the *tribe*, and the *clan* within the tribe, and, indeed, which was the ground of the familial sense of belonging which distinguished the early *City States*. The first social bond was one of obligation rooted in *feelings* – of loyalty, duty, and affection within the disciplined demands and regulations of kinship; of sentiment, attachment, belonging, the sense of community; and this has remained perhaps the most powerful bond of all, in all societies, and continues to be so today. Indeed, the family, with its closest kin, can be said to be the one remaining area of *community* experienced in all *societies*, no matter how complex they may have become. But the family and kinship also formed the origins of human society in a more strictly *institutional* way.

It is not too much to say that the entire regulatory system of social institutions (the whole pattern of custom – 'sanctioned usage') in the simpler societies was rooted in, reflected and sustained, the system of families and interrelated kindred within them. Religion and morality rested largely on kinship taboos and totemic systems of ancestry. The 'law' was sustained by the 'blood feud', again resting on kinship. 'Political' authority was sustained by a 'council of elders' (with or without a chieftain) for the people as a whole. 'Property' – chiefly the allocation of land – again rested on the divisions of kinship: tribe, clan and individual family. The bonds of family and kinship, the ties of blood, formed the institutional basis of human society – and the historical development of society, from that time to this, has largely been a process of *differentiation* and *specialization* of particular institutions and their functions from this early context of a close community of kindred. The historical *sequence* of human society as a whole has been of this nature and, in every particular society, the recognition of the bond of ancestry (even of its *sanctity*) has remained important. In a way deeper than we may nowadays suspect, it is the *veneration of ancestry* which lies at the very heart of a society's order and continuity.

But, closely connected with all this, indeed as a part of it, there is also a second sense in which the family may be said to be the origin of human society (though perhaps it is more correct and precise to say that it is the most basic group for originating fundamental values and ensuring the preservation and continuity of society) and that is: that it is the original, primary, *domestic group* into which all children are born, and through which all individuals are, over a number of their most impressionable years, introduced to their society and learn to become members of it. It is the context for the *origin* of social feelings, perceptions, judgments, and values in all individuals. The intimacies of sexual relations between husbands and wives, of mutual care and mutual aid in the experience of intimate needs among all those who are dependent upon each other, of the mutual and shared responsibilities of prolonged parenthood, seem to have dictated the existence – everywhere – of small domestics groups within which such detailed and inter-personal matters can be experienced and fulfilled. No other kind of group, it seems, can cater for these needs. For satisfactory personal lives, for the satisfactory exploration of all dimensions of personal experience, men, women and children need *homes* – as a basis for their continuing life in the wider society and their own personal fulfilment. All this, clearly, is especially true for *children*. For them, their home and family is the taken-for-granted context of familiarity – of all their physical, emotional and mental growth and development – during those early years of complete dependence before any other kind of group is encountered. Their basic emotional bonds, sentiments, attitudes, orientations to society and life, are established here; and all of these are the basis – good or bad – in which all that is to follow will be rooted and out of which it must grow. Here are a child's beginnings.

The family (the small domestic group) is the most impressive, influential and important agency of what is now called 'primary socialization'. Without thinking of this by any means in a completely *deterministic* way (i.e. thinking of the child's nature as being totally *moulded* by society), it is obvious that the most simple physical skills – of grasping, manipulating, walking, toilet-training, dressing, fastening buttons and laces; the most basic proprieties of conduct (politeness of speech and manners); the most basic awareness of language, vocabulary, dialect; the earliest establishing of emotional responses, attitudes, qualities of character; indeed, the earliest establishing, in the individual person, of his or her own consciousness and conception of 'self'; all take place within the family. *The child first becomes a social person there* – and this, again, may be for good or ill, to a considerable extent influencing (if not in some ways and to some extent determining) much that happens later.

This importance of the family as an agency of primary socialization has obviously two clear aspects: it is important both for the *individual person* and for *society*. What happens during these earliest years of experience within the family will affect a person for the rest of his or her life. But also what is established then – in the form of basic habits, attitudes, sentiments, beliefs – will be of the most fundamental importance for preserving orderly behaviour and desired qualities of social life throughout the adult life of society at large, and another point becomes evident here, so important as to be emphasized separately.

'Human nature': the 'Self' and 'Society'

We tend, usually, to think of 'human nature' entirely in terms of what is inherited from our parents. We think of ourselves as one biological species among others (though different and distinct from other species as they are distinguishable from each other), and of 'human nature' as the particular endowment of our own species. There is a strong ground for supposing, however, that this conception is too limited, and that – because our 'human nature' is such as to need *social* regulation and *social* stability for the prolonged care of dependent children, and since such social intercourse is *psychologically creative*, some of the basic and universal features of our 'humanity' are, in fact, *social* in nature. It was C. H. Cooley and G. H. Mead, the American sociologists, who most clearly emphasized and analysed this, and there were two particularly

28

important elements in their conception and formulation of it: (1) the importance of *communications* in the making of 'human nature', in the making of the human 'self' (particularly the intimate nature of communications in the primary group of the family); and (2) the importance (as the child encountered social customs and institutions during his or her growth) of the establishing of *sentiments* in the 'self' during the sequence of growth and development of the individual from birth to adulthood: in the making of individual character and the instilling of a core of values for an inner regulation of responsible conduct in society.

Usually, we think of communications as something taking place *between* people, but both Cooley and Mean insisted that communications were not only important but *essential* in the *making* of people. The 'self' was something taking shape within the intimate influences of 'society', and the first context of such influences – the first and most influential primary group – was the family. Cooley put the matter like this:

A little reflection assures us that the individual has his being only as part of a whole. What does not come by heredity comes by communication and intercourse.... By communication is meant the mechanism through which human relations exist and develop – all the symbols of the mind, together with the means of conveying them through space and preserving them in time.... All these taken together, in the intricacy of their actual combination, make up an organic whole corresponding to the organic whole of human thought; and everything in the way of mental growth has an external existence therein. The more closely we consider this mechanism (i.e. communication), the more intimate will appear its relation to the inner life of mankind, and nothing will more help us to understand the latter than such consideration.... Without communication the mind does not develop a true human nature, but remains in an abnormal and nondescript state neither human nor properly brutal.[1]

Mead was equally clear:

Our contention is that mind can never find expression, and could never have come into existence at all, except in terms of a *social* environment; that an organized set or pattern of social relations and interactions (especially those of communication by means of gestures functioning as significant symbols and thus creating a universe of discourse) is necessarily presupposed by it and involved in its nature.[2]

This means that 'human nature' – in addition to universal features of man's biological endowment (anatomy, physiology, instinct, emotion, modes of perception, etc) – could also be:

'a social nature developed in man by simple forms of intimate association or "primary groups", especially the family and neighbourhood, which are found everywhere and everywhere work upon the individual in somewhat the same way. This nature consists chiefly of certain primary social sentiments and attitudes, such as consciousness of one's self in relation to others, love of approbation, resentment of censure, emulation, and a sense of social right and wrong formed by the standards of a group. This corresponds very closely to what is meant by "human nature" in ordinary speech. We mean something much more definite than hereditary disposition, which most of us know nothing about, and yet something fundamental and wide-spread if not universal in the life of man, found in ancient history and in the accounts of remote nations, as well as now and here. Thus, when we read that Joseph's brethren hated him and could not speak peaceably to him because they saw that their father loved him more than all the rest; we say, "Of course, that is human nature". This social nature is much more alterable than heredity, and if it is "pretty much the same the world over", as we commonly say, this is because the intimate groups in which it is formed are somewhat similar. If these are essentially changed, human nature will change with them.'[3]

The view here maintained is that human nature is not something existing separately in the individual, but a *group-nature or primary phase of society*, a relatively simple and general condition of the social mind. It is something more, on the one hand, than the mere instinct that is born in us – though that enters into it – and something less, on the other, than the more elaborate development of ideas and sentiments that makes up institutions. It is the nature which is developed and expressed in those simple, face-to-face groups that are somewhat alike in all societies; groups of the family, the playground, and the neighbourhood. In the essential similarity of these is to be found the basis, in experience, for similar ideas and sentiments in the human mind. In these, everywhere, human nature comes into existence. Man does not have it at birth; he cannot acquire it except through fellowship, and it decays in isolation.'

'Where do we get our notions of love, freedom, justice and the like?' Not from abstract philosophy, surely, but from the actual life of simple and widespread forms of society, like the family or the play-group.... A congenial family life is the immemorial type of moral unity, and source of many of the terms – such as brotherhood, kindness, and the like – which describe it.[4]

I have quoted Cooley (in particular) at such length on this matter for three reasons, all important.

First, his work dwells upon a point – and a truth – which is all too infrequently made: emphasizing so clearly the importance of the family for the full development of 'human nature' in ourselves as individual persons. Second, it explains the universality of many of the social and moral characteristics of human nature despite the wide diversity of societies and their 'cultures' which we have briefly mentioned; showing, as it does, that human *sentiments* share much similarity and agreement throughout the world because they take shape within universally similar *primary groups.* No matter how widely different the large-scale structures of societies and civilizations have been, and still are, the characteristics of familial and neighbourhood groups remain in many respects the same. And third, it does imply (as, in fact, Cooley says) that if these basic groups were ever to become essentially changed, then 'human nature will change with them.' This is in close agreement, too, with a particular view of Edward Westermarck's (to which we shall come much later), and in the closing section of this book I shall suggest that many of our present-day problems are rooted in this one essential fact alone: that, within the new collective conditions of our modern societies, it is the system of communications which has been transformed in such a way as to disrupt not only the relationships of people in their primary group, but also, and because of this, the actual making of personal character there. The modern 'world of mass-communications' has invaded the primary group of the family, and so displaced and disrupted the primary group communications which, in all societies of the past, have existed within the family hitherto.

But, these several points aside, one other fact which deserves central emphasis can be seen quite clearly in all this.

(iii) The family – and marriage

This (the conclusion also emphasized by Edward Westermarck in his book *The History of Human Marriage*) is: '*that the family is not rooted in marriage, but marriage is an institution rooted in the family*' (my italics). It appears a simple point, but important considerations arise from it. After a very extensive comparative study of the characteristics of marriage and the family in many societies, Westermarck concluded:

> it is originally for the benefit of the young that male and female continue to live together. We may therefore say that marriage is rooted in the family rather than the family in marriage. Indeed, among many peoples true married life does not begin for persons who are formally married or betrothed, or a marriage does not become definite, until a child is born or there are signs of pregnancy; whilst in other cases sexual relations which happen to lead to pregnancy or the birth of a child are, as a rule, followed by marriage or make marriage compulsory.[5]

On the grounds of comparative sociology Westermarck's statement holds good. Marriage does not exist in and for itself, but is an institution whose *raison d'être* is the foundation and maintenance of the family. In any society it is one regulation in the whole organization of a particular family type.

The central consideration in this establishment of a mating relationship is the having and rearing of children, and the family provides for the over-all satisfaction of the needs of children during their years of complete, and then partial, dependence. The family therefore inhabits a common house, a 'home', in which, in conditions of relative privacy and security, this intimate and prolonged provision for the needs of its members takes place. In addition to the care of dependent children, the family usually cares for the dependent aged, and, indeed, for any of its members who may become temporarily or permanently dependent owing to various vicissitudes.

It follows clearly from these characteristics that the family, as a group, is inevitably limited in size. Indeed, it is the smallest of the formal associations in society, and it is just because of this that it is one of the most influential and important. Because its members comprise only a small number of people, living together in great intimacy over a long period of time, the family makes more constant, concrete, intense, and subtle demands upon its members than does any other kind of group. It should also be noted that, for the children especially (but, to varying degrees, for the parents too), the family is an *involuntary* grouping. The particular family of which they are members is not of their own choosing, and they cannot – at least for a very long time (if even then in any real and effective sense of the word) – contract out of it. Consequently, the many compulsive situations of family life must be expected to give rise to frustrations and resentments as well as fulfilments. To use a term familiar in psychology, our experience in the family is necessarily 'ambivalent'. We experience both love and hate, both fulfilment and frustration, both loyalty and rebellion, towards the same people, objects, and situations; and because of this continual – sometimes harmonious, sometimes conflicting, but always intense – complexity of demands in the family, some of the deepest and most abiding human sentiments are set up within it.

This, of course, was the ground for the emphasis of Cooley, Mead and others on the importance of the family for instilling the primary group sentiments and primary group ideals as a strong abiding core of values for the inner regulation of personal life and conduct. We know from our experience that these sentiments – whether worthwhile or regrettable, noble or petty, pleasant or painful – prove to be of abiding importance in the characters and personalities of the members of a family; influencing, indeed in great part determining, their directions of taste, belief, interest, and effort throughout their lives.

Enough has been said to show that the family is, in fact, a community in itself: a small, relatively permanent group of people, related to each other in the most intimate way, bound together by the most personal aspects of life; who experience amongst themselves the whole range of human emotions; who have to strive continually to resolve those claims and counter-claims which stem from mutual but often conflicting needs; who experience continual responsibilities and obligations towards each other; who experience the sense of 'belonging' to each other in the most intimately felt sense of that word. The members of a family share the same name, the same collective reputation, the same home, the same intricate, peculiar tradition of their own making, the same neighbourhood. They share the same sources of pleasure, the same joys, the same sources of profound conflict. The same vagaries of fortune are encountered and overcome together. Degrees of agreement and degrees of violent disagreement are worked out amongst them. The same losses and the same griefs are shared. Hence the family is that group within which the most fundamental appreciation of human qualities and values takes place – 'for better for worse': the qualities of truth and honesty, of falsehood and deceit; of kindliness and sympathy, of indifference and cruelty; of cooperation and forbearance, of egotism and antagonism; of tolerance, justice, and impartiality, of bias, dogmatism, and obstinacy; of generous concern for the freedom and fulfilment of others, of the mean desire to dominate – whether in overt bullying or in psychologically more subtle ways. All those values, and all those discriminations and assessments of value, which are of the most fundamental importance for the formation of adult character are first experienced and exercised by children in the context of the family. Furthermore, these qualities are not 'taught' or 'learned' in any straightforward or altogether rational way; they are actually embodied in people and their behaviour. The child perceives them and appraises them in concrete and demanding situations, and in direct face-to-face relationships with people who matter supremely. In this way, the family is an *educative* group of the most fundamental kind, and these 'educative' characteristics of the family deserve a little further consideration.

As a community, the family is, as we have seen, the earliest and most impressive social situation (or social environment) in the context of which the character of the child is moulded. But the family is not *only* a community in itself, and it is certainly not an *isolated* community. It has its being in the context of a wider grouping of kindred, a wider neighbourhood, and in a wider and more complicated society. For the child, therefore, the family is a kind of 'avenue' through which it comes gradually to an experience of these wider social groupings, and, in so doing, to full adulthood and responsible citizenship. The family provides an 'introduction', as it were, to the wider structure of society – to the knowledge of the wider pattern of kinship; the various groups and characteristics of the neighbourhood; the more detailed economic, governmental, educational, and religious organizations in society. In sociological terms the family is that most important 'primary' group of society which gradually introduces the child to the complicated 'secondary' groups of society – that complicated fabric of social organization with which it will have to come to terms and within which it will have to work out the course and pattern of its life. Through this introduction, the family provides the child with those values and modes of behaviour which are appropriate for life in the wider society. In a fuller sense than we suggested earlier, then, the family is – for the child – the first, and perhaps the most important, agency of education in society.

This might be more clearly illustrated in Diagrams 1 and 2.

34

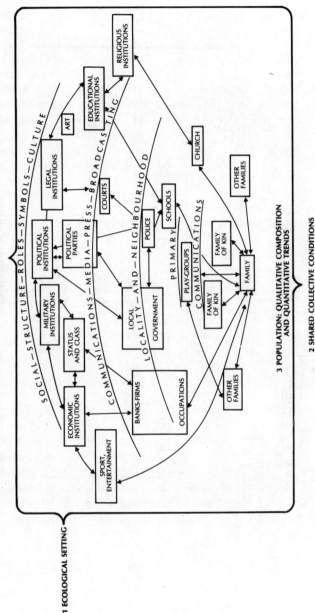

4 THE SOCIAL FRAMEWORK OF
EXPERIENCE AND BEHAVIOUR

SOCIAL—STRUCTURE—ROLES—SYMBOLS—CULTURE

COMMUNICATIONS—MEDIA—PRESS—BROADCASTING

LOCAL—LOCALITY—AND—NEIGHBOURHOOD

PRIMARY COMMUNICATIONS

RELIGIOUS INSTITUTIONS

EDUCATIONAL INSTITUTIONS

ART

LEGAL INSTITUTIONS

POLITICAL INSTITUTIONS

POLITICAL PARTIES

COURTS

MILITARY INSTITUTIONS

STATUS AND CLASS

LOCAL GOVERNMENT

POLICE

SCHOOLS

CHURCH

ECONOMIC INSTITUTIONS

BANKS-FIRMS

OCCUPATIONS

PLAY-GROUPS

FAMILY OF KIN

FAMILY

OTHER FAMILIES

SPORT, ENTERTAINMENT

OTHER FAMILIES

FAMILY OF KIN

1 ECOLOGICAL SETTING

3 POPULATION: QUALITATIVE COMPOSITION
AND QUANTITATIVE TRENDS

2 SHARED COLLECTIVE CONDITIONS

1 Society as objectively observed (Sanctions, sentiments, values: The core of social institutions and 'individuals' alike)

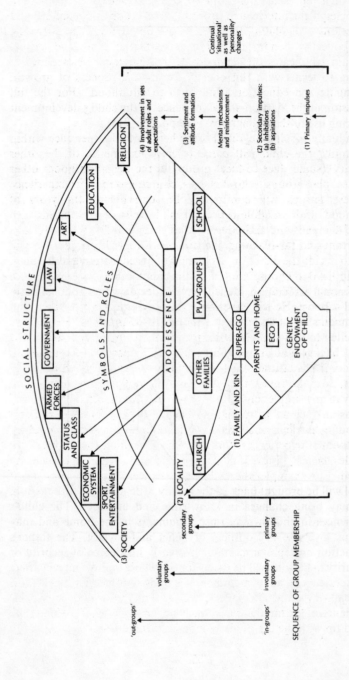

2 Society as subjectively perceived and experienced (The social framework of experience and behaviour)

Diagram 1 represents the framework of social structure existing in any society – the interrelated forms of all its groups, associations and institutions – regulating the lives of the population who share the same collective conditions within its particular ecological setting. Diagram 2 indicates the *sequence* of the individual's experience in coming to terms with this society during the process of growth, upbringing and education from birth to adulthood. (For the full discussion of the 'natural-social sequence' of the child's development – making use of these diagrams – see pp. 186–218).

Gradually moving beyond his (or her) earliest experience within the family, the child will come to have experience of the other 'primary' (small, face-to-face) groups in the neighbourhood: other families, play groups, school classes, church groups. His experience of these groups will continually broaden during the years of childhood, until, in adolescence, he will have to come to terms with all the demands and activities of adult society and will have to take important and far-reaching decisions with regard to them. He will have to decide the direction and extent of his education and training. He will have to choose a job, and probably join a trade union or a professional association. He will have to decide which political party he will support. He will experience the demarcations, pressures, and curtailments of class, privilege, and status distinctions. He may be compelled to undertake service in the armed forces, and so on. His family background, throughout this experience, will be a central influence in the attitudes he forms and the decisions he adopts.

It is clear, however, that the family is not an 'introduction' to society in any simple sense of the word; neither should it be regarded *only* as an 'avenue' to something beyond it. The family is rather a continuing 'nucleus' of shared experience and behaviour, a 'pooling' of individual experiences, through which medium the impressions, attitudes, beliefs, tastes, of all its members are interdependently being formed. For example, the child's experiences in play groups or at school will be brought back to the family, will give rise to discussion, and may bring changes in knowledge and attitudes. The child's experiences in church may raise arguments in the home and may perhaps give rise to conflicts of belief and loyalty. The father's satisfaction or depression about his work, his degree of security or insecurity in his job, will be issues for the whole family and will affect the experience of all its members. His trade union commitments, his political views and allegiances, will all enter into and colour the experience of the family as a whole. The family is therefore integrally bound up with the life of all its members in the wider society. It is a community which reflects and, in its own particular way, digests, the experiences of its members in all their other forms of association, and it is in the context of this ongoing complexity of experience that children grow up into adulthood and into adult citizenship.

It seems clear that for any wise upbringing of children, neither the 'avenue' nor the 'community in itself' conception of the family should dominate to the exclusion of the other. Both require balanced emphasis. If the family is treated only as an 'avenue' to something beyond it, a child may be treated only as a potential adult, with reference to what it is desired that he should become in future; and he may never enjoy consideration as a person, at the moment, in and for himself; he may never enjoy a child's life, satisfying and important in itself, within a settled home life. But, alternatively, if the family is treated only as a 'community in itself', the child may suffer from too great a degree of family-containment, of dependence upon the family, and he may be handicapped later by never having been brought to terms with the demands of the wider world in which he must live. The home may become too much of a 'retreat'. It is clear that both aspects of the family are of importance and require due consideration, and there are some of us, at any rate, who appear to emphasize only one or the other. Indeed, how to balance the two is one of the most difficult (if not impossible) tasks of parenthood at a time when the very nature, the social, economic and political conditions, and the boundaries of 'childhood' and 'adulthood' are being substantially changed by legislation and public policies.

It is clear that it is these general points about the nature of the family in society which makes possible the clear summary outline-statement of its more obvious and important functions we have already noted (p. 3). The same points make it clear, too, that there at least two reasons why the family is of crucial importance, both for the social scientist (for purposes of social analysis) and for the statesman (for purposes of practical social policy).

First, the family is that association specifically formed for and specifically focusing upon the *reproduction of the population* and the rearing of each new generation. Any social policy concerned with the quantity and quality of the population must therefore take into account, and operate upon, the families in society. This, of course, is a crucial matter for the very survival and the sustained quality of the entire political community. Second, since it is that association within which the earliest character-formation of individuals takes place – within which the earliest and deepest pattern of sentiments, attitudes, beliefs, ideals, and loyalties is established – the family is one of the most important agencies making for the *continuity of the social tradition*. And there is much (and obvious) evidence to show that this importance of the family is recognized beyond the bounds of social science in the realm of practical affairs, which leads to a final point: that the family is demonstrably so important a social group, so powerful a nucleus of interests and loyalties, and so fruitful a source of individual variety, that it is always very conspicuously and strictly regulated by the central agencies of authority and control in society – the State, the law, and religion. These seem good grounds, too, for believing in the continued strength of the family in society – so many factors suggest that it is indispensable – and, despite all the changes of the modern world, Westermarck, for example, after what is perhaps the most searching inquiry that has ever been undertaken, concluded:

> There is every reason to believe that the unity of sensual and spiritual elements in sexual love, leading to a more or less durable community of life in a common home, and the desire for and love of offspring, are factors that will remain lasting obstacles to the extinction of marriage and the collapse of the family, because they are too deeply rooted in human nature to fade away, and can find adequate satisfaction only in some form of marriage and the family founded upon it.[6]

Later, we shall come back to this conclusion. It was not Westermarck's last word!

This, however, completes the preparatory considerations which I have felt it necessary to outline by way of introduction. Strictly speaking, it has been a laying of foundations for the detailed arguments which are to come later, and their full significance will then be seen.

I cannot resist, however, one final and more general comment.

4

Family? or wider social causation?

(i) The example of war

When one stops to reflect, even for a moment, does it not seem remarkably strange that – bearing in mind all the massive disasters which have inflicted their damage upon our own society, other societies, and the world at large during our conflict-ridden century – social critics and moralists alike should focus both their attention and their blame upon *the family*? Looking again at the denunciations of the critics of the 1950s and early 1960s after a period of some twenty-five years or so, I can only say that I find this fact strange almost beyond belief. And here I will mention only one consideration, by way of example, though I shall return to it and dwell on it later. It is about *war*.

Later, I shall want to place very strong emphasis on what I shall call 'the long tentacles of war' as one of the most important grounds for the understanding of much of our behaviour since 1945. Here, however, I want only, and quite simply, to call attention to this one stark fact: that, looming like a great storm-cloud over all other considerations, our twentieth century has been a *century of war*. It is the century which has witnessed – through the troubled experience of two succeeding generations – the two most destructive and all-encompassing *world wars* mankind has ever known. The second of these, furthermore, was a *total war* – in which armies, navies, air forces, were recruited by a compulsory (if selective) conscription which covered the entire population; in which the urgent demand for 'war-work', 'work of national importance', was met by a compulsory direction of labour; and in which cities and civilians – as well as the armed forces – were subjected to deliberate and often undiscriminating mass destruction.

Almost every war-memorial in England (perhaps in every participating land) – these monuments to human sacrifice – tells the clear story of the changed nature of these two world wars. Commemorating the First World War is the massive list of servicemen slaughtered in the trenches. Commemorating the Second World War is the very much shorter list of servicemen who lost their lives, but also the much longer list (ie. compared with that of the First World War) of the *civilian* dead. The First World War was entered into in a blaze of the most genuine idealistic patriotism – gradually subsiding and turning into a sickness at heart as many of the pointlessly continued horrors of the trench warfare became known. The Second World War – one of stark but expected aggression met, ultimately, by the meting out of stark vengeance – was entered into as, at best, a matter of necessity: resignedly, stoically, reluctantly; so that one who was later to become England's 'Poet Laureate' (Cecil Day Lewis) was unable to speak of it with anything approaching enthusiasm.

> *Where Are the War Poets?*
> They who in panic or mere greed
> Enslaved religion, markets, laws,
> Borrow our language now and bid
> Us to speak up in freedom's cause.
>
> It is the logic of our times,
> No subject for immortal verse,
> That we who lived by honest dreams
> Defend the bad against the worse.[1]

Dostoevsky had long ago pointed out that the greatest evils and crimes against humanity – the worst, most wanton, most insensate cruelties, indecencies, and indiscriminate licentiousness of behaviour (in looting, raping, general sexual abandonment, as well as in killing) – were unleashed, countenanced, and ruthlessly pursued by the 'great leaders', the 'great men', the 'heroes' of nations, in *war*. Beside these evils, the worst crimes committed by individuals in times of peace seemed to pale into insignificance. Who was the greater criminal? – a Napoleon? – a Caesar? – or a man who deliberately rid the world of a foul old woman money-lender in an attic, a woman who brought misery to everyone she held in her grip? That was Dostoevsky's question. During the experience of two generations, millions of people in the populations of Europe, Russia, America, and elsewhere in the world had been subjected to these evils. The second war, too, ended with the use of a weapon which brought a threat of warfare more terrible than anything which had been known before. The very energies of the world were sucked up into the mushroom cloud which then hung over the world: a terrible harbinger of peace. But ... peace did not come. After the war, during the 1950s and 1960s (and continuing still), wars and rumours of wars have continued – civil wars and wars between nations – the noise of their ever-worsening barbarism echoing continually throughout the world. The prospect for the remaining decades of our century remains one under the threat of a globally destructive war far more terrible than anything of which mankind has ever dreamed. In our time – no longer in a passage of literature, but in day-to-day actuality – the whole population of the world lives and moves through the valley of the shadow of death.

In Britain, as in the other countries of Europe, two entire generations were torn out of the settled contexts of their families and communities and subjected to the disruptive influences of these two world wars. The generation which had suffered, but survived, the vast losses and destructiveness of the First World War had also suffered the even more cynical disillusionment of the peace which followed: the lamentable story of the making of 'the Land Fit for Heroes to Live In'. The disillusionment coming with the 'Lloyd George' of the peace – the dole queue at the Labour Exchange and the 'national assistance' – had bitten perhaps even more deeply into the minds and spirits of the British people than the disillusionment which had slowly gathered behind the Lloyd George of the protracted war of the trenches – which, in itself, had led even committed soldiers like Siegfried Sassoon and Wilfred Owen to turn away, sickened, disgusted, from the supposed 'glories' of war; outraged at the 'leaders' who perpetuated it. And the following generation of that generation's children – having, during their own growth to young manhood and womanhood, witnessed the slowly developing story of the débâcle of the Treaty of Versailles, the League of Nations, and its supposed policy of 'Collective Security' – faced war again: a war the 'great leaders' of nations had allowed to happen despite warning after warning from critics as to the probable outcome of the policies they were following and the undertakings they had promised but were neglecting to uphold. Two generations were torn out of the settled lives they were gradually building in peacetime – and thrown into war.

In the armed forces, in the civilian services, on farms and in factories, in the organized movements of men and women between nations and within each nation, and of their children 'evacuated' from their homes and sent to safer places outside major cities, the life of two entire generations was disrupted in the most radical way by the usurping demands of total war. The disruption, disordering, dissolution of relationships and patterns of behaviour which had just been becoming stable, was the rule – the very general experience. The breaking of long-founded, long-developed relationships and being thrown into the close working proximities of new, incidental, short-lived relationships under conditions of uncertainty and instability, was the rule – the common situation. And after this entire dislocation, if not destruction, of their social and personal worlds, men and women had then to return to the task of re-making their lives in a world of peace again. But it is deeply doubtful whether, after several years of modern war, anyone ever goes back home. Those who go back, and those to whom they return, are not the same people. The same home – despite appearances – is not there.

Though it is all too easy to exaggerate – by the use of an image – it was, in a way, like having to rebuild a living community in the hollow of an empty volcano, when the heart of it, on the only recently established and apparently settled ground, had been spewed out yet again in a great eruption, when the floor and walls – which now, again, seemed familiar and firm – were not yet still, were vulnerable to moving and sliding, and a continuing apprehensiveness of new possible disruptions to come was part of the prevailing atmosphere. Everyone though, spoke, behaved, as though the grounded world they had left – despite the cataclysm which had shaken it – was firm again. But it was not so. And this, ever since, has been the actual, realistic context of our lives. The life of a generation, the lives of individuals within it, are short – shorter than they themselves appreciate during the living of them – and what have they been able to believe? – in what have they been able to place their confidence? – within this century's context? Is disillusionment, cynicism, a shrugging off of all long-term care for the future, surprising? Again, a poet who long ago saw these impending evils looming on the horizon, could well be speaking for us now.

> We are getting to the end of visioning
> The impossible within this universe,
> Such as that better whiles may follow worse,
> And that our race may mend by reasoning.
>
> We know that even as larks in cages sing
> Unthoughtful of deliverance from the curse
> That holds them lifelong in a latticed hearse,
> We ply spasmodically our pleasuring.

And that when nations set them to lay waste
Their neighbours' heritage ...
And hack their pleasant plains in festering seams,
They may again – not warely, or from taste,
But tickled mad by some demonic force ...
Yes. We are getting to the end of dreams.[2]

In the 1950s no less a person than Lord Shawcross, in a speech to the Royal Society of St George in London, reported in *The Times*, 4 May 1962, asking whether the Welfare State was not 'making the British people too soft', and fearing the destruction of 'the great permanencies hitherto deeply ingrained through all the generations of our people', said: *it is the parents who frighten me most* (my italics). The 'great deeply ingrained permanencies of the past'? The sure religious beliefs? The firmly founded moral ideals? The established principles of judgment and conduct? Where were they, and what were they, in these great and quickly repeated conflagrations? What did they say then for the regulation of our conduct? – for the conduct of our leaders? – for the judgment of those in the churches and other high places who spoke for them? Where are they, and what do they say, now? Surely we are walking still through a valley of the shadows of great doubts and perplexities? And surely we have not known, and still do not know, where we are going? '*Where do we come from? What are we? Where are we going?*' The title of Gaugin's haunting painting surely haunts us now – coming to the close of our century of total war?

But I write like this, in this introductory fashion, only to reiterate the one simple question.

Does it not seem strange almost to the point of perversity, almost to the point of disbelief, that – in the aftermath of these cataclysms of war, within the context of the relatively short span of years following these massive disruptions of human experience, following this radical disturbance of values, behaviour and relationships – these self-appointed judges of the conduct of their fellows (these clergymen, judges, educationists, politicians) – should blame *the family* for all the ills of our society? – for the behavioural incoherence and disorder of our time? Is it not strange that – having forgotten, it seems, these recent and many-sided disasters of war – they should lay the blame for all our social ills at the door of *the family*? – itself so obviously improved within the Welfare State? That they should turn their accusations against such reforms as improvements in the status of women, efforts towards securing equality of opportunities for children in health and education, attempting some redistribution of wealth and welfare, and seeking an improved material well-being for all? Just to take one other similar judgment by way of example, and with this background of war in mind, how could a man like Dr Leslie Weatherhead (obviously himself a good man in a thousand and one ways) persuade himself that the nation was 'in dire moral peril' owing to the spread of 'sexual depravity' which, to modern youth, was '*a greater danger than nuclear war*' (letter to *The Times*, 20 September 1961, my italics)? Was this not (as part of a criticism of the condition of the family in society) an almost unbelievable judgment – coming from a Christian clergyman of the highest reputation?

I can only confess that the more I reconsider these relatively recent condemnations of the family, the more absurd, the more lacking in any serious sense of perspective, they seem to be. If a grave and restless disorder, a profound disorientation, a decline of conviction in beliefs, principles and morality, assailed – and continues to assail – our society, it does not seem to me at all surprising. During a time in which every secure foundation of every society in the world has been thrown into a vast vortex of war and social change, when the entire order of civilized thought in the world is undergoing a process of rapid transformation the outcome of which we cannot yet foresee, how can it be even remotely sensible to make *the family* the butt of our criticisms? The very highest levels of supposed authority – in international affairs, in other societies, and in our own society – rock with uncertainty, indecision, and unprincipled manipulation. The doctrines of all religions, including those of our own national church, are riddled with doubts, cleavages, illogicalities, and even downright simple-mindedness. The realities of public corruption are only occasionally and partially glimpsed (though now with increasing frequency), but none the less very revealingly so, in the pages of the press and the procedures of the courts. And yet, for some curious reason, it is *the family* which is the scapegoat. It is '*the breakdown of the family*' within the supposed '*laxities of the Welfare State*' – or it is '*the reactionary strength of the family*' and the pernicious influences of '*the intensity of its too-private world*' – which is blamed for our bad behaviour! But surely, if anything seems true in all this, it is that the family in society, and all its members, have been the *victims* of society's disasters, not their *causes*?

To this, however, I shall return because there is much more to be said.

But now – let us turn to an examination of the facts and an attempt to explain them.

Part I

The Family in Britain: After the Divorce Reform Act

Facts and interpretations

What, then, are the facts? What has happened since the coming into operation of the 1969 Divorce Reform Act in 1971, and what does the factual evidence itself reveal? Has there been a continued and popular observance of the institution of marriage? – or has it been rejected and abandoned? Has there been an increasing breakdown and decline of the family? – or has it been retained as the basic domestic group in our society? Do the facts demonstrate a growth of more casual and irresponsible attitudes towards both marriage and family relationships – between husbands and wives, parents and children, younger adults and the aged? – or a continuity of reciprocal family concern? Let us take each item of information in turn, and, since marriage (as an institution) and the family (as a domestic group) are clearly not the same, let us begin with the questions concerning divorce and marriage and consider the family afterwards. This should provide a picture of 'then' and 'now' and clarify the trends of the past fifteen years. First of all, too, we will look at the facts in the form of the naked statistics, keeping interpretation to the bare minimum of pointing out the indications of the statistics themselves and the interconnections between them. Then we can consider other kinds of evidence which are factual none the less, and support certain very specific interpretations and judgments.

(i) Divorce

We saw that even during the formulation of the 1969 Act, it was generally known that a substantial increase in divorce would immediately follow its coming into effect. In itself, therefore, this would signify no other trend than that already established – bringing before the courts the 'backlog' of petitions from marriages which had been 'irretrievably broken' before this time. This increase did, in fact, occur. The graph 3 shows the increase in divorce up to 1964; graph 4 (incorporating the earlier figures) shows the trend since that time.

The 1971 increase is very plain. Since this seems like a sudden increase in marriage breakdowns, and therefore a sudden deterioration, it is most important to remind ourselves very clearly that it was not this at all. On the contrary, it was an essential stage in the rectification of the long-standing problem of marital re-adjustment which it had been impossible to resolve under the old law, and it is worthwhile to recall one of the aims of the 1969 Act. Moving the second reading of the Bill, Mr William Wilson said:

> Any Bill which seeks to reform the divorce law must provide a means whereby existing stable illicit unions can be regularised. How many of these unions actually exist no one knows. The children born each year to these unions are estimated as between 10,000 and 20,000. One thing is certain: there is a substantial number of them. They are not temporary alliances. They are stable. They are marriages in everything but name. The children of those alliances generally must remain illegitimate. The point can be made that the vast majority of the persons involved in these unions are anxious to remarry. They do not necessarily want to avoid their responsibilities to a spouse from whom they parted 10, 20, 30 or even 40 years ago.[1]

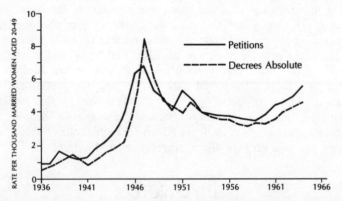

3 Dissolutions and annulments of marriage: new petitions filed and decrees made absolute per 1,000 married women aged 20–49, England and Wales, 1936–64.

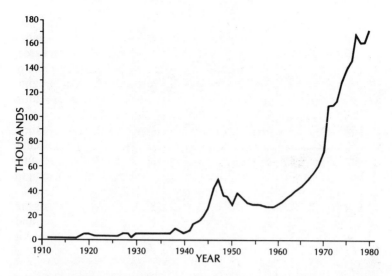

4 Petitions filed for dissolutions and annulments of marriage in England and Wales, 1910–80. Data from the Office of Population Censuses and Surveys[2]

The large increase during the early 1970s was therefore *not* a sudden increase in marriage breakdowns and in the *rate* of divorce; it was a major re-adjustment, a great improvement in itself – putting a long-intolerable situation to rights. It was a great measure opening the way to the legitimation and regularization of the many illicit unions then existing, and two other important points deserve note. First: it made possible the regularization of the family situations of a large number of children (and was therefore likely to be to their benefit), and second: it was an obvious prelude to an equally noticeable increase in the number of *re-marriages* – a fact to which we shall return.

What is also plain, however, is that, far from 'levelling off' when the immediate back-log was over, the number of divorces continued to increase for a few years. This continued into the second half of the 1970s, fell a little, and increased again – seeming, now, to have arrived at a plateau. The figures in Table 5 show these more recent trends very clearly.

It will be seen that although the number of decrees *made absolute* in 1984 was almost double that in 1971, the larger increase shown in 1976 and onwards incorporated the increase in the number of *petitions filed* then under the new law. To some extent (a fact to

5 Divorce statistics, England and Wales, Scotland, and Northern Ireland, 1961–84

	1961	1971	1976	1979	1980	1981	1982	1983	1984
Petitions filed (thousands)									
England & Wales									
By husband	14	44	43	46	49	47	47	45	49
By wife	18	67	102	118	123	123	128	124	130
Total	32	111	145	164	172	170	174	169	179
Decrees nisi granted (thousands)									
England & Wales	27	89	132	140	151	148	149	150	148
Decrees absolute granted (thousands)									
England & Wales	25	74	127	139	148	146	147	147	145
Scotland	2	5	9	9	11	10	11	13	12
Northern Ireland	0.1	0.3	0.6	0.8	0.9	1.2	1.4	1.5	1.6
United Kingdom	27	80	136	148	160	157	159	162	158
Persons divorcing per thousand married people									
England & Wales	2.1	6.0	10.1	11.2	12.0	11.9	12.1	12.2	12.0
Percentage of divorces where one or both partners had been divorced previously									
England & Wales	9.3	8.8	11.6	14.7	15.7	17.1	18.5	20.0	21.0

Source: Office of Population Censuses and Surveys; Lord Chancellor's Department

which we shall return) there was an obvious 'carry on' effect of the 1969 Act. It may be of considerable significance, too, that under the Family Law Reform Act of 1969 the age of majority was reduced from 21 to 18, changing the position – both for marriage and divorce – of younger women. Also, the sudden increase in petitions filed in England and Wales in 1984 came later in that year when the law was changed to allow petitions after only *one* year of marriage. And it is to be noted, too, that the decrees *granted* in England and Wales have been gradually *decreasing* since 1980. *Some* aspects of this trend are therefore explicable in terms of changes in the law itself, and, in particular, the sharp increase in the early 1970s can be fully explained in these terms. What seems to require *new* explanation is the continued increase in divorce from the early 1970s to 1980, and the continuation of a high divorce rate from then onwards, even though something of a plateau did then seem to have been reached. It deserves note, too, that the number of persons divorcing per thousand of married people in England and Wales has remained remarkably constant from 1980 to 1984. A part-explanation will suggest itself when we consider the parallel trend of marriage, but, before this, some aspects of these divorce figures do seem particularly significant.

THE POSITION OF WOMEN

First, it cannot be without significance that the number of petitions filed in England and Wales by *husbands* for the whole period between 1971 and 1984 has remained remarkably constant, whereas that filed by *wives* has enormously increased between 1971 and 1980 (though remaining *relatively* constant since that time). (The sharp increase in petitions filed by *both* men and women in the early 1970s is to be explained by the changes in the law already mentioned.) Plainly, the major increase in petitions for divorce has come from *wives*, and this must surely reflect changes in the position, conditions (domestic and otherwise), and attitudes of women. What might these changes be? Women now enjoy a greater degree of equality, have greater opportunities to work (whether part-time or full-time), can claim a greater degree of support from the social services and social security, and have, therefore a greater measure of independence. They are also independent at an earlier age. They may well, now, have considerably higher expectations of marriage. Having enjoyed personal freedom and certain standards of living before marriage,

51

they may well be the more reluctant to lose them after marriage. These probabilities seem also to be borne out by other facts.

One indicator lies in the *grounds* given for divorce. Graph 6 is given in the 1986 issue of *Social Trends*.

Until 1971, the grounds given for divorce were adultery, desertion and cruelty. Up to that date (from 1950) the adultery of the wife was the ground increasingly given by husbands, the cruelty *and* the adultery of husbands the grounds increasingly given by wives. A significant difference took place after 1971, when the 'irretrievable breakdown of marriage' became the sole ground for divorce (with the five reasons given for the breakdown: desertion, separation for 2 years, separation after 5 years, adultery, and unreasonable behaviour). In this new situation, the chief reason given by husbands for the irretrievable breakdown of their marriage was still the adultery of their wives, but for wives, the chief and increasing reason given was 'unreasonable behaviour'. In 1984, 43 per cent of husbands cited their wives' adultery; 46 per cent of wives cited the unreasonable

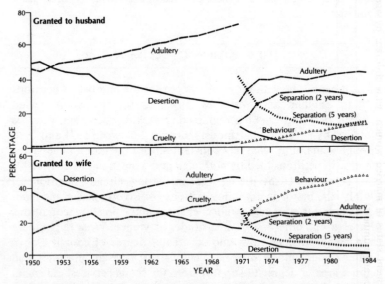

Source: Secular changes in divorce in England and Wales by class of decree – a socio-legal analysis, John Haskey, *Biology and Society*, vol. 3, 1986

6 Divorce – party granted decree: by grounds, England and Wales

7 Employment status of married women[1] with children: by age of youngest dependent child, 1973–81 (Great Britain, percentages and numbers)

	1973	1976	1979	1980	1981
Youngest dependent child aged 0–4 (percentages)					
Mother – not working	76	74	71	70	75
– working part-time	18	21	23	23	19
– working full-time	6	5	5	6	6
Sample size (= 100%) (numbers)	1,831	1,694	1,390	1,376	1,458
Youngest dependent child aged 5–9 (percentages)					
Mother – not working	38	40	39	38	43
– working part-time	44	44	45	48	45
– working full-time	17	16	16	14	12
Sample size (= 100%) (numbers)	1,144	1,156	1,030	1,030	1,029
Youngest dependent child aged 10 years or more (percentages)					
Mother – not working	33	31	27	29	30
– working part-time	38	41	47	43	45
– working full-time	29	28	25	28	26
Sample size (= 100%) (numbers)	1,135	1,308	1,261	1,349	1,367
Dependent children of all ages (percentages)					
Mother – not working	53	51	47	46	50
– working part-time	31	34	37	37	35
– working full-time	15	15	15	16	15
Sample size (= 100%) (numbers)	4,110	4,158	3,681	3,763	3,854

[1]Women aged 16–59.
Source: General Household Survey

8 Employment status of married and lone mothers: by age of youngest dependent child, 1981–3 (Great Britain percentages and numbers)

Employment status (percentages)	Married mothers–age of youngest dependent child				Lone mothers–age of youngest dependent child			
	0–4	5–9	10 or over	All ages	0–4	5–9	10 or over	All ages
Mother – not working	75	43	31	51	82	52	43	58
– working part-time	19	44	45	35	11	29	28	23
– full-time	6	12	24	14	7	19	28	19
Sample size (= 100%) (numbers)	3,838	2,465	701	10,004	434	336	562	1,332

Source: General Household Survey, combined data for 1981–3 inclusive

behaviour of their husbands. The choice of these two reasons as against the other three may have much to do with the fact that both of them entitles the petitioner (man or woman) to an *immediate* decree nisi. Even so, there must be some significance in the different ground claimed by the two sexes, and the 'unreasonable behaviour' claimed by wives does suggest higher expectations of marriage and a lowered threshold of tolerance of conditions of domestic life they find unsatisfying and unsatisfactory. Once women had to endure the domestic life within which their marriage had placed them. Now – it is not so.

The facts of womens' *employment* also point to an increasing (though not great) independence of wives. In 1951, 22 per cent of wives were in employment, in 1966, 38 per cent, and in the early 1980s about 58 per cent. The table 7 shows the employment situation of married women with children during the greater part of the 1970s. It will be noticed that the increases were chiefly in the category of mothers working *part-time*.

The same picture emerges from the employment of *both* married *and* lone mothers during the years 1981–83 (table 8).

The limited degree of the changes, however, can be seen in the comparison (figure 9) of the economic activity of married women during the first four years of the 1980s with that at the end of the 1970s.

Over the whole period, *self-employment* rose from 2 per cent to 4 per cent. From 1983 to 1984, *part-time* employment rose from 22 per cent to 24 per cent. It was found, too (in 1984), that women were returning to work more quickly after having a baby, and increasingly returning to work *between* births.

It seems, then, that at least *some* of the explanation of the higher rate of the termination of marriages lies in the changed position and expectations of women. It must be noted, however, that in these same figures there is little evidence of *irresponsibility in motherhood*. The great majority of married and lone mothers alike do not work at all when they have dependent children under the age of 5. Indeed, a slight majority – having children of *all* ages – do not work at all. The greatest proportion of work is of a *part-time* nature. This increases with the age of the children, and (as many studies have pointed out) is undertaken *for the benefit* of the children, not at their expense. In her book *Ask the Family*, Jeanette Longfield's finding was that: 'more than 2 out of 5 people believe it is wrong for mothers of young children to go out to work,' but that 'there would be 4 times as many families in poverty if women didn't work outside the home.'

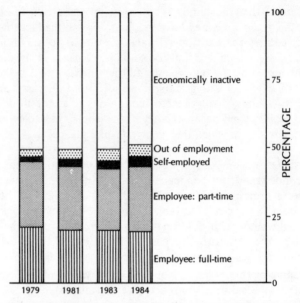

Source: *Labour Force Surveys*, Department of Employment

9 Economic activity of married women, 1979–84 Great Britain

DIVORCE AND RE-DIVORCE

Turning back to table 5, however, it will also be seen that *one* other conspicuous factor in the *continuing* high rate of divorce (even during the 1980s, when the plateau seems to have been reached – and it is noteworthy, again, that the *number of persons* divorcing per thousand married people in England and Wales has remained remarkably constant during this period) is the marked increase in the number of divorces of previously divorced and *re*-married people. People who have been divorced and have then re-married are more prone to subsequent divorce than people (of similar ages) marrying for the first time. The number of *re*-marriages is *increasing*, as against that of *first* marriages which has been *decreasing*, and it is the continual increase in the divorce rate of those *re*-married which contributes in particular to the *over-all* increase – so sustaining the high rate of divorce. Chart 10 shows the trends from 1961 onwards.

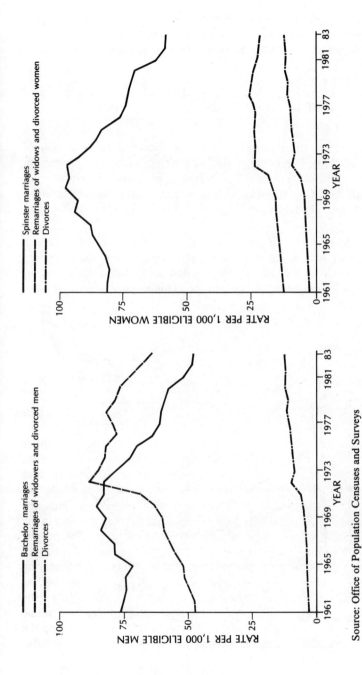

Source: Office of Population Censuses and Surveys

10 Marriage, remarriage, and divorce: rates 1961–83 (Great Britain)

There is, clearly, a *direct relationship* between the rate of *divorce* and the rate of *marriage*, and we shall return to this point very soon. First, however, two other aspects of the trends in divorce must be noted.

DIVORCE AND DURATION OF MARRIAGE

One concerns the relation between divorce and the *duration* of marriage. This, in most respects, is little changed from the situation in the mid-1960s. The graph (11), first of all, shows the clear trend, through the 1970s, towards divorce at shorter and shorter durations of marriage. The latest available table (12) provides the figures up to 1983.

The fact which emerges is that the higher rate of marriage breakdown is, and has consistently remained, among the marriages which are shortest-lived; and this, by and large, means the marriages of those in the younger age-groups. This implies, too, that such

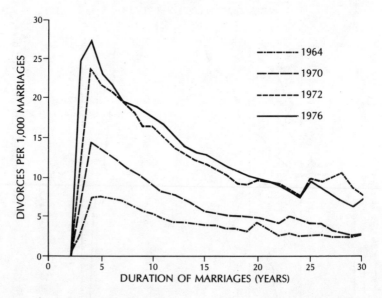

11 Divorce by duration of marriage, selected years, England and Wales, 1964–76.
Data from the Office of Population Censuses and Surveys

12 Divorce: by duration of marriage, 1961–83 (Great Britain percentages and numbers)

	Duration of marriage (completed years)								All divorces (× 100%) (numbers)
	0–2	3–4	5–9	10–14	15–19	20–24	25–29	30+	
Year of divorce									
1961	1.2	10.1	30.6	22.9	13.9	13.9	21.2		27,018
1971	1.2	12.2	30.5	19.4	12.6	9.5	5.8	8.9	79,249
1976	1.5	16.5	30.2	18.7	12.8	8.8	5.6	5.9	135,386
1979	1.2	17.4	30.4	19.0	12.4	8.9	5.2	5.6	147,539
1980	1.3	17.8	30.4	19.3	12.5	8.6	5.0	5.0	158,831
1981	1.5	18.0	30.1	19.4	12.7	8.6	5.0	4.7	155,608
1982	1.5	19.0	29.1	19.6	12.8	8.6	4.9	4.5	157,986
1983	1.3	19.5	28.7	19.2	12.9	8.6	5.2	4.7	160,717

Source: Office of Population Censuses and Surveys; General Register Office (Scotland)

marriages are the most likely to be childless. In 1984, two thirds of the couples who divorced within the first 3 years of marriage were childless. But this leads to a further important point.

CHILDREN

Earlier, in the late 1950s and early 1960s, it seemed that the number of children exposed to risk through divorce was a remarkably constant proportion. Now, it is clear beyond doubt that a *larger number* of children have become involved, though the number is not continually increasing. The chart (13) shows the picture clearly – bearing in mind, again, that the sharp peak in the very early 1970s followed the 1969/71 Act and therefore did not signify a *new* situation for the children in these cases, but was a recognition of a situation of long standing to which they may already have become adjusted. Following this, there were other peaks in 1978 and 1980 (of about 163,000), falling, then, to 149,000 in 1984.

It is interesting to note, however, that in 1983, 29 per cent of divorcing couples had no children and just over 13 per cent had children who were over 16. Only 58 per cent, therefore, had very young children particularly at risk. This, however, is not said to gloss over the situation. The sheer number of children suffering from broken homes has increased, and this, perhaps, presents the most serious aspect of the entire situation. In 1957 the total number of children of marriages dissolved or annulled was just under 31,000. In 1984 it was just under 149,000. From any point of view, this is an alarming figure, and, of course, it cannot simply be supposed that children *over* the age of 16 remain unaffected by the parting of their parents. Adolescence, no less than infancy, is a critical period of personal development, prone to its own kinds and degrees of intensity.

QUALIFICATIONS – FOR INTERPRETATION

All these facts concerning terminated marriages and broken homes clearly give grounds for anxiety, but some points must be entered by way of interpretation as it is all too easy to slip into a completely negative – and, indeed, false – appraisal. The extreme claim is often made (e.g. implied by Robin Blackburn in his 'Brief Guide to

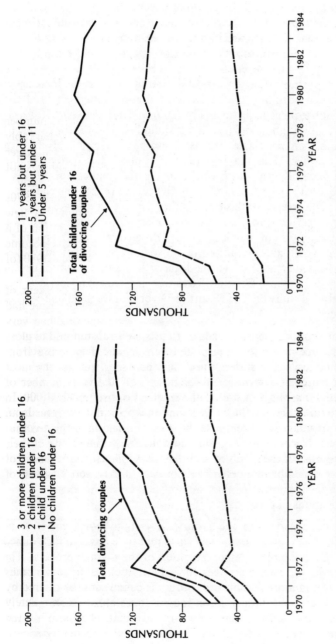

13 Divorcing couples: by number and age of children, 1970–84 (England and Wales)

Source: Office of Population Censuses and Surveys

Bourgeois Ideology', *Student Power*, Penguin Special, 1961, and shared by some of the earlier critics), and is sometimes simply assumed, that the increase in divorces demonstrates a '*rejection of marriage as an institution*' (my italics). It can be said quite firmly, however, that – whatever else is true – *this* is not!

It is important to remember, first, that in so far as the increase in divorce is a corollary of the changed divorce law itself (and the several subsequent adjustments of it), *it is what we want*! If we *do* believe that it is good and just that it should be possible for people to terminate their marriages because these have 'irretrievably broken down', rather than having to rest upon, and prove, some 'matrimonial offence' – with all the adversarial implications of this – then we must expect the number of divorces to reflect this change in the law. The essence of this point is that a *high* divorce rate (i.e. high relative to earlier times) may be a corollary not of a *lower* but of a *higher* conception of marriage. A high divorce rate may be an index of changed collective conditions in our society, but also of our higher standards, expectations, and the legal articulation of our values. A long time ago (1958) Griselda Rowntree and Norman Carrier, after their detailed study of 'The Resort to Divorce in England and Wales', concluded:

> Nothing in our material leads us to predict a substantial fall in the divorce rate in the immediate future ... and if spouses and children are not to suffer unnecessary hardship, it calls for a more complete acceptance of the institution of divorce as a part (whether we like it or not) of the fabric of our social life at all occupational levels. Such a recognition would involve procedural reforms designed to complete the democratization of the divorce process. It would involve, too, more flexible social service provisions for the divorced and their dependants. Reforms of this nature would be more effective, however, if they were based on a much fuller knowledge than we now possess of the social implications of divorce.[3]

This conclusion and the grounds for it do not seem to have changed. The changes in the law since that time have, in fact, aimed at 'the more complete democratization of the divorce process'. The changes in the social services have been such as to make more adequate and more flexible provisions. The many studies of divorce, marriage and the family have sought to establish more reliable knowledge and sounder perspectives of judgment. The essential point here, however, is that all have rested on the recognition of a continued high rate of divorce as part of our society. As Rowntree and Carrier suggest, divorce has been recognised as 'an institution', which is, in fact, the other side of the coin of our improved social actuality of 'the institution of marriage'. If we want high standards of marriage, we must expect – it seems – the corollary of a high rate of divorce. And this, though many will still interpret it as such, is by no means the negative resignation, the defeatism, that it seems.

A second point of interpretation stems from the fact that a very large proportion of divorces are of marriages among the youngest age-groups. Here is at least one identifiable area where (perhaps) some of our chief problems lie. With research, education, and appropriate social action, it is possible that the misery of broken marriages among the young might be minimised. Sir George Baker, when President of the Family Division of the High Court, frequently called for a better *education* and *preparation* for marriage, and this might well be more seriously undertaken. The significance of this is well known and can be seen in the relation between age at marriage and the risk of divorce. In 1985, the official comment accompanying the statistics was:

> Age at marriage is strongly associated with the likelihood of divorce, the chance of marital breakdown generally declining the older the spouses are when they marry. In 1982, 13% of divorces involved couples where the husband was under 20 at marriage, and the corresponding proportion where the wife was under 20 at marriage was 37%. In fact spouses who marry in their teens are almost *twice* as likely to divorce as those who marry between the ages of 20 and 24.[4]

With preparation, and, indeed, with a mere deferring of marriage for a number of years, a substantial proportion of divorce and its problems might be overcome. This seems even more evident, too, when the clear correlation is seen between age at marriage, divorce, and social class. In 1979, for example, the rate of divorce for husbands of all ages in unskilled manual occupations was more than *four* times that of husbands in professional occupations. But in the *younger* age-group – of 20–29 (and relatively few men marry before the age of 20) – it was *five-and-a-half* times higher. It is among these lower income groups that the most severe problems are likely to follow broken homes, so that, again, a simple deferral of marriage might well make a big difference. We must be careful in our judgment even here, however, for these marriages have, at least, fewest dependent children, and at least one writer has referred to such young, quickly ended marriages as a 'married form of "pre-marital" cohabitation', and suggested that they might even stabilize later marriages in which children *are* produced (M. P. M. Richards, *Relating to Marriage*, National Marriage Guidance Council, 1984, p. 167). It must be noted, too, that these young marriages have begun, recently, to decline. But it is a third consideration of interpretation which is the most important.

We noted earlier that there is a *direct relationship* between the rate of *divorce* and the rate of *marriage*. It is *just because* marriage itself is so *popular* – especially among the young, but also among all age-groups – that problems of divorce arise, and it is necessary, now, to look closely at the facts of *marriage* itself.

Meanwhile, it deserves reiteration that though many questions are to be asked about divorce, and though anxiety about it is right and proper, what is *certain* is that the increase in divorce over recent decades has *not* meant a rejection of marriage, and we must consider this point in some detail later.

(ii) Marriage

The first fact to be emphasized is that – if the divorce rate is high – so is the rate of marriage itself. The statement that 'marriage is more popular now than it has ever been before' has become a commonplace in arguments about the statistics, but it is still very largely true. The trends in the total number of marriages, and the proportions of first and second marriages, are shown in Table 14.

This table, too, makes some more specific facts seem clear. The halting of the overall increase, and the steadying of the rate of first marriages, during the 1920s and the early 1930s may well be accounted for by the 'slump' conditions of those years; just as the considerable increase in the rate of first marriages from the 1950s to the 1970s may be explained by the increased 'affluence' of that period and the general extension of opportunities for people in all age-groups. Graph 15 shows that throughout this latter period the general increase in marriages paralleled the increase in divorce, and particularly, too, that marriage was increasing among the younger age-groups (carrying the higher risk of divorce).

To turn back to the table, however, from the mid-1970s three things are noticeable. First, the total number of marriages seemed to be declining, but has recently begun to rise again. (In 1982 the

14 Marriages: 1901–84

	1901	1911	1921	1931	1951	1961	1971	1976	1981	1983	1984
Total (thousands)	291	307	360	344	402	397	459	406	398	389	396
First for both parties	253	272	307	307	329	340	369	282	263	255	259
First for *one* party only	28	25	40	28	51	36	54	70	74	73	74
Second (or later) marriage for *both* parties	10	9	13	10	22	21	36	54	61	61	62

Source: Office of Population Censuses and Surveys

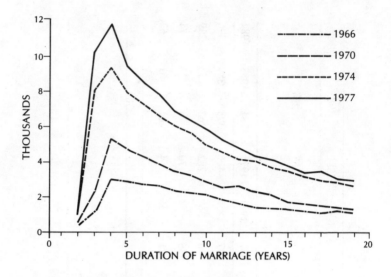

15 Marriages in England and Wales, 1966–77
Data from the Office of Population Censuses and Surveys.

number had fallen to 387,000 but then rose to 389,000 in 1983 and 396,000 in 1984). Second, though a constant reduction in the number of first marriages for both parties seemed to be taking place, even here this seemed to be increasing again in 1984. There is no way, then, in which the facts can be interpreted as a 'flight from marriage' or a 'rejection of marriage'. Marriage has retained, and still retains, its wide popularity. The third very noticeable fact, however, can be seen in the break-down shown in table 16 of the numbers of those marriages which were *second* marriages for either one or both parties.

What becomes clear is that the most conspicuous increase has been that in the rate of *re-marriage* between parties *both* of whom have been divorced. The official comment was:

The *remarriage* rate increased substantially for both men and women between 1961 and 1983, *the major* increase coming in the early 1970s after the Divorce Reform Act 1969 came into force in England and Wales in 1971.... In 1983 nearly 100,000 men remarried in Great Britain, compared with 95,000 women. In 1984 the corresponding figures were 101,000 and 96,000. The difference in rates between the sexes is due mainly to there being more widows and divorced women than widowers and divorced

66

16 Marriages, 1961–84 (United Kingdom thousands and percentages)

	1961	1971	1976	1981	1983	1984
Marriages (thousands)						
First marriage for both partners	340	369	282	263	255	259
First marriage for one partner only						
Bachelor/divorced woman	11	21	30	32	32	32
Bachelor/widow	5	4	4	3	2	2
Spinster/divorced man	12	24	32	36	37	38
Spinster/widower	8	5	4	3	2	2
Second (or later) marriage for both partners						
Both divorced	5	17	34	44	45	46
Both widowed	10	10	10	7	7	6
Divorced man/widow	3	4	5	5	4	5
Divorced woman/widower	3	5	5	5	5	5
Total marriages	397	459	406	398	389	396
Remarriages[1] as a percentage of all marriages	14	20	31	34	35	35
Remarriages[1] of the divorced as a percentage of all marriages	9	15	26	31	32	32

[1] Remarriage for one or both partners.
Source: Office of Population Censuses and Surveys

men, especially among the older section of the population, so the eligible populations are different.[5]

This one fact has several aspects.

It reinforces the interpretation that it is not marriage *itself* which divorced people rejected, but the particular marriage they found intolerable. About three-quarters of them try marriage again – some very quickly. In this, however, the close tie between the statistics of marriage and those of divorce becomes increasingly clear. The great *popularity* of marriage, spreading to men and women in the younger age-groups as their opportunities grew, in itself entailed the higher incidence of divorce – especially in the earlier years of marriage, and made more possible by all the facts we have touched upon earlier: the new attitudes, the extension of legal aid, the changing position of women, the supportive provisions of social security, etc. Strange though it may seem when stated so directly, it is none the less true that *the very popularity of marriage* has been (and is) one large reason for the high incidence of divorce. But – once established and thereafter – the close relationship continues. The high rate of divorce after a short duration of marriage leads to a higher rate of re-marriage. Re-marriages, however, are themselves at greater risk of divorce than are first marriages, and so ... this in turn, increases the rate of divorce.

There is a strange way in which the statistics (and the underlying actualities) of marriage and divorce feed upon each other – each following upon the other's heels. It seems almost as though the big increase did, in fact, take place between 1971 and 1976 – following the new Act – and that the high subsequent rates of both marriages and divorce were sustained through re-marriage and re-divorce. The *certain* thing that emerges, however, is that the facts of both, taken together, give no evidence whatever of an overall *rejection of marriage as an institution* in our society.

It is often said that 1 in 3 marriages in Britain will end in divorce. Even in itself this still means that, within all the changing collective conditions of our time, 66 per cent of our marriages do *not* end in divorce. The great majority of marriages remain firm. But – going beyond this simple statistic – other facts are to be noted.

We have seen that it is the marriages of the younger age-groups which are most at the risk of divorce. One marked fact in recent years, however, is that people have been tending to marry *later* in life. This picture has been clearly shown between 1971 and 1980 (i.e. throughout the 1970s).

17 Median age at marriage: by previous marital status, 1971 and 1980 (Great Britain, years)

	1971				1980			
	Previous marital status of partner				Previous marital status of partner			
Previous marital status	Single	Widowed	Divorced	All	Single	Widowed	Divorced	All
Bridegroom								
Single	23.1	41.4	28.5	23.3	23.6	39.8	28.2	23.9
Widowed	56.0	63.2	55.2	59.9	53.2	65.5	54.6	59.9
Divorced	33.3	49.2	39.4	36.8	32.2	49.8	38.3	35.5
All	23.4	56.9	34.9	24.0	24.2	57.3	34.4	25.6
Bride								
Single	21.2	44.4	25.4	21.4	21.5	40.3	24.5	21.8
Widowed	44.5	59.7	48.5	53.9	43.1	61.4	48.7	55.0
Divorced	29.6	47.1	35.1	32.9	29.8	45.9	43.9	33.1
All	21.4	53.4	30.5	22.0	22.0	54.9	30.9	23.1

Source: Office of Population Censuses and Surveys; General Register Office (Scotland)

But it is interesting to see that the reduction in the number of first marriages since the 1970s has chiefly been among the younger age-groups. During the 1970s, the annual number of spinsters marrying in their teens about *halved*, and since 1981 the continued reductions have been of the order of 9 per cent *or more* in any one year. In 1984, only 1 in 6 spinsters marrying was a teenager. In 1974, the comparable proportion was just over 1 in 3. Even marriage rates for persons aged 20 to 24 were over a third lower in 1980 than in 1971. There seems, therefore, to have been a change and delay in the *timing* of marriage, and this must have a long-term implication for the rate of divorce – probably implying a long-term reduction. But coupled with this there has also been an increase in *cohabitation* (whether as a pre-marital 'experiment', or as a relationship in its own right independent of marriage), and, on the face of it, this does seem an abandonment of marriage on the part of *some*. This, however, presents a complicated picture and needs some detailed consideration because – marriage aside – it has important implications for any appraisal of *the family*.

(iii) Cohabitation

The facts of cohabitation are complicated, knowledge of them is limited, but three things, it seems, can be said.

First, there has been – particularly since 1970 (again following the coming into force of the 1969 Act) – an *increase* in pre-marital cohabitation, and in relation to both first and second marriages (table 18).

This survey shows that, in the case of first marriages, at the end of the 1970s, 18 per cent of women under the age of 50 had lived with their husbands before their wedding. At the beginning of the 1970s, this had been only 6 per cent. In second marriages the increase was larger: 58 per cent having lived with their husbands before marriage – which was more than *double* the proportion of those who had married during the 1960s. This suggests some degree of caution and 'trial marriage' before the full commitment to marriage itself. But in the case of second marriage (though these considerations might still apply) it might to some extent simply mean a matter of waiting until a previous marriage was dissolved and subsequent marriage became possible.

But second, it is clear that cohabitation is chiefly prevalent among those whose earlier marriage has, for whatever reason, been ended.

18 Proportion of women aged 16–49 in 1981 who had lived with their husband before their current or most recent marriage: by first or subsequent marriage, age at marriage, and year of marriage (Great Britain, percentages and numbers)

	Year of marriage					
	1960–4	1965–9	1970–4	1975–6	1977–8	1979–80
First marriage of both partners – age of woman at marriage (percentages)						
16–19	3	3	6	9	21	19
20–24	2	2	6	9	13	15
25–49	7	3	8	⎫ 18 ⎬ (1975–6 to 1979–80 combined) ⎭		
All aged 16–49	3	2	6	10	16	18
Sample size (= 100%) (numbers)						
16–19	263	313	302	101	97	86
20–24	450	480	460	143	158	152
25–49	85	96	145	⎫ 125 ⎬ (1975–6 to 1979–80 combined) ⎭		
All aged 16–49	798	889	907	281	304	277
Second or subsequent marriage for one or both partners						
All aged 16–49 (percentages)	⎫ 26 ⎬ (1960–4 and 1965–9 combined) ⎭		43	71	51	58
Sample size (= 100%) (numbers)	⎫ 120 ⎬ (1960–4 and 1965–9 combined) ⎭		214	97	129	122

Source: General Household Survey, 1981

Table 19 shows that 18 per cent of widowed, divorced or separated women between 18 and 49 were cohabiting in 1980–1 compared with 9 per cent of single women, and this difference was even more marked in the age-group 18 to 24. It is interesting to note, too, that of *all* the non-married women between the ages of 18 and 49, 11 per cent were cohabiting. And third, the trends from the end of the 1970s to now can be seen in terms of *age* alone (table 20). It is interesting to see, here, that there is a decrease in cohabitation in the younger age-group just at the time that *marriage* begins, again, to increase.

But three other facts seem necessary to interpret the overall situation.

(iv) Family size, illegitimacy, adoption

First, the earlier decline in *family size* has continued. During the period from 1961 to 1981, the average *household* size fell from 3.09 to 2.71. One fact giving rise to this has been the fall in the birth-rate since the middle of the 1960s, leading to *smaller families*. In part, at least, this results from more efficient *contraception*, and the general statistical facts have been supported by more limited qualitative studies which

19 Proportion of women aged 18–49 cohabiting[1]: by age and marital status, 1980–1 (Great Britain percentage and numbers)

	Marital status		
	Single	Widowed, divorced, or separated	All single, widowed, divorced, or separated women
Age group			
18–24	7	20	8
25–49	11	17	15
All aged 18–49	9	18	11
Sample size (= 100%) (numbers)			
18–24	1,764	94	1,858
25–49	718	956	1,674
All aged 18–49	2,482	1,050	3,532

[1]Living with a man (other than husband) as his wife.
Source: General Household Survey, combined data for 1980 and 1981.

20 Percentage of women aged 18–49 cohabiting: by age (Great Britain percentages and numbers)

	1979	1980	1981	1982	1983
Age group (percentages)					
18–24	4.5	4.5	5.6	6.1	5.2
25–49	2.2	2.5	2.6	3.2	3.2
All aged 18–49	2.7	2.9	3.3	3.8	3.6
Women in sample (= 100%) (numbers)					
18–24	1,353	1,404	1,517	1,250	1,191
25–49	4,651	4,790	5,007	4,246	4,094
All aged 18–49	6,004	6,194	6,524	5,496	5,285

Source: General Household Survey

demonstrate that people do now have the size of family they *want*. In a survey reporting a five-year follow-up study of 350 couples married in Hull, for example, John Peel revealed the accuracy of birth-control, and concluded quite decidedly that:

> people now have almost complete control over their behaviour in family planning. . . . The results clearly demonstrate that not only attitudes but also actual behaviour can be viewed as rational in the area of family planning . . . couples are now having the families they want rather than making the best of what they get and indulging in subsequent rationalizations about the result.

The overall facts show that cohabitation has not entailed (any more than marriage) larger family groups.

Necessarily, however (i.e. as a matter of sheer definition), there has been an increase in illegitimacy, and with the growth in the proportion of cohabitation and one-parent families, illegitimate births have become a growing proportion of *all* births. The trend from 1961 to 1984 has been as shown in table 21.

What is especially interesting is the last line of figures, but some comments are necessary here – even if rather perplexed and undecided – on the very complicated relationships between contraception, illegitimacy, and abortion, if only because it is in these areas, in particular, that moral judgments arise most hotly and most frequently. The statistics have demonstrated (as we have implied) a continued and consistent use of all methods of contraception over

21 Live births: by legitimacy, 1961–84 (England and Wales)

			Live births (thousands)			
	1961	1971	1976	1981	1983	1984
Legitimate live births to women married once only	746	698	504	515	490	485
Legitimate live births to women in second or later marriage	16	19	27	39	40	41
Total legitimate live births	763	717	531	554	530	526
Total illegitimate live births	48	66	54	81	99	100
As a percentage of total live births	6	8	9	13	16	17
Percentage of illegitimate births registered in joint names	38	45	51	58	61	63
Total live births	811	783	584	634	629	637

Source: Office of Population Censuses and Surveys (simplified table)

the past decade; IUD and oral contraceptives being the methods most widely used, and oral contraceptives being by far the most popular. One important aspect of this which must have had a great effect on sexual relationships is that contraception has plainly passed, to a considerable extent, into the control of the woman – giving her a greater degree (if she so wishes it) of sexual freedom and autonomy – though slight variations seem to have varying effects. A slight reduction in the use of oral contraceptives came about in 1984 after the wide publicity given (late in 1983) to the possibility of health hazards. But this reduction may have had wider influences. The number of vasectomies performed, for example, had previously declined from 20,700 in 1978 to 14,800 in 1982, but in 1984 this increased again to 17,100. Was there some slight switch then towards male responsibility? Similarly, in 1984 there was a marked increase in abortion – clearly shown in table 22 – among the age-groups in which abortion predominantly occurs.

But a few specific points seem important – chiefly to indicate the complex nature of the situation.

First, it will be noticed that the number of abortions among *married* women, especially those with children – and with moderately sized to larger families – has gone *down*. Presumably, here, more efficient contraception has displaced abortion. The number among widowed, divorced and separated women has gone *up*, but not greatly. The great increase has been among single (never married) women – this proportion increased from 46 per cent in 1971 to 60 per cent in 1981 – the largest number being among *childless* women. One's immediate assumption is that a large proportion of this number represents the termination of *first*, accidental conceptions. Over a *quarter* of abortions in 1984 were carried out on girls under the age of 20. This suggests a lack of knowledge about contraception, or carelessness in its use, or the sheer falling into mistakes, but – given the wide availability of contraceptives, and the much wider knowledge of them and their use, coupled with the (evidently) general accuracy in their use – the relationships between contraception, abortion, and illegitimacy are by no means clear, and other factors complicate the matter. For example, the number of conceptions outside marriage in *Great Britain* during the ten years from 1971 to 1981 rose by some 47,000, but – said the official statistician – this reflected 'an increase of about a quarter in the population of single women aged 14 to 44 rather than an increase in the *rates* of extra-marital conception.' Clearly, the gross facts cannot be taken at what *seems* their face value. Also, the proportion of

22 Legal abortions[1], 1969–84 (Great Britain, thousands and percentages)

				Women resident in Great Britain					
	1969	1971	1973	1976	1980	1981	1982	1983	1984
Age of women (thousands)									
Under 16 years	1	2	3	4	4	4	4	4	4
16 to 19 years	9	19	25	26	34	34	34	33	36
20 to 34 years	32	60	68	61	79	80	79	79	86
35 to 44 years	10	17	19	16	19	19	19	18	19
45 years and over	–	1	1	–	1	1	1	–	–
Age unknown	1	2	2	2	–	1	–	–	–
Place of abortion (thousands)									
NHS hospitals	37	60	63	58	68	70	71	71	74
Private hospitals and clinics	16	41	55	51	69	68	66	65	72
Total number of abortions (thousands)	53	101	118	109	137	138	137	136	146
Marital status and number of previous children (percentages)									
Single women									
No children	40	42	42	44	47	46	47	49	50
One or more children	4	4	5	5	6	6	7	8	8
Total	44	46	48	50	54	54	56	58	60

22 (*cont.*) Legal abortions[1], 1969–84 (Great Britain, thousands and percentages)

					Women resident in Great Britain				
	1969	1971	1973	1976	1980	1981	1982	1983	1984
Married women									
No children	3	3	3	4	4	4	4	4	4
One to three children	29	30	30	29	26	25	24	23	22
Four or more children	14	11	9	6	4	4	3	3	2
Total	47	45	42	39	34	33	31	30	28
Widowed, divorced, and separated women	9	9	10	11	12	13	13	12	12
Total	100	100	100	100	100	100	100	100	100

[1]Legal abortions carried out under the Abortion Act 1967.
Source: Office of Population Censuses and Surveys; Scottish Health Service, Common Service Agency

legitimate births conceived before marriage *fell* from 38 per cent in 1971 to 20 per cent in 1981, whilst, over the same period, the proportion ending in abortion *rose* from 26 per cent to 43 per cent. On the face of it, women were increasingly choosing to avoid *both* the births they did not want *and* the pressured marriages they did not want. This was particularly marked among teenage girls. In *England and Wales* in 1972, the proportion of legitimate births conceived before marriage was 27 per cent; in 1982 this had fallen to 14 per cent. In 1972, 21 per cent of teenage conceptions ended in abortion, in 1982 this had risen to 32 per cent. These facts do seem to imply that abortion itself has increasingly been used as a method of birth control – especially among women in the 16–34 age-groups – and it may be significant that the number of abortions carried out in private hospitals and clinics has very considerably increased. In 1969, a good deal fewer than *half* of the total abortions were carried out in private establishments, by far the greater number being carried out in NHS hospitals. By 1984, the proportion had become about *equal*, and in both cases with a very much larger number. Yet we are told about the 'category' of abortion: 'The reason given for a legal abortion is usually "risk of injury to physical or mental health" of the woman', and that this accounted for almost 90 per cent (89 per cent) of all the cases in England and Wales in 1984. (Only a small proportion was due to a substantial risk of the *child* being born abnormal.)

But these trends in legitimate births conceived before marriage, and in abortion, must be seen, too, in relation to the trends in *illegitimacy*. Illegitimacy too, as we have already noted, has increased. The proportion of conceptions ending in illegitimate births was 19 per cent in 1972 and had become 33 per cent in 1982. The official comment was: 'This rise reflects both the greater number of cohabiting couples in 1982 and also the rise in one-parent families since 1972.' Given the decline in legitimate births conceived before marriage and the increase in the number of abortions, coupled with the comment above ... this suggests, perhaps strangely, that illegitimate births are increasingly wanted (i.e. that many women who conceive before marriage are deciding neither to legitimate the births by marriage nor terminate the conception by abortion, but to have, keep, and care for their child), and, furthermore, that illegitimate children may increasingly be being born into *families*. We shall come back to this point in a moment, but for now it is enough to see that the connections between all these facts are extremely difficult to see and disentangle. Some interpretations, however, do seem plausible.

(1) There seems to be no clear and easy-to-establish connection between the readiness to practice contraception and illegitimacy. (2) Among young unmarried women particularly, there seems to be a greater readiness to turn to abortion as a method of preventing unwanted births. This suggests (3) a diminished readiness either to have an unwanted child or to be pressed into marriage by an unwanted pre-marital conception. (4) At the same time there has been an increase in illegitimacy coupled with a greater readiness and ability to keep and care for the child. The question arises whether illegitimacy has not become increasingly deliberate (i.e. deliberately preferred to the other choices); whether, indeed, the very nature of illegitimacy may not in large measure have changed? And it is here that the last line of figures in table 21 (showing the trend in illegitimate births) can be seen to be of particular interest.

What is quite clear is that a large and growing proportion of the parents of illegitimate children are registering the births in their joint names. This suggests at least two things: first, that the stigma of illegitimacy is – in social and moral fact – diminishing (whether or not it is so in the law), and is no longer of any great concern to parents. Second, however, and more important, that the parents of illegitimate children are deliberately (and jointly) acknowledging their parenthood and accepting responsibility for them – suggesting that their relationships of cohabitation possess some degree of stability and permanence; suggesting, in short, that these illegitimate children are being born into *families* even though these have not been founded through the formal institution of conventional marriage. (The official comment is even broader than this, saying: 'that although a single woman who becomes pregnant may not get married before the birth of her child, she might nevertheless *maintain a stable relationship with the father outside marriage*' (my italics). Such stable relationships could, of course, not necessarily involve *cohabitation*. And this does, in fact, seem to be borne out by the further fact that fewer illegitimate children are being put forward for *adoption*: mothers clearly, now, being more prepared to keep them and care for them themselves. The trend from 1970 to 1982 can be seen in chart 23. The slight up-turn shown in 1981 has since returned to the prevailing downward trend as shown in the 1984 position (Chart 24), together with the chart's accompanying comment:

The number of adoptions in Great Britain has fluctuated recently: 11,000 in 1981, 12,000 in 1982, falling to 10,000 in 1983, and 9,000 in 1984, thereby resuming the downward trend of the

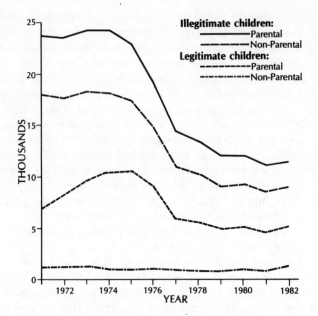

Illegitimate children:
———— Parental
———— Non-Parental
Legitimate children:
------- Parental
--·--·-- Non-Parental

23 Annual number of adoptions, 1972–82 (Great Britain thousands)
Source: Office of Population Censuses and Surveys; General Register Office (Scotland)

last decade; the number is now less that half the 1971 total of 23,000. This trend contrasts with the increase in illegitimate births over the same period, and it could be that lone parents have become more willing and able to support their children themselves rather than have them adopted; in an increasing proportion of cases both parents are actually involved in caring for the child even though they are not formally married (for over *three-fifths* of illegitimate births, both parents now register the births).[6]

This comment and its detailed implications are highly significant, and all these facts pertaining to cohabitation, coupled with all those we have noted concerning marriage and divorce, now lead to what is perhaps the most central and important point of all. They lead us to consider the facts about the family, and to ask the simple question: whether – perhaps surprisingly – it might not be the case that the much publicized statistics about marriage and divorce (about

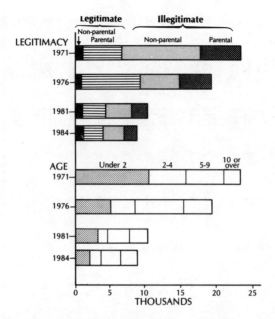

24 Annual number of adoptions, 1971–84 (Great Britain)
Source: Office of Population Censuses and Surveys; General Register Office (Scotland)

marriage breakdown) have been such as to be actually misleading with regard to the condition of the family in Britain?

(v) The family

Stated quite baldly, the crucial point is that however much the facts about marriage, divorce and cohabitation may seem (to some) to suggest a lessening concern for marriage, there is no doubt whatever that *the family* is not only what the great majority of the people of Britain actively *want*, it is also what, in fact, they actually *have*. The truth is that the vast majority of the people in Britain do actually live in 'nuclear' families within private households. The wide publicity given to the incidence of marital breakdown has become a distorting smoke-screen hiding the underlying fact that the nuclear family is the firm, desired, and actual experience of by far the greater part of the population. If we consider some of the facts about families, we shall see that this one point has some curious twists and turns.

81

25 Households: by type (Great Britain percentages and thousands)

	Percentages						Thousands		
	1961	1966	1971	1976	1980	1981	1961	1966	1971
No family									
One person									
Under retirement age[1]	4	5	6	6	8	7	726	890	1,122
Over retirement age[1]	7	10	12	15	14	15	1,193	1,682	2,198
Two or more people									
One or more over retirement age[1]	3	3	2	2	1	2	536	463	444
All under retirement age[1]	2	2	2	1	1	2	268	251	304
One family									
Married couple only	26	26	27	27	27	26	4,147	4,377	4,890
Married couple with 1 or 2 dependent children	30	27	26	26	26	26	4,835	4,602	4,723
Married couple with 3 or more dependent children	8	9	9	8	6	6	1,282	1,452	1,582
Married couple with independent child(ren) only	10	10	8	7	8	8	1,673	1,746	1,565
Lone parent with at least one dependent children	2	2	3	4	4	4	367	400	515
Lone parent with independent child(ren) only	4	4	4	4	4	4	721	755	712
Two or more families	3	2	1	1	1	1	439	317	263
	100	100	100	100	100	100	16,189	16,937	18,317

[1] 60 and over for women, 65 and over for men.
Source: Office of Population Censuses and Surveys

As to the nature of present-day 'nuclear' families themselves, and the effects marital breakdown might have had upon them, we will consider, in a moment, direct evidence other than that of a purely statistical kind. But let us think, for the present, about the overall facts concerning the households of Britain – including those of one-parent families and cohabiting couples (and bearing in mind the emphasis of the Rights for Women Group and some Womens' Lib views on 'extended families', 'collectives', and 'communes'). Table 25 shows the distribution of types of households between 1961 and 1981.

It will be seen that in households where there is *no* family, the greatest proportion consists of lonely people over retirement age, and any growth in this proportion is accounted for by (a) larger numbers surviving into old age as widows and widowers, and (b) to a very much lesser extent, to more young people living on their own. The number of households of a lone parent with dependent children doubled during the 20 years – but was still only 4 per cent (becoming 5 per cent in 1983), and it was *this* category which chiefly reflected the growth in divorce, the larger number of illegitimate births, and the fact that fewer such children were put forward for adoption. No fewer than 76 per cent of households, however, are of married couples with or without their children, and those without children are chiefly older couples whose children have left home. When, in addition, the actual number of *people* are taken into account, the picture given of people living in families is even more convincing. In 1981, for example, approximately 80 per cent of the people of Britain lived in households consisting of a married couple with or without children (20 per cent of these being married couples alone, 60 per cent being couples with their children.) The picture from 1961 to 1983 is shown in chart 26.

The family, then, as the stable domestic group within a private household is the widely prevailing experience of the great majority of people in modern British society; and if this seems astonishing, it is no less astonishing that the much emphasized and publicized statistics of marital breakdown should have been allowed to spread so false a picture as that of a decline of the family in Britain.

But other interesting aspects of this lead us back to what I said earlier about the spread of 'half-baked' conceptions of marriage on the part of some, and to the distinction which seems necessary between *marriage* and *the wedding*. Consider these facts.

When people (mistakenly) claim the status of 'common law wife' or 'husband'; when they claim the right to the same treatment from society as those who are married (in their rights of parenthood,

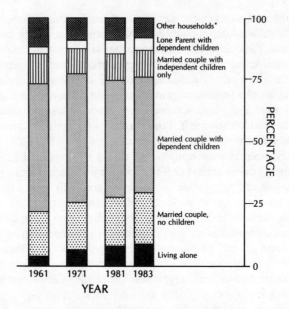

26 People in households: by type of household and family in which they live
(Great Britain percentage)*

*The official explanatory note to the table is: '"Other households" include:
households containing two or more unrelated people; households with more than one
family; and lone parents with independent children only, which would include people
caring for an elderly dependent parent. The chart excludes people not living in private
households such as those in hotels, schools, hospitals, and other institutions, or
camping or sleeping rough. This group numbered 1.4 million persons in Great Britain,
or 2½% of the population, on census night in 1981.'

Source: Office of Population Censuses and Surveys

treatment of joint property, etc., etc.); when, though not marrying,
they jointly register their children's births and assume responsibility
for them, whilst at the same time deriding marriage as being 'only a
piece of paper' ... what, really, are they doing? Why should they
want to use the expressions 'common law *wife*' or '*husband*' at all?
They are, in fact, insisting on what they take to be the essential
nature of a marital relationship for themselves. They are, in fact,
referring in their disputes and claims to the law pertaining to
marriage, insisting that this law should apply also to them. They are,
in fact, in wanting the same treatment in such reciprocal claims,
conceding that marriage as an institution contains within its nature

and provisions the essential and reasonable ingredients for regulating a committed relationship of cohabitation and parental relationships. Their dismissal of marriage as being 'only a piece of paper' is no more than a mistaken identification of marriage with the public wedding and the mere form of its registration. They have a misguided impatience with the formal procedures, thinking them not essential. But in insisting on their natural or common law rights as cohabiting partners and parents, they are doing so, none the less, in relation to the reciprocal claims it is right and justifiable that they should make on each other, and, in particular, with regard to the care of their children. We shall come back, later, to consider the full conception of marriage, of which the ceremony of 'solemnization' and public registration are the institutional forms, but, for the present, it is enough to see that this misconception of marriage, and the ignoring of it on the part of some, in no way invalidates the importance of the family as a unit of social life, as the primary domestic group in society, for the great majority of people.

The actuality of the matter is that most of the people of Britain still

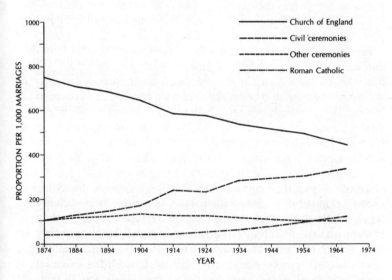

27 Manner of solemnization per 1,000 marriages at ten-year intervals: England and Wales*

*Source: *Britain in Figures*, Penguin Books, 1971; Church Information Office, *Facts and Figures About the Church of England*, No. 3; Registrar General's *Statistical Review*, 1967.

live in families. Family life, the 'nuclear' family, in a household giving them their own family privacy, is what they both want and have. It is only that – for themselves – *some* (though relatively few) believe that the public celebration and registration of their partnership is of no consequence; though this, clearly, is mistaking the procedural forms for the human actuality. And it is interesting to wonder how far this impatience with apparently religious forms and traditional proprieties might be only a more extreme extension of the general *secularization* of marriage which has certainly been a marked fact of our time. Graph 27 shows this very plainly.

The large and consistent increase in *civil* marriage (in the solemnization of marriage in the register office) is clear, as is the equally large decline in marriage according to the rites of the Church of England. A similar, but smaller, decline has taken place among other denominations and the Jews. Only marriages in the Roman Catholic Church have increased, but even here a decline seems evident in recent years. The detailed facts for each denomination can be seen in table 28.[7]

This may signify many things in terms of a widespread decline in religious beliefs and membership of the various religious bodies, but among all these things one is certain. Without suggesting at all that marriage has been reduced to the bare level of a 'contract' – commensurate with other kinds of civil contract (it is more than this, and many of those without religious convictions can believe so) – it must be the case that, in the minds of an increasing number of people, it has ceased to be regarded as a *sacrament*, and is conceived, instead, as a voluntary union between a man and a woman of a purely human, civil, secular nature. As in many other areas of social thought and behaviour, there has unquestionably been a growing secularization of marriage. It is difficult to know what (if anything) this signifies in terms of the quality of family life which follows. In December 1985 the report of the Registrar General for Scotland showed that the divorce rate for couples marrying by civil ceremony was more than double that for church marriages. On the other hand, though one might suppose that a sacramental union (entered into before, and involving, God) would hold dimensions of a kind deeper than those of a purely human commitment, in the late 1970s a report by a Catholic working party set up by the Canon Law Society of Great Britain and Ireland expressed its concern over their finding that the average duration of marriages involving a Roman Catholic was shorter than the national average. 'The old attitudes have gone,' was the report's comment. 'The beliefs, and the sanctions which

28 Marriages by manner of solemnization, 1844 to 1967, England and Wales

Year	Civil marriages per 1,000 total marriages	Church of England and Church in Wales	Roman Catholic	Marriages according to the rites of denominations shown per 1,000 marriages with religious ceremonies						
				All	Other denominations					Jews
					Methodists	Congregationalists	Baptists	Others		
1844	26	932	18	49	–	–	–	–		1
1864	81	851	52	95	–	–	–	–		2
1884	131	813	49	134	–	–	–	–		3
1904	179	782	49	160	–	–	–	–		9
1919	231	776	67	150	73	30	25	21		7
1924	238	759	72	160	79	32	26	22		9
1929	257	756	80	154	76	31	25	23		9
1934	284	747	91	153	73	30	25	25		9
1952	306	714	136	142	69	29	22	22		8
1957	280	689	160	145	69	27	24	26		7
1962	296	673	175	145	69	26	24	25		6
1967	341	681	170	143	69	26	22	26		6

accompanied the beliefs, have dwindled.' Even the fact of the increase in the Roman Catholic solemnization of marriages, then, may reflect more of a certain forcefulness of custom and habit, or of family and social pressures among the members of that church, than of spiritual conviction. Secularization may well have crept into experience and behaviour even there (as, indeed, seems to be the case in connection with the practice of artificial contraception among Roman Catholics). The present-day rift over the growing demand for divorce in Ireland seems indicative of the same tendency.

It cannot be assumed at all, however, that the movement towards civil marriage signifies *irresponsibility*, even if a more extreme impatience with the form of some social institutions has come in its train. It may, on the contrary, reflect a growing insistence on integrity in not pretending religious belief when it is not there, in refusing to observe the ritual when its words have become meaningless, and the question arises whether the statistical facts, as such, can make any useful revelations at all about the *qualitative factors* involved in marital breakdown, divorce, and their consequences. We have already touched on some suggestions arising from the statistics – the changes reflecting changes in the law itself (to which could be added the changing provisions of legal aid), the changing position of women (wives), the curious relationship between marriage, divorce, re-marriage and re-divorce, changes in the age of majority and in the conditions, affluence and opportunities of the young, and – perhaps – a changed and secularized conception of marriage itself – but do the facts throw up any other such suggestions?

(vi) Factors in divorce?

The facts, as such, cannot be expected to reveal much. The weight we give them is always likely to reflect our own desired interpretation. Even so, some do seem to stand up like pointing fingers. Some suggestions are deliberately mentioned in the course of presentation of the official statistics (i.e. by way of carefully guarded comment), and some facts, in themselves, do seem to be irresistible as statistical *indicators* pointing to specific areas as being the probable sources of qualitative *causes* of noticeable trends and problems.

At least one author, for example, has raised the question of the relevance of war. In an article exploring the effects in the experience of children of the facts of 'Separation, Divorce and Remarriage', Dr Richards writes:

> Given the clear links between marriage, divorce and war in 1914–1918 and 1939–45, it is interesting to speculate how present wars and the nuclear balance of terror influence attitudes and actions. There is some evidence that fears concerning nuclear warfare are highly significant for young people in at least some European countries, and it seems unlikely that the growing conflict about policies for nuclear weapons and the increasing involvement of young people in the related political action will not have repercussions in family life.[8]

I placed much emphasis on this earlier, and shall come back to it later as I believe that the continuity and growth in scale of *war* throughout our century possess a far greater significance than has yet been understood or conceded. Despite Leslie Weatherhead's almost unbelievable judgment mentioned in our earlier pages (p. 43), perhaps it is 'nuclear war' far more than the 'nuclear family' which threatens the order and quality of our human life. But ... there are more specific, more limited factors than this.

It has become clear during recent years that marriage breakdown has at least some correlation with *social class* generally, and, within this context, with particular kinds of *occupations*. Table 29 shows that the numbers of divorces per thousand among all husbands aged 16 to 59 was four times greater for men in unskilled manual occupations than for those in professional occupations, and that this difference was even greater for the 20 to 29 age-group. Indeed, it will be seen that by far the greater number of divorces come from *all* the manual grades of occupation taken together.

Closely related to this must be the fact that earlier ages at marriage are found among the lower social classes, and that divorce is more probable with earlier age. What is even more evident, however (though this same qualification would still apply) is that the rate of divorce is (over-all) more than *all* of these among the *unemployed*. This is similar to the unskilled manual grade in the first two age-groups specified, but it is interesting to see that it is considerably higher among men aged between 50 and 59.

A number of more specific factors are probably embedded in these gross facts. These are difficult to disentangle, but the facts themselves do seem to lead to certain suggestions.

The unskilled level of occupations and the condition of being unemployed clearly, alike, suggest low levels of status and of self-

29 Divorce rates[1]: by age and social class of husband, 1979 (England and Wales, rates)

	Age of husband at divorce				
	20–29	30–39	40–49	50–59	All aged 16–59[2]
Social class of husband					
Professional	10	10	7	4	7
Intermediate	17	17	11	5	12
Skilled non-manual	19	20	15	10	16
Skilled manual	23	18	11	5	14
Semi-skilled manual	22	23	15	6	15
Unskilled manual	55	37	25	9	30
Unemployed husband	43	36	28	23	34
All husbands[3]	23	19	12	6	15

[1]Divorces per thousand husbands in each age group, based on a representative national sample of 2,164 divorces in 1979.
[2]A few husbands in the sample were aged under 20 at divorce, insufficient to derive reliable estimates of divorce rates.
[3]Based on all divorces in England & Wales in 1979.
[4]Estimate not made because rate based on fewer than 10 divorces.
Source: 'Social class and socio-economic differentials in divorce in England and Wales', John Haskey, Population Studies, 38

esteem – among both the men themselves (of themselves) in a highly competitive and status-conscious society, and among their wives in their estimation of their husbands. Coupled with this may well be (though not necessarily among some of the unskilled) a relatively low level of income, a low level of future prospects and a limited level of material life possible on this basis – contrasted with the awareness of ever increasing affluence and ever improving prospects of other sectors of the community, and the attractive range of consumers' goods and activities available for the better-off perpetually flaunted before their eyes by television advertising. The gap between what is available and what is possible is bound to be great, and sometimes hopelessly great. These factors are almost bound to be coupled, too, with the new position and expectations of women mentioned earlier: of wives who may no longer be prepared to accept indefinitely limited and low-level standards. Bearing in mind the large increase in the number of petitions filed by wives, and the fact that the chief reason given for their marital breakdown is 'unreasonable

30 Divorce: by age of wife at marriage, 1961–84 (Great Britain percentages and numbers)

	Age of wife at marriage							All divorces (= 100%) (numbers)
	Under 20	20–24	25–29	30–34	35–39	40–44	45 or over	
Year of divorce (percentages)								
1961	31.8	46.2	13.4	4.5	1.9	1.0	1.1	27,018
1971	37.9	45.3	10.0	3.2	1.6	0.8	1.1	78,922
1976	39.0	44.3	9.5	3.3	1.6	0.9	1.4	134,823
1981	37.7	43.2	10.4	3.9	2.1	1.2	1.6	155,608
1983	36.0	42.9	10.9	4.7	2.3	1.4	1.7	160,717
1984	34.8	43.3	11.4	4.8	2.5	1.4	1.7	156,416

Source: Office of Population Censuses and Surveys

behaviour,' the ages at which women marry and divorce seem significant. Table 30 shows that the greater number of divorced women married before their mid-twenties.

May there be a close connection, then, between low status, low income, low self-esteem and low esteem of one's spouse, on the one hand – and inflated, even inflammatory, expectations on the other? It is interesting to note, too, that in 1984 just over half the divorces were to men aged between 20 and 29 (and comparatively few men marry before the age of 20). Does one large possible explanation lie in the fact that a large proportion of the population – which is relatively youthful – is condemned to the experience of low status, a limited standard of life, poor, insecure and perhaps hopeless prospects – but is continually bombarded and titillated by advertisements leading to relatively lavish and unsettling expectations? And might this be a connection between social facts and influences which is growing in size and extent (with unemployment) throughout all the industrialised nations?

All of these factors, obviously, would be exaggerated in the experience of unemployment, and this seems particularly apparent in the relatively high figure for men between 50 and 59. Here – redundancy, perhaps a part-dependency on his wife, and little hope of future employment, will transform the situation and self-esteem of a man: not only reducing the status he has known in his occupation and in the community, and his economic effectiveness in supporting his family, but also stripping from him every contextual element of personal and social standing to which, over a long working family life, he has come to attach meaning, significance, dignity. It is noticeable here, too, that there is a particularly high rate among the *skilled* non-manual – where the loss of status might be supposed to be the more extreme, and felt more extremely. The world and society are no longer the same for such a man. He is a changed man. And perhaps, within this new context, his marriage, too, is changed and rendered more vulnerable.

It seems highly probable, too, that it is among the lower social strata that the many other features of economic, social, and cultural deprivation lie. It may be that not all unskilled occupations, nowadays, are marked by low wages, but, even so, it is here that cultural levels are likely to be most limited, and – especially after marital breakdown – where there are likely to be poorer housing, poorer neighbourhood conditions, greater economic difficulties of debt and insecurity, greater intensities of deteriorating personal relationships. (To this must be added the fact that a large proportion of those marriages broken and divided by 'separation', rather than by divorce, are also from families, and leave behind families, in very straitened circumstances.) These are the areas of problems, in short, where the 'problem families' are likely to be located: where the baby-battering, the wife-beating, the violence between step-parents and children not their own, are likely to occur; where children are more likely to be 'in care'; where social workers with unmanageable 'case-loads' are most likely to be in evidence.

But these facts have recently received an even more detailed (though as yet inconclusive) analysis. Within these levels of social class and income-groups, differences have been thrown up between specific kinds of occupations. This has been studied particularly by J. Haskey, and table 31 is one of his tables showing the crude divorce rates and his more sophisticated measure – the 'Age-Standardized Divorce Ratio' (SDR).

It is impossible to say what factors in each occupation lead to the differences in marriage breakdown, but one particular conclusion seems both clear and important. It is that though we can correctly speak of a general form of the family in Britain – that shaped by the many reforms and legislative and social changes – we should, within this over-all context, place a much sharper emphasis upon families in Britain. There may, in short, be differing types of family in society, each possessing its own significantly different collective conditions. Perhaps the particular conditions, the stresses and strains, of each occupation pose different situations for the particular type of family whose livelihood and style of life is based upon it, and the causes of family breakdown might well lie in the different conditions in each case. In literary, artistic and sports occupations, in 'Selling', in personal services occupations, for example, it may be that a wide range of personal contacts is continually being made and experienced, in freer, varying, more personally manageable conditions of work, whereas in processing, painting, repetitive assembly (and the like) there may be no range of contacts, and conditions of work may be completely unchanging and restricted. The many unskilled, labouring occupations may impose similar restrictions and limitation, but here there may also be the dissatisfactions of never-to-change low income, prospects, status, and personal level of esteem.

When all these facts are drawn together, and considered in relation to the fact (as we have seen) that the great growth in divorces has

31 Number of divorces, median age at divorce of husband and standardized divorce ratio, SDR, by occupation order of husband

Occupation order of husband	Number of divorces	Estimated median age of husband at divorce	Crude divorce rate* per thousand married men	SDR*
(1) Professional and related supporting management; senior national and local government managers	68	35	9	59
(2) Professional and related in education, welfare and health	71	36	11	77
(3) Literary, artistic and sports	30	32	28	174
(4) Professional and related in science, engineering, technology and similar fields	77	33	10	64
(5) Managerial occupations	189	38	12	89
(6) Clerical and related occupations	87	37	11	79
(7) Selling occupations	101	35	21	135
(8) Security and protective service occupations	80	33	25	156
(9) Catering, cleaning, hairdressing and other personal service occupations	74	35	24	177
(10) Farming, fishing and related occupations	25	36	15	100
(11) Materials processing; making and repairing (excluding metal and electrical)	133	32	14	92

31 (*cont.*) Number of divorces, median age at divorce of husband and standardized divorce ratio, SDR, by occupation order of husband

Occupation order of husband	Number of divorces	Estimated median age of husband at divorce	Crude divorce rate* per thousand married men	SDR*
(12) Processing, making, repairing and related (metal and electrical)	340	33	13	90
(13) Painting, repetitive assembling, product inspecting, packaging and related occupations	47	36	9	68
(14) Construction, mining and related occupations, not identified elsewhere	107	34	16	105
(15) Transport operating, materials moving and storing and related occupations	231	34	17	115
(16) Miscellaneous occupations (foremen, labourers & unskilled workers not elsewhere classified)	135	33	46	338
(17) Inadequately described occupations and not economically active	369	34	—	—
All occupation orders (sample)	2164	32	15	100
(All occupation orders (E & W)†	138706	34	15	100))

†Based on all divorces in England and Wales in 1979.
Source: 'Social Class and Socio-economic Differentials in Divorce in England and Wales', *Population Studies*, 38 (1984), pp. 419–38

stemmed from wives on the ground of 'unreasonable behaviour', a certain coherence seems to lie behind the several figures. But the one conclusion is certain: that, in future, we should begin to think more precisely (especially where research and causal explanations are concerned) not of *the family* in Britain but of *families* in Britain. If, to this consideration, is added the obvious cultural diversity of the family-types of immigrant groups, its forcefulness becomes even more clear. In seeking an understanding of marriages, marital breakdown, and the problems facing families, we should now be considering *different kinds of family in their differing kinds of community conditions* – and this consideration leads directly to one kind of family which has increasingly figured in the statistics and which has raised questions about the growth (or otherwise) of casual attitudes and irresponsibility. What are the facts about 'single-parent families'? – and what do they suggest?

(vii) Single-parent families

The growth in the proportion of single-parent families throughout the ten years to 1981 can be seen in table 32 from the 1981 General Household Survey. The over-all proportion clearly increased during the period, the chief increase being in the number headed by single women and divorced women.

The household circumstances of single-parent families – brought a little further up to date – can be seen in the comparison between 1973 and 1983 given in table 33.

In general there has been a trend for all categories of women to live increasingly alone with their children, rather than with their parents or relatives – something which most probably reflects changes in both attitudes and circumstances; but again the chief increases are those in the number of single parents and divorced parents living alone, though the proportion of divorced parents living alone with their children is considerably greater. The comment in *Social Trends* (1986) is that:

> of all one-parent families with dependent children in Great Britain, 38% were headed by a divorced mother, a proportion which had risen from 27% since 1973–75. Of these divorced women 84% lived with their children only, compared with 56% of all single mothers. Single (that is never-married) mothers were more likely to be living

32 Family types: with marital status of lone mothers, 1971–81

Families with dependent children*

Family type	1971–73	1973–75	1975–77	1977–79	Great Britain 1979–81
	%	%	%	%	%
Married couple[+]	91.8	90.7	89.8	88.9	88.1
Lone mother	7.1	8.0	8.8	9.7	10.4
single	1.2	1.3	1.5	1.7	2.2
widowed	1.8	1.9	2.0	1.9	1.7
divorced	1.9	2.5	3.2	3.8	4.1
separated	2.1	2.2	2.1	2.3	2.4
Lone father	1.2	1.3	1.3	1.3	1.5
Base = 100%	1405	13655	13972	13178	12984

*Persons aged under 16, or aged 16–18 and in full-time education, in the family unit and living in the household.
[+]Including married women whose husbands were not defined as resident in the household.
Source: General Household Survey 1981

33 One-parent families: by household composition[1], 1973–5/1981–3 (Great Britain, percentages and numbers)

| | Marital status of lone mothers | | | | | | | | | | | | All lone fathers | | All one-parent families | |
| | Single | | Widowed | | Divorced | | Separated | | All lone mothers | | | | | | | |
Household composition	1973 –75	1981 –83	1973 –75	1981 –83	1973 –75	1981 –83	1973 –75	1981 –83	1973 –75	1981 –83	1973 –75	1981 –83	1973 –75	1981 –83	1973 –75	1981 –83
Living alone	36	56	88	88	74	84	78	80	72	77			70	82	72	78
Living with parents	49	32	7	3	15	5	13	8	18	11			11	8	17	11
Living with relatives	7	5	4	7	4	3	3	4	4	4			8	3	5	4
Living with non-relatives																
Male	7	4	2	3	7	7	5	5	5	5			1	2	5	5
Female	1	2	0	0	—	2	1	3	—	2			10	5	2	2
Sample size (= 100%) (numbers)	182	298	256	196	350	579	302	287	1,090	1,359			183	165	1,273	1,524

[1]Based on relationship of lone parent to other family heads.
Source: General Household Survey, combined data for 1973–5 inclusive, and 1981–3 inclusive.

with their own parents or other relatives, while widowed mothers were the most likely to be living with just their children. The proportion of one-parent families headed by a father declined from 14% in 1973–75 to 11% in 1981–83.[9]

It is interesting to note that the slight increase shown in table 32 in the number of one-parent families headed by a *father* was later reversed.

Of all one-parent families, 55 per cent have dependent children, but this figure can be broken down a little: 98 per cent headed by a parent under the age of 30 have dependent children; 88 per cent headed by a parent aged between 30 and 44; and 32 per cent headed by a parent aged between 45 and 64. Roughly half of all one-parent families are headed by either a divorced or a separated mother, and it deserves note that about three-quarters of all lone-parents live alone with their dependent children – though this ranges from about 90 per cent for widowed mothers to only 56 per cent for single mothers. But most other single mothers live with their own parents in a three-generation household. In all cases, then, there seems to be no general demonstration of any abandonment of child-care, and the official comment is: 'about half the people who get divorced in any one year remarry within five years – so many lone-parent families will not remain as such for long.' If we take into account the pattern of cohabitation, too, it may well be that families will soon exist though marriage has ceased, before re-marriage takes place, and even if re-marriage never takes place. But it is here, of course – as in broken homes among the unskilled and unemployed – that conditions of poverty and stress, domestic conflict, violence, child abuse, and all the many evils known to social workers are more likely to arise – from the jealousy of subsequent step-mothers or -fathers, or from 'common law husbands' or wives.

These, then, baldly stated, are the chief statistical facts indicating the trends in marriage, the family, and family breakdown since 1971, and it seems possible, now, to set out a clear summary statement of the main points which have emerged.

Summary conclusions

(1) The coming into force of the 1969 Act in 1971 was, in fact, immediately followed by the large increase in the number of divorces which had been expected, and this, as we have seen, was *not* an increase in marriage breakdowns but the remedying of a long-standing and

unsatisfactory situation – making possible the regularization of many illicit unions. However, a high rate of divorce continued after that time (no doubt variably affected by the changing provisions of legal aid) but has seemed now, since the end of the 1970s, to have reached a plateau. It is almost as though the period of the 1970s was the decade of a slowly worked-through re-adjustment to the new law which had marked its beginning.

(2) This increase did not, however – and obviously – constitute a 'flight from marriage'. The rate of marriage itself (including that of re-marriage) also continued to be very high, and even the rate of first marriages (which seemed to be declining) has again, over recent years, begun to increase.

(3) Since 1971, too, the rates of *both* marriage *and* divorce have been closely related to each other in such a way as mutually to sustain their high levels. The high rate of marriage (especially – for a long time – among the young) has meant a high rate of divorce. The high rate of divorce (given the continued popularity of marriage) has meant a high and increasing rate of re-marriage. The higher rate of re-marriage (re-marriage being more at risk) has meant an increasing rate of re-divorce. The large 1971–6 increase therefore had a curious and cumulative 'carry-on' effect, though this may now be levelling off.

(4) With the larger numbers of broken marriages since the initial increase, however, larger numbers of children have become affected, and many – given other changes – are members of single-parent families, or are illegitimate.

(5) These rates have also been complicated by several other facts of a legislative and also a merely numerical kind. The lowered age of majority, the improved standards of life and opportunities for young people (over at least a large part of the period), the increase in marriages at younger ages and consequently in divorces at shorter durations of marriage, the legal change allowing petitions for divorce after only one year of marriage, an increase in the number of women aged 14–44, etc., must have exerted some influence. There seems now, however, to be a steadying of the rate of first marriages at younger ages, and a general trend towards marrying later.

(6) Undoubtedly, however, the factor which comes most conspicuously to the fore in the tracing of these trends, is *the changed position of women*, and this, in itself, has many aspects.

(i) By far the largest increase in the petitions for divorce has come from wives.

(ii) The reason chiefly and increasingly given for the 'irretrievable breakdown' of their marriages has been 'unreasonable behaviour'.

(iii) This suggests higher standards of single life, higher demands upon life, higher expectations of marriage, and a diminished readiness to continue with a relationship or situation found unsatisfactory.

(iv) The increased opportunities for employment (chiefly part-time), coupled with various kinds of support from the social services and 'Social Security', have given women a greater degree of economic independence and personal autonomy; a greater readiness and ability to manage their own single-parent family situations.

(v) At the same time, the pattern of such employment indicates no abandonment (or diminution) of child-care, but, on the contrary, a general continuity of responsibility in motherhood.

(vi) Contraceptive practices, too, have passed increasingly within the control of women; have become practised with increasing accuracy – reducing the average size of families and households; and seem, too, to be replacing abortion as a method of controlling family size among married women.

(vii) The increasing resort to abortion by single (never-married) women, the decrease in the number of legitimate births conceived before marriage, and the increase in illegitimacy (with an apparently changed nature) suggest a growing degree of control on the part of women over their sexual, marital, and parental destinies. Unwanted births and unwanted marriages are prevented – by abortion. Marriages are less frequently entered into to legitimate pre-marital conceptions. Illegitimacy seems increasingly to be becoming a matter of deliberate preference – often with the joint responsibility of partners.

(viii) In single life, and in their situations following divorce, separation, or widowhood, women are increasingly assuming responsibility for 'single-parent families', though (with the registration of illegitimate births in the joint names of the parents) evidently maintaining some stable relationship with their partners – with or without some sort or degree of cohabitation.

(ix) Increasingly, women are deciding to *keep* their illegitimate children – fewer and fewer of them being put forward for adoption.

(7) Despite the continued popularity of marriage, there has been an increase in cohabitation (pre-marital and otherwise). Some men and women at least – though wanting family and domestic life – no longer set any store by the formal procedure and status of marriage; though, at the same time, tending to lay claim to the law pertaining to marriage when their rights have to be asserted or protected, or when situations arise between them when claims and counter-claims have to be made upon each other. Though some such relationships are no doubt sound and responsible, it is within this area that 'half-baked' notions about the

nature of marriage and the implications of cohabitation may arise, and on the basis of which unfortunate and unhappy situations are all too easily, casually, and unguardedly entered into. But this tendency to disregard the significance of the form of marriage may be a concomitant (or extension) of one other fact.

(8) There has been a marked secularization of marriage (whatever this may or may not imply for religious beliefs, sentiments, and values.) For an increasing number of people, marriage has lost its sacramental dimensions. It is a human commitment, solemnized by a civil ceremony and registration, only.

From all these facts, one conclusion emerges very clearly: though marriage unquestionably remains a firm and popular institution for the vast majority of people (*and*, for those (an increasing number) re-marrying without children, or without the prospect of children, *an institution in its own right* – not only as a procedure for the founding of a larger family), on the part of some it has come to seem *inessential* as a way of entering into stable domestic relationships and forming a family group. Even so, our critical survey of all the facts of marital breakdown has revealed with equal clarity another – and perhaps surprising – conclusion.

(9) The vast majority of people in Britain (at least 80 per cent) still live in 'nuclear' families of married couples with or without dependent children (some with independent children) within households which give them the family privacy they desire. The family, without any doubt whatever, remains the primary domestic group in British society: the most intimate social group possessing closely shared feelings of community and meeting the most profound and reciprocally demanding personal needs – within the larger and more impersonal institutional framework of society. It is the basic group which the majority of people both want and have, and which they are predominantly concerned to preserve and improve. It remains the basic social unit of British society in that almost all the legislative, administrative, economic requirements and regulations of personal life, inter-personal responsibilities, and the provisions of the social services are focused upon it, with the over-all aim of protecting its conditions of life and the security and rights of its members.

Marriage, then, as an institution, may have diminished in significance in the minds of a minority, but the family remains the basic unit of personal and social life for almost all – and those who lack it are chiefly either the old who have now left it behind (through the death of their partners), the young who are starting out in adulthood and setting up households for single life, or the unfortunate who lack all roots and all security.

(10) The facts of marriage breakdown also serve to indicate those specific problem areas where the most unfortunate deprivations, inter-personal difficulties, and unpalatable kinds of behaviour may lie (I mean where the general cultural equipment of people to deal with their problems – as well as their economic resources – will be at its lowest), and these, too, have various aspects.

(i) Most marriage breakdown takes place at the lowest levels of the scale of social classes and at that of the unskilled manual occupations.

(ii) This high incidence of breakdown is even more marked among the unemployed.

(iii) It is at these (class and employment) levels that marriage at younger ages chiefly takes place.

(iv) Despite high wages among some unskilled occupations (though on short, weekly contractual terms – and therefore vulnerable), it is at this level that economic insecurity and general educational and cultural deprivation will be most marked, and where marriage breakdown may lead to the most difficult situations of economic stringency – if not outright poverty, unsatisfactory conditions of housing and other accommodation, and poor qualities and conditions of neighbourhood life – within which the poorest levels of personal life and care and the worst intensities of domestic and neighbourhood violence may occur. This is the socio-economic context within which the most overt social and personal deprivations and problems may lie (although, of course, marital and family breakdown may well leave unhealed scars at any and every level of social, economic, and cultural life).

Clearly, then, there are some quite definite aspects of the overall situation which provide ample grounds for anxiety and concern. The chief of these lie in considerations of: (a) the large number of children involved; (b) the broken families whose members are trapped in the most deprived and distasteful situations – of a material, social, and inter-personal nature – and who are having to confront and endure the most vicious of conditions and relationships; and (c) the sheer numbers of individuals involved despite all that can be said (concerning the majority of the population) about statistical rates. To give only one example: only 2½ per cent of the British population (as recorded on census night, 1981) do *not* live in private households, and are accommodated in 'hotels, schools, hospitals, and other institutions' or are 'camping or sleeping rough'. It is an extremely small percentage, but the *number of persons* involved was 1.4

million, and anyone who has seen (for example) only 30 old people sitting round the edges of a hotel lounge in Leicester, or the same number of people 'sleeping rough' under the bottom arch of Charing Cross bridge, knows how much misery and distress such a number must entail.

But in pointing to such specific problem areas, these conclusions drawn from the statistical indicators have also the virtue of pointing (a) to what it is unwise to try to do, and (b) to what might most effectively be done. It would seem futile and unwise, for example, to seek to eradicate divorce, and to deny the justice and correctness of the reforms which have changed the provisions for it – as though divorce, in itself, was a bad and unfortunate thing. Given high expectations of personal life and high standards of marriage and the family, divorce must be accepted as an institutionalized corollary of these values in our society. But there are specific problem areas, specific avenues, into which it seems that efforts and resources might most profitably be directed to minimize marriage breakdowns and to ameliorate the unfortunate consequences following those which do occur; for example: (i) in educating children and young people about the whole of personal life and life in society, and the whole of family relationships, and about sexual life within this whole context; (ii) in persuading them (on grounds of health, morality, and as constituting the most likely way towards adult happiness) to consider carefully the wisdom of delaying sexual experiment and experience, and marriage itself, in the realization that it seems to be in early, ill-considered mistakes that most subsequent traps and misery lie; and (iii) in studying more closely those most difficult problem areas where the lowest standards of behaviour may be – and therefore the worst kinds of violence, cruelty, and abuse.

The conclusions of this survey of the facts since 1971 reveal a scene, therefore, which is by no means untroubled, but, equally, is by no means one of instability, disintegration and decay. The basis of annoyance and criticism of many of the newer more radical critics ('The Abolitionists') was right in this one thing at least: that the family is most certainly a group of great strength, resilience and tenacity, of which no revolution in the world is easily going to rid society. Despite all the changes in the collective conditions of our time – in legislation, degrees of liberalization, and the like – the family remains completely firm, even though marriage (for some) has come to be thought not essential for its foundation. But the criticisms have been wrong in almost all other respects – for the 'nuclear family', in its own household, with its own privacy, is quite clearly what the people of Britain want, still have, and have no intention of abandoning.

Social commentators (both journalistic and academic), having come to this conclusion, tend to speak of the British family in terms suggesting that it has somehow survived though its nature has changed. Some, for example, speak of 'serial monogamy', some of 'the Neo-Conventional Family'. But such terms are misnomers. What people want, and what exists, is *monogamy* – and, furthermore, monogamy with a higher standard of consideration and expectation. If it fails them once, or they fail it, they seek it again. What people want, and what exists, is *the family* – as it has long existed in British society, but now, again, with higher standards of consideration and expectation. The changes that have been made in it have been such as to ensure that the families which exist in society are, in fact, *wanted* families – not those fastened together and enduring because of an oppressive law; and that – within it and beyond it – its members (husband, wife, children, alike) enjoy better material and social conditions, a more secure protection of their rights, greater degrees of chosen freedom. We are back, in short, at what Geoffrey Gorer concluded after his repeated investigation at the beginning of the 1970s: that the men and women of Britain take marriage and the family seriously and that the kind of domestic union and relationship they now want is a 'marriage of good friends'. As against superficial notions of 'romantic love' or of sexual gratification isolated from other feelings and commitments, he found it necessary (in *Sex and Marriage in England Today*, 1970) to emphasize:

> the great importance for English men and women of *the institution of marriage*, and the seriousness with which they consider it. It is *marriage itself* which is important, not, I think, love or sexual gratification; and marriage is living together, making a home together, making a life together, and raising children (my italics)

– in fact, making and enjoying a home and a family. And Gorer continued:

> I think I discern quite a new pattern ... the roles and characters of husband and wife are given little emphasis; what is emphasised is doing things together, going out together, helping one another, and above all talking together.

This it is that he calls 'The Marriage of Good Friends'.

The facts surveyed so far, however, have been no more than the 'naked statistics', and it is important to see that the findings of many other studies are such as strongly to support the conclusions we have drawn from them.

Related studies and qualitative evidence

We have already noted those studies appearing at the end of the 1960s and the beginning of the 1970s which – reporting facts of a qualitative kind – supported the conclusions about the condition of the family and marriage in the early 1970s (when the 1969 Act was just about to come into force) stated in the introduction. Some were *direct* studies of the family, some *indirect* in that – concerned with quite different areas of social life and problems – they none the less found it necessary to place great emphasis upon the nature and strength of the family. The family forced itself upon their attention; intruded into their fields of enquiry. It could not be ignored. It is necessary, now, to say a little more about these, because they continue to be relevant to all that has happened between 1971 and now, and were followed by additional and similar studies which came to both supplement and reinforce their findings.

Geoffrey Gorer's investigation of *Sex and Marriage in England* (1971) was a repeated survey of the *qualitative attitudes* of men and women, revealing the values which lay at the heart of their character (which directed their aims and efforts in life), and the qualitative aspects of their sexual, marital and family life. His findings revealed not only the degree of seriousness with which English people concerned themselves about their marriages and the life and conditions of their families, but also the changes which had taken place – over a period of twenty years – in the nature of their domestic relationships. Many things had remained the same. Having a home of one's own, enjoying relative financial security and prosperity, enjoying a satisfactory sex-life, wanting and having 'give-and-take', understanding, love and affection, shared interests, and children ... all these remained the same and had even become more taken for granted – as though they were commonly expected, available, and not even questioned now. There was, however, one marked change. It was in the emphasis placed on *companionship, comradeship, doing things together*, and – with particularly strong emphasis – on enjoying continual and close *communication* with each other. Confidence in close companionship, articulate communication with each other, *being together in the life they shared* ... these, in 1970, were the qualities most emphasized, and, in particular, they were wanted, enjoyed, and stressed as being most important by the *young*.

'The Marriage of Good Friends' – this was the picture of the modern partnership in marriage painted by Gorer, and it is interesting to see that this included shared and caring parenthood, and, indeed, that this was especially so on the part of men. In both the 1950s and the 1970s surveys:

> it is interesting that men, particularly men of the working class, mention the importance of children much more frequently than do women; tender fatherhood seems to bring more conscious rewards than does motherhood, because, as can be easily understood, mothers are much more aware of the work and the limitation of outside interests inherent in the care of young children than are the fathers.[10]

Gorer points out that in 'Parents and Family Planning Services' (a survey based on interviews with young parents carried out by Ann Cartwright) it was also found that more fathers (54 per cent) than mothers (47 per cent) hoped they would have more children, and that more fathers than mothers were pleased at the latest pregnancy. *Fatherhood*, it seems, no less than motherhood, is an ingredient of central importance in the modern British family.

The same picture also emerged clearly from the findings of Mark Abrams, and these rested on very systematic and carefully designed surveys. The naked statistics, as we have seen, can provide quantitative indicators as to where qualitative problems (and causal explanations) might lie. Realizing this very fully, Mark Abrams wanted to dig deeper to try to establish subjective indicators (his papers were entitled 'Subjective Social Indicators') which would point to the significant dimensions in the experience of the people of Britain. In which areas of personal and social life do the people of Britain find their greatest degrees of satisfaction? Abrams measured these subjective judgments by the method of rating (respondents were asked to weight their degree of satisfaction in particular areas of social life on a scale of 1 to 7). The entire procedure was worked out within the Survey Unit of the Social Science Research Council (of which Abrams was the Director),[11] and surveys were repeated in 1971, 1973 and 1975. (Pilot surveys were carried out by Research Services Limited (of a sample of 213 people aged 16 and over, in March, 1971) and, subsequently, by Social and Community Planning Research (of 593 respondents, in November, 1971.) This latter was a quota sample of people in the 7 largest conurbations in Britain.) In the first study (reported in 1973), the satisfactions people felt in eleven *domains* of social life were rated, and among all of these, *family life, friendship* and *personal health* stood out

34 Levels of satisfaction in each domain (of social life), Mark Abrams

	Mean	Scale rate[1] (percentages)							Don't know	Number[2] (=100%)
		1	2	3	4	5	6	7		
Marriage	6.5	1	1	*	1	7	22	68	*	424
Family life	6.1	1	2	1	3	14	26	51	2	593
Job	6.0	1	1	2	5	18	32	41	—	303
District	5.7	2	1	3	5	20	40	29	—	593
Health	5.7	4	2	4	8	12	28	40	2	593
Being a housewife	5.7	4	3	4	8	13	26	42	—	182
Spare time	5.5	3	3	4	8	22	25	31	4	593
Housing	5.4	4	1	3	12	26	27	27	—	593
Standard of Living	5.1	3	3	7	15	27	25	18	2	593
Education received	4.9	7	4	6	16	26	21	20	—	593
Religion	4.8	—	11	12	22	19	15	21	—	467
Democratic standards	4.7	4	6	8	22	28	17	11	4	593
Average	5.5	3	3	4	10	19	26	34	1	593

*Less than 0.5%.

[1] Range of assessment: 1 is low satisfaction: 7 is high satisfaction.

[2] In some cases the base is less than 593, since for some respondents the question was not relevant—e.g. those not married, not going out to work, not a housewife etc.

quite clearly as being those most highly rated. (The first domains were: family life, friendship, health, housing, job, district, leisure, children's education, police and courts, welfare services, financial situation. The second were those of table 34.) Following this (in 1975), the domains were slightly altered (to number 12 in all) in such a way as to include four more: marriage, being a housewife (obviously for married women only), religion, and the quality of democracy in Britain today. The detailed ratings of the new range of domains were as shown in table 34.

It will be seen that those with extremely high scores were *marriage, family life*, and *job*, and – perhaps surprisingly to some – *being a housewife* was one of the most highly rated within the group of average to high scores. The importance to British people of their marriage and family was even more plain when the respondents were asked, more specifically: 'Which 3 items on the list do you think are the most important for you personally in determining how satisfied or dissatisfied you are with your life in general these days?' The result was as shown in table 35.

Mark Abrams's comment was perfectly plain.

Of the total sample, 72% were married, 14% single, and 14% either widowed, divorced or separated. The first of these groups gave an overall satisfaction rating of 6.5 when asked about their own marriage – *easily the highest rating accorded to any of the domains of life dealt with in the interview.*

The statement subsequently made about the qualities which (in the judgment of the respondents) formed the most important basis for a

35 Three most important domains

	Percentage as voted	Importance order	Satisfaction order
Marriage	54	1	1
Family life	51	2	2
Health	44	3	4
Standard of living	38	4	8
House	33	5	7
Job	27	6	3
Spare time	14	7	6
District	13	8	4
Religion	13	9	10
Democracy	7	10	11
Education	5	11	9

happy marriage also entirely bore out Gorer's own findings. They focused on *four* chief ingredients: tolerance, absence of money worries, love and affection, and understanding; and again – understanding was especially emphasized by the *younger* people. There seems little doubt that the older generations of married people were accustomed to regarding the life of the husband and the life of the wife as being to a considerable extent distinct from each other, in two different compartments, lived within two different spheres: of work, for the husband; of home, for the wife; whereas younger married couples thought much more in terms of a shared life together (though this earlier distinction, at least to some extent, would obviously have to continue.) We shall see, in a moment, that work itself may well have changed its nature – becoming much less of a thing in itself within a world of its own, and increasingly seen as something instrumental to the enjoyment and betterment of the life of the family in the home.

The 1975 survey showed that the 1971 and 1973 order of all these ratings had remained unchanged.

One other point, however, is extremely interesting. After all that has been noted about the rate of marital and family breakdown in America (i.e. in the reports of some of the 'New Feminist' writers), it may be astonishing to see that the ratings of men and women in the United States were almost exactly the same as those in Britain. The SSRC survey used the same scale as the Survey Research Centre of the University of Michigan, so that a clear comparison could be made (table 36).

36 Mean satisfaction scores

	Britain		U.S.	
	Mean score	Rank order	Mean score	Rank order
Marriage	6.5	1	6.3	1
Family life	6.1	2	5.9	2
Job	6.0	3	5.7	5
Health	5.7	4	5.8	3
District	5.7	4	5.8	3
Leisure	5.5	6	5.6	6
House	5.4	7	5.6	6
Standard of living	5.1	8	5.3	8
Education	4.9	9	4.7	9
Overall life satisfaction	5.7		5.5	

After all that has been widely publicised about family breakdown, it is strange to see that it is in marriage and the family that the people of both nations find their greatest degree of satisfaction. 'In both,' said Abrams, 'the highest levels of satisfaction are for marriage and family life.'

This same kind of qualitative study was carried out later by Roger Jowell (Co-Director of Social and Community Planning Research) and his colleague Colin Airey, but this was now extended to cover a wide-ranging survey of 'British Social Attitudes'. Some of these, however, still focused upon aspects of family life, and, again, the findings were in agreement with those of Gorer and Abrams, and therefore need not be repeated. One finding, however, is particularly interesting. Despite all that has happened since the Second World War in moving towards the equal status of women, despite all that has been said about moving away from the traditional roles of husband and wife, the surprising thing is that – from the 1950s to the 1980s – the traditional division of labour within the household has remained almost unchanged. The tables of 1984 were extended and printed (as in table 37) in *Social Trends* of 1986.

The conventions have remained the same. Might it not be that there *is* some underlying difference between the sexes? – some close interconnection between their biological and social natures? – which accounts for this? One is reminded of Elaine Morgan's conjectures (in her book *The Descent of Woman*) about the establishment of the family as a group in primitive times: of the child-bearing woman at the heart of the lair, and of the childhood and then adult relationship of the male to all this. Is there some primitive basis here which continues unaltered under all the varieties of the world's civilizations? It is interesting to see that the same findings were borne out in another 1984 study – *Women and Employment: A Lifetime Perspective* – undertaken by J. Martin and C. Roberts, and, again, that exactly the same continuity of the traditional division of labour was found in America, in two studies covering approximately the same period: from 1955 to 1971 (*Social Change in a Metropolitan Community*, O. D. Duncan, H. Schuman, and B. Duncan, Russell Sage Foundation, New York, 1973, a study of Chicago and Detroit in 1955 and 1971). Jowell's comment was:

> Very little change was found to have occurred in the 16 years between the two surveys ... it appears plausible that the answers we obtained from married couples would not have been greatly different had we asked the same question at any time during the last 30 years or so.

111

37 Household division of labour: by marital status, 1984 (Great Britain, percentages)

Household tasks (percentage[3] allocation)	Married people[1]						Never-married people[2]		
	Actual allocation of tasks			Tasks should be allocated to			Tasks should be allocated to		
	Mainly man	Mainly woman	Shared equally	Mainly man	Mainly woman	Shared equally	Mainly man	Mainly woman	Shared equally
Washing and ironing	1	88	9	—	77	21	—	68	30
Preparation of evening meal	5	77	16	1	61	35	1	49	49
Household cleaning	3	72	23	—	51	45	1	42	56
Household shopping	6	54	39	—	35	62	—	31	68
Evening dishes	18	37	41	12	21	64	13	15	71
Organisation of household money and bills	32	38	28	23	15	58	19	16	63
Repairs of household equipment	83	6	8	79	2	17	74	—	24

37 (cont.) Household division of labour: by marital status, 1984 (Great Britain, per centages)

| | Married people[1] | | | | | | Never-married people[2] | | |
| | Actual allocation of tasks | | | Tasks should be allocated to | | | Tasks should be allocated to | | |
	Mainly man	Mainly woman	Shared equally	Mainly man	Mainly woman	Shared equally	Mainly man	Mainly woman	Shared equally
Child-rearing (percentage[3] allocation)									
Looks after the children when they are sick	1	63	35	—	49	47	—	48	50
Teaches the children discipline	10	12	77	12	5	80	16	4	80

[1] 1,120 married respondents, except for the questions on actual allocation of child-rearing tasks which were answered by 479 respondents with children under 16.
[2] 283 never-married respondents. The table excludes results of the formerly married (widowed, divorced, or separated) respondents.
[3] 'Don't knows' and non-response to the question mean that some categories do not sum to 100 per cent.
Source: British Social Attitudes Survey, 1984, Social and Community Planning Research.

Changes are made ... but, somehow, some things stay the same!

It is worthwhile to remind ourselves, too, that the reports of building (housing) surveys, such as that undertaken in 1968, showed conclusively that people wanted a home and garden which gave their families *privacy*. *That* does not change either, and all our subsequent and actual experience of the architecture and town-planning schemes of the enormous blocks of flats of the inner cities (including the high-rise flats) has borne the same point out in terrifying fashion, filling our television screens with pictures of physical and human dereliction which are like some bizarre underworld picture of the decaying and the dead drawn on cinema by Jean Cocteau.

In 1971, too – on a different theme – Rhona and Robert Rapoport published their study of *Dual Career Families*. Starting out from the conviction that the kinds of family existing in modern society were 'more complicated and variable' than was yet realized, they focused their attention on the type which interested them: that in which *both heads pursued careers*. On the basis of five detailed case studies (selected from a larger number – but all, however, of middle-class professional people) they made many diagnoses and proposals – regarding the dual-career family as one conspicuous and adventurous example of the creation of a new kind of family in which familial values remained firm, but within which the individual partners in marriage could still freely pursue their own professional and personal fulfilment. For our purposes, however, it is enough to see that the detailed studies of *all* these families demonstrated the high value placed upon both marriage itself and upon the quality of family life within this – showing, too, a very special and sensitive concern for their children; something (even in these most 'progressive' of families) which runs completely counter to Germaine Greer's picture of 'the West' (in *Sex and Destiny*) as being 'profoundly hostile to children' and having an 'anti-child thrust'. On the contrary: 'At the core of modern civilization is a concern for the well-being of children, emotional as well as physical. *All* of the parents studied in the dual-career families had this as a major concern.'[12]

In the pursuit of personal freedom, then, there was no abandonment of marriage and the family and no evidence whatever of such a trend. On the contrary, there was a desire (whether misplaced or not) to enrich and extend the life which was possible on that firm foundation.

Studies continued, too, of the *history* of the family in Britain, accumulating more and more evidence in support of the perspective already established in the early work of Laslett, and which was already there to be seen – though not overtly and deliberately stated – in the work of the earlier social historians. Laslett followed *The World We Have Lost* with other books and essays – *Household and Family in Past Time*, 'Family Life and Illicit Love in Earlier Generations', etc. – and all reinforced, beyond doubt, the truth that the nuclear family had, for centuries past, been the norm in British society, and that the widely held view that there had once existed some culturally rich context of an 'extended family' within a close community from which the modern impoverished family had stemmed, was false. He shows conclusively that from the time of the Stuarts at least, and perhaps from a time earlier than that: 'the independent nuclear family, that is, man, wife and children living apart from relatives, was the accepted familial unit.' But Laslett made many more specific points in describing the 'Characteristics of the Western Family' (the title of one of his essays.) It is a mistake, for example, to think that girls in the sixteenth century commonly married at a very early age – in their teens. Most, in fact, married in their middle or late twenties, so that children were chiefly being born to women in their late twenties or early thirties. The family of the past was much more like the family of the present than casual and untested generalizations have led us to suppose. Indeed, when he has pointed out all the ways in which marriages and families were broken in times past (and within the scale of the expectation of life existing then) Laslett concludes that high industrial society in the 20th century is not *more* likely but *less* likely to leave children without their natural parents than was pre-industrial England – and perhaps not even the 'problem of the parentally deprived child' is especially, or peculiarly, modern. We shall find much agreement with this judgment, in a moment, in the work of Anderson.

The historical perspective, then, was continually being improved; demonstrating ever more clearly the myth of the general notion of the movement from the extended family and close community of the past to the nuclear family of the present (indeed, to the nuclear family of 'industrial capitalism'). It may just be added that J. H. Plumb, in particular, has also pointed, time and time again, to the gross misconceptions we all tend to harbour unthinkingly about the nature of the pre-industrial past – the horrors of which (in the experience and circumstances of the majority of people) he has so graphically described.

But perhaps more intriguing than all this is the fact that these direct studies of the family were buttressed by the findings of quite different investigations from which no one had initially expected anything of consequence about the family in society to arise. One such area of study was that of education. The early studies by J. B. Douglas and his colleagues (*The Home and the School*) were followed up and extended by the same team, and – without any doubt whatever – all the findings in them proved the enormous strength of the many influences of the home, the parents, the family, on the subsequent educational career of the child (progressive or retrogressive) within the schools, colleges and universities. This remains a vitally important emphasis in education, but is now so well known as to need no further detail here. It is equally well known that the subsequent studies by Basil Bernstein and his colleagues of the importance of language for the educational progress of the child also emphasized very powerfully the importance of the home, parental background, and the conditions and culture of the family within those of its local community context. Indeed, the research found it necessary to devise a special 'maternity communications index' because of the crucial influence of the nature and attitudes of the mother in the family. The family – particularly the mother – was found to be of the most basic importance. But this same *indirect* demonstration of the centrality of marriage and the family in the experience of the British people came also – and perhaps more surprisingly – from the study of *industrial life* in relation to possible changes in orientations of attitudes within the class-structure of society.

We have already noted *The Affluent Worker*[13] by David Lockwood and his colleagues. Concentrating, again, on attitudes and behaviour within the context of industrial work, and questioning how far their new experience of relative affluence moved workers towards the attitudes and behaviour of the middle classes, this study, too, found that the family – indeed, the nuclear family – was the most powerful focus of attention, effort and enjoyment in their social life. The life of the home and the family now competed with work itself. Work, the nature of work, the nature of the place of work, had become increasingly *instrumental*. Little attachment was felt to work itself, and the place of work. Work was a means of earning money, and money was chiefly wanted to improve the conditions and experiences of home and family. This interestingly parallels Abrams's findings – in which 'job' and 'financial considerations' were all subordinate, as sources of satisfaction, to marriage and family life. The home and the family were clearly the direction in which wealth chiefly went. This, of course, may well be connected with a change in the nature of work, and changes in the relationship of authority and subservience between owner/manager and worker, and these may have had their influences upon the diminished extent to which the world of the husband and the world of the wife is divided. Work is no longer, for many, as it once was, an established trade for life, a special long-earned skill, within a world of application having its own customs and qualities, and to which a man was attached by loyalty and pride; neither, indeed, is it still the province of men alone. 'Push-button' work within a mechanized or even computerized system may well reduce the extent to which work is a source of creative satisfaction to a man, whereas marriage, the family, and his home – especially within improved material and social conditions – are increasingly a context for his many individual and shared activities which bring satisfaction. And this seems to be borne out in the experience of unemployment in the areas of the older industries which seem to be going out of existence for ever. The family within its local community is the context to which attachment is felt – so strongly, indeed, as to preclude moving elsewhere in search of other employment. Time after time, this particular study finds itself having to point its comments decidedly in this direction:

> our respondents referred frequently to their overriding commitments to their families.... Family life is looked to as a major source of expressive and affective satisfactions, while little is expected or sought from working life other than the wherewithal for the pursuit of extrinsic ends....
> The majority of the workers in our sample appeared to concentrate their aspirations on securing a continuing improvement in their standard of domestic living rather than on advancement of any kind in their occupational lives....
> The most widespread kinds of aspiration held by our affluent workers were those which related to increased consumer capacity and to higher standards of domestic living....
> The majority of our respondents were led to adopt a style of life which was decisively centred on the home and the conjugal family. Their major emotional attachments ... were made in their relationships with their wives and children, and these relationships were in turn their major source of social and psychological support.... Work tended to be devalued in other than its economic aspects; the family, rather than work, was for these men their central life interest....
> As a factor of greater potential importance (i.e. than the effects

of technology in determining attitudes to work and the structure of work relationships) we would again refer to ongoing changes in working-class life outside work, and most notably in this respect to changes *within* the family. In consequence of the conjugal family assuming a more 'companionate' or partnership-like form, relations between husband and wife and between parents and children would seem likely to become closer and more inherently rewarding; certainly more so than could generally have been the case under the economic and social conditions of the traditional working-class community. If workers are better able to satisfy their expressive and affective needs through family relationships, it may be anticipated that those men at least who enjoy no special occupational skills or responsibilities will less commonly regard their workplace as a *milieu* in which they are in search of satisfactions of this kind. Rather, time spent in work-based association will more probably be seen as detracting from time available for family life and thus as representing social cost.[14]

It will be noted especially in this quotation that – fully agreeing with Gorer, Abrams, and others, and with Laslett's historical perspective too – it supposes, very clearly, that the changes from the economic and social conditions of the traditional working-class community of the past to the collective conditions of modern society, with its modern technology, have, in fact, been parallelled by a qualitative improvement in family relationships, and this, very decidedly, is one of the central conclusions of the entire study:

> It is possible for work not to be a central life interest and to be given largely instrumental meaning without the individual being thereby virtually deprived of all social activities and relationships which are rewarding in themselves. Rather, as we have seen, the readiness to adopt an orientation to work of the kind in question would appear often to indicate a commitment to the interest of *one primary group – the conjugal family – which is of an overriding kind.*[15]

That is a very positive evaluation of the nature of the modern British family to emerge from a study of industrial life. But, without question, it fully supports the other judgments we have noted, and it is enough for our purposes to note that studies of a like kind followed on the heels of all these during the 1970s and 1980s – all coming to the same conclusions, and, strangely enough, almost all declaring their intention to rid the whole subject (i.e. the family and marriage) of the mythical judgments which had been held about it in the past. *Ask the Family*, by Jeanette Longfield (1984) deliberately adopted the sub-title *Shattering the Myths about Family Life*,[16] and went on to uphold the qualities of affection, reciprocal care, and shared effort in meeting problems, she had found in all areas of family relationships: the stability of families despite the figures of divorce; the caring for children – in one-parent as well as in conventional families; the attention of young people to the care of the elderly; the desire of the elderly to preserve their independence and prevent themselves from becoming burdens upon the young. The interesting preface claims that:

> What this book does is blow a much needed and highly
> refreshing blast of truth through a miasma of myth. Anyone who
> reads it and emerges still telling himself and anyone else who will
> listen that 'People don't look after their elderly relations the way
> they used to', or that 'Young people have no respect for their
> parents – that's why there's all the trouble', or that 'the Welfare
> State looks after the disabled nowadays – families have been
> spoilt – they just don't take on their responsibilities any more', is
> a fool or a knave. Or both.

All such surveys, then – direct or indirect – into the qualitative aspects of family life in Britain – the qualitative facts – have been such as to bear out and supplement the conclusions to which the quantitative statistics point. Since the mid-1970s, too, more detailed and highly specialized studies have been undertaken for particular bodies responsible for family advice or administration. *Marriage Matters* – the report of a Working Party set up in 1975[17] by the Home Office – concerned itself with an adequate basis of knowledge for reliable marriage counselling, education about marriage, etc. and, though centrally concerned with 'marital disharmony', was none the less quite clear that, despite changes (especially that of the status and position of women):

> There is no evidence that marriage is dying out. It is no longer
> fashionable to predict that marriage, in any recognizable form, is
> about to give way to radically new forms of sexual relationships.
> Marriage has never been more popular, even if it has never been
> more risky.

(In this, they were borrowing from a newspaper headline (*The Times*, 17 August 1976) – 'Marriage – never more popular, never more risky'

– which was, itself, the title of an article reporting on the latest edition of *Social Trends*.)

Similarly, the Marriage Guidance Council itself has held conferences and produced publications of a very high standard of analysis, comment, and discussion, and again the same balanced view of all the other qualitative studies has been borne out. One of the best of these is *Relating to Marriage* (1985) – offering papers and group discussions on many aspects of family life and marital breakdown. The list of such qualitative studies could be very long indeed, but one other source of very informative articles is particularly important.

During the 1970s and 1980s a great deal of research, critical analysis and comment has been increasingly undertaken in relation to the official records and statistical work of Government departments. Until the late 1960s and early 1970s, a volume of 'Commentary' always accompanied the Registrar General's annual 'Statistical Review of England and Wales', but since the early 1970s, government departments have increasingly provided their own statistical reviews and appraisals of trends within their own fields (though these have still, selectively, been centrally gathered together in *Social Trends*). The important point is that *individuals* (sometimes with official funding) have been able to contribute their own essays – offering qualitative analysis, diagnoses, judgments, and possible explanations, of the quantitative facts which are being presented. Indeed, some of the official publications are themselves of this specialised nature: for example – *People and their Families* (1980, by the Central Policy Research Staff and Central Office). These contributions already cover a wide range, and we have already mentioned those of Mark Abrams, Roger Jowell, etc., but there are many others. (See bibliographical details (pp. 278–9) for John Haskey, Richard Leete, in particular, but for many other contributions, and details, see the list of contributors to the 1983 conference on 'The Family' held by the British Society of Population Studies.) Among them all, however, perhaps two are of special significance.

The first is Kathleen Tiernan (of the Centre for Population Studies, London School of Hygiene and Tropical Medicine), who contributed a paper (pp. 17–36) on 'The Structure of Families Today: Continuity or Change' (her emphasis proving to be decidedly on continuity.) Having considered in detail first marriages, cohabitation, child-bearing within and outside marriage, marital breakdown, re-marriage, single-parent families, and similar matters, it is interesting to see that she, too, in formulating her conclusions, finds it necessary to challenge the widespread 'myths' of earlier judgments. Pointing to the aspects of marriage and the family most widely publicised – the 'declining marriage rates, increased divorce, people living together outside marriage, decreased popularity of childbearing within marriage, and increased number of single-parent families', and the fact that 'many authorities regard these trends as signalling the demise of the family' – she none the less claims:

> Even a cursory glance at the literature on marriage and the family shows that the demise of the family has been thought to be imminent at many periods throughout this century....
>
> Most people in Britain still marry, the majority of couples still produce at least one child, the majority of children are still reared by their natural parents and the majority of marriages are still terminated by death and this is likely to remain so for the foreseeable future. This is not the stuff of media discussion, nor of academic and political debate; the uncontroversial seldom is.

And many of her conclusions are of a similarly positive kind. Noting, for example, that it is marriage which has most changed, that fewer people are marrying in the youngest age-groups, that more are divorcing after shorter durations of marriage, and that there is more cohabitation, she is none the less convinced that 'young people today still see marriage as part of their future' though the 'long term trend towards progressively lower ages at marriage has ceased'. (For the attitudes on which she rests her judgment, see Study Commission on the Family, 1983.) This, too, is coupled (in her considerations) with the trends in cohabitation, but not negatively so:

> Young women who married in their teens and early twenties are increasingly likely to have cohabited before their marriage. One could speculate that young couples, having decided that they wish to marry, organise their future home and are increasingly likely to live together before the nuptial ceremony instead of living apart with their respective parents or paying two rents. Such a pattern of behaviour may account for the fact that the time spent cohabiting before marriage is relatively short.

She also shows a positive, as against a negative, interpretation in her judgment that this delay in marriage could well be of a beneficial kind.

All too frequently the declining marriage rates of the 1970s have been viewed as reflecting either a downgrading or a rejection of marriage; rarely have they been viewed as a positive trend. Yet, the time spent in one's teens and early twenties acquiring additional education, labour market experience, and accumulating savings and wealth can represent an investment in human capital which could provide the basis for a stable and productive family life.

(It should be noted that all this was written before the very recent increase in the rates of marriage, including that of first marriages, but that, even so, marriages are taking place at a later age.) She sees quite clearly, too, that the improvement in the status of the individual partners in marriage had made marriage more demanding, had made for higher standards of reciprocal consideration, and had therefore made affection, not the compulsion of an oppressive law, the basis of the marriage bond. The personal functions of marriage, she says, have been increasingly emphasized:

Marriage is the primary source of love, affection and emotional support for the majority of adults. According to popular ideology partners are regarded as being of equal status and the foundation and maintenance of the relationship is based on mutual affection and understanding. Such relationships are intrinsically intense affairs based on personal choice, responsibility, and mutual consideration which may be potentially more rewarding but are also potentially more unstable. Over time, increased value has been placed on the marital relationship, and in some senses just as the advent of safe and effective methods of contraception liberated coitus from procreation, so the conjugal bond has been separated from any necessary connection with the generational nexus. With such increased emphasis upon the personal functions of marriage, it is perhaps not surprising that when the needs of partners are not met, the conjugal bond is more likely to be dissolved and that young people are less hasty in making such a commitment.

It will readily be seen that this judgment is in entire agreement with that outlined earlier in this book, and, interestingly – and surely not as a matter of coincidence, but of complete agreement – she concludes with those judgments of both Herbert Spencer and Edward Westermarck which our own judgment had come to support. From Spencer, she quotes:

increased facilities for divorce point to the probability that whereas, hitherto, the union by law was regarded as the essential part of marriage and the union by affection as non-essential; and whereas at present the union by law is thought to be more important and the union by affection the less important; there will come a time when the union by affection will be held to be of primary moment. (See '*The Family and Marriage in Britain*', 3rd edition, p. 248.)

And that day, she claims, has come. Her own full statement of conclusions also reiterates the position of Westermarck:

we started by emphasising the continuity of family life: the fact that most young people in Britain will marry, that most marriages will survive, that most married couples will have children and the majority of these children will be brought up by their natural parents. In other words, the family based on a married couple with children committed to a permanent relationship is still the norm today. There have also been changes. The family as we see it in the early 1980s will probably continue to experience the changes evident over the last decade. Late marriage, later childbearing and both parents working are patterns of behaviour that are likely to continue and the increase in the diversity and the vulnerability of conjugal unions is likely to persist. But the demise of the family is far from imminent as the current debates and controversies surrounding the family might lead us to believe. There is every reason still to hold to E. Westermarck's thesis, which in essence states, that the family founded upon some form of marriage, which is based on deep-rooted sentiments both conjugal and parental, will last as long as these sentiments last.

This last qualification – on the lasting nature of conjugal and parental sentiments – is one to which we shall return later as being of quite crucial importance, but, for the moment, it is clear that this qualitative analysis of the facts is in complete agreement with our interpretation of the quantitative statistics, as it is with our over-all judgment of the nature of the family in Britain today. Marriage has been questioned, but by no means generally or destructively so, and, without any doubt, the family remains intact.

The other significant contribution is on the matter of our perspective on the history of the family and what this reveals about the condition of the family today, and is such as completely to bear out the picture drawn by Laslett. In an essay 'What is New about the

Modern Family: an historical perspective', Michael Anderson of the University of Edinburgh, too, begins by questioning – indeed rejecting – the myths which have been held about the nature of the family in Britain in past times. The central myth contrasts the modern situation of: 'isolated, small, readily disrupted and conflict-ridden families, living out their private lives in isolation from any close and meaningful wider social relationships' with a quite different image of the past: 'full of affectively close and stable families, in which uncontrolled fertility produced large numbers of children within marriage (while strong morality inhibited their birth outside it), a past in which the population lived in large and complex households, set in stable communities and surrounded by large numbers of close and more distant relatives.' All recent research, Anderson claims, has significantly modified this view. The more detailed our knowledge of the past becomes, the more it becomes clear that such stable communities 'in which most of the population grew up and grew old together, living out their whole lives in one place' were *very rare*, at least (he states in *People and their Families*, 1980) 'since medieval times'. Quite specific facts are reported about the nineteenth century:

> work on a national sample from the 1851 Census of Great Britain suggests that well under half of the whole population was living in the place where they had been born, that around two fifths had moved from their place of birth by the time that they were 15 and that one child in every six had been geographically mobile by the time of his or her second birthday.

The rates of population turnover were such that 'the likelihood that people would have had many relatives living in the same village as themselves was quite low right into the 20th century – even if they had the living relatives to live near.' And – no doubt astonishing to some – we are told:

> Contrary to the popular view it was in the 20th century that rent restriction, council housing and a fall in population growth rates produced in many areas more stable communities than had probably been found for hundreds of years.

When the vast changes in travel and communications which have taken place between then and now are taken into account – vastly improved roads and road transport, the railways, the postal service, bicycles, cars, telephones – it is clear that keeping in touch with kinsfolk at any distance has become easier, not more difficult. But, in terms of residence patterns, Anderson's conclusion is that 'as far as relatives were concerned the picture for the more distant past looks not unlike today's'.

Many aspects of the family life of past and present are then put under the scrutiny of exacting historical analysis – and facts become plain. It is *not* true that there was a better and more sensitive care of the elderly in families of the past. It is *not* true that family relationships in the past were more marked by warm affection and altruism. It seems, indeed, *not* true that even the high rate of marital breakdown is new. We compare the present rate (says Anderson) with that of the earlier part of our own (twentieth) century, when the rate of breakdown was temporarily low. But before our century, it seems that 'at most marriage durations, marital breakup rates closely parallelled modern ones.' Similarly, it seems not true that the rate of illegitimacy has been markedly higher in modern than in mid-Victorian times, and, qualitatively, as we have seen, the nature and conditions of modern illegitimacy (as well as the sheer numbers involved) have much changed. 'The recent rise in the ratio (from an early 1960s figure at about the mid-19th century level) is clearly much more a function of the drop in legitimate fertility than it is a reflection of a collapse in family life.'

But Anderson's analysis is much more telling than this in his exploration of many other facts of past and present which have transformed the nature and experience of the generations, married partners, parents, and children in the British family of our own time.

For example, the straightforward facts of age, death, longevity, and health have had qualitative influences upon experience – in many respects – which are difficult fully to appreciate. Consider the fact that:

> it was only in *the early 1770s* that half of any marriage cohort could have even celebrated a 'silver wedding'. At that date about 2% of children were total orphans (had lost both parents) by age 10, 4% by age 15 and 12% by age 25.... The approximate estimated median age of a child at the death of his or her father was 32 and of his or her mother 34....
>
> A child born in *1861* stood a 1% chance of orphanhood by age 10 and 6% by age 25, with father dying when he or she was 35 and mother at 36....
>
> But of the 'median' children of the *1921* cohort only 2% lost both parents by age 25 and such a child would have been 41 by the time father died and 47 by the death of his or her mother....

Of the cohort born in *1946*, around 1% can expect to have lost one parent by age 25 and the median child of the first generation a majority of which has any expectation of inheriting a substantial sum (as a result of the spread of owner-occupancy in the 20th century), has to wait until age 45 for death of father, 53 for death of mother and 56 for death of both. (my italics)

This brief mention of 'inheritance' throws up many considerations which clearly deserve further exploration. For example, young people coming to adulthood after having experienced a long childhood and youth within a context of high standards of home life, are nowadays faced with a situation in which, if desiring complete personal independence, they will not possibly be able to achieve and enjoy the same standards for a long time, and will have no prospect of inheritance, either, for many years to come. Longevity, health, affluence – all desirable things; things on the basis of which we should rightly be counting our blessings – none the less pose new problems, in new life-situations, for the young, and we will touch on other aspects of this problem in a moment.

Similarly, the facts of age, health and longevity lead to a different experience between the generations. For example (slightly simplifying Anderson's figures) in 1681 a grandmother would have been dead 13 years before her last grandchild was born. In 1861, she would have lived for five years after the birth of her last grandchild. But now:

Even men can expect ... to live some 14 years after the birth of their last grandchild and women can expect another 23 years of life; this is just long enough to see all their grandchildren married if they marry at the median age. Modern levels of life expectancy give a woman around 30 years of life after the marriage of her last child, compared with just 3 for the 1681 cohort and only 6 for the cohort born in the early 1830s.

The situation for modern families has been transformed. Anderson himself makes the point, here, that the very possibility, need for, and nature of a '3 generational system of child and grandparent care' has vastly changed, and, of course (with falling family size) the number of children in these family situations has also changed.

The same facts also make, obviously, for longer marriages. 'How many people on marriage consciously realise that "till death us do part" is now likely to mean 45 years?' And this, too – again a consequence of many improvements – can clearly be one factor in the vulnerability and long-term instability of marriage.

Anderson offers far too many detailed and important observations to be possibly taken into account here, but one last specific point can be touched upon because it is one on which I want to lay much emphasis later. Describing the way in which, during the nineteenth century, children at early and later ages left their homes and families – to go into service, to live with kin, to become living-in apprentices and shopmen, to be living-in workers on farms, to go into lodgings – Anderson shows clearly the *protracted* nature of the passage from childhood to an adulthood which carried with it the headship of an independent household. For a considerable period, young people could not hope for such independence. This situation too has now been transformed. Figures are quoted for 1979:

> At age 17 almost all were still living in households headed by a parent and none were heads. . . . By age 24 almost three quarters had left home and almost 70% were heads. By age 30 over 90% had left home and around 90% were heads. The average age gap between leaving home and entering headship was one year.

Later, I shall come back to this when considering the situation we have created by lowering the age of majority to 18 and raising the school-leaving age to 16, something which has very many important implications for the problems now facing the young, the influence of their parents over them, and their behaviour.

Many other – and equally telling points are made, but, though very guarded in his judgments and careful to say that economic changes during the 1980s could greatly change things – perhaps even for the worse – Anderson none the less concludes:

> a more stable economic position (and, in general, a more predictable environment) plus a rising emphasis on individual rights at a societal level do seem to have been associated, especially perhaps in the years after the Second World War, with some shift of emphasis towards a family system providing a context for the pursuit of the personal happiness and achievement of its members as a prime goal.

This conclusion, too, is clearly in agreement with the picture we have presented before, but – perhaps even more important than the agreement itself – is the implicit and explicit position adopted in Anderson's analysis, namely: (a) that the casting aside of historical myths and faulty perspectives can give us an altogether different and more positive appraisal of the nature of marriage and the family today, but (b) that a clarification of the improvements which have transformed our situation is by no means such as to present a scene which is trouble-free. On the contrary, (c) improvements bring about new problems, and (d) even though once achieved, cannot be guaranteed. Changed collective conditions can – again – bring new changes in them, and any responsible approach to the working out of social policies should clearly have this problematical perspective of judgment in mind.

For now, however, we have been able to see quite clearly that the studies of the qualitative facts since the early 1970s have, in fact, produced findings which are closely in agreement with the quantitative facts and their indications, and which support the interpretations we drew from them. On this basis, and with all of these facts in mind, we can now move into the very difficult area of seeking causal explanations, and considering the implications of these for our final judgment and the most advisable courses of social policy and social action which we might adopt.

*　*　*　*　*

Part II

A World in Transformation: Progress and Crisis

Explanations and Conclusions

Introduction

Claiming that the new critics of the late 1960s and the 1970s could now be safely laid to rest with the old critics of the 1950s, we have now seen that the study of the facts from 1970 onwards bears out – indeed supplements – our estimation of the family at the end of the 1960s outlined in the Introduction. In discussing all the issues involved, we have moved through many twists and turns of argument and looked at the facts from all sides. To what firm explanations and conclusions can we now arrive? In this final drawing together of all our foregoing considerations, I want to explore the many dimensions of our knowledge, uncertainty and anxiety in as comprehensive a manner as possible – and for one simple reason. Whatever our own appraisal of the various arguments leading to a judgment about the family, it is clear that – in some way or other – we are profoundly ill at ease over our estimation of the present condition of our society and of the family within it, and nothing can possibly be gained by avoiding problems. No good can come of oversimplifying in any direction – bending considerations towards apparent certainty for the sake of seeming to have proved an argument – if certainty, really, is not there. It is better to end with a clear exposition of doubts and unresolved questions than to profess conviction if such conviction possesses even the slightest degree of pretension. And doubts and unresolved questions most certainly remain. We have seen clearly enough that *any* sound judgment about the nature of the family and marriage in Britain today must concede that since mid-Victorian times very decided improvements have been made. At the same time, it must equally acknowledge that disturbing problems still exist, still giving rise to this sense of unease and anxiety. Furthermore, this apparent contradiction, this curious split at the heart of our judgment, is by no means only a slight or marginal matter. It is profound. Strangely, improvements or no improvements, we feel ourselves to be in a condition of crisis. Improvements or no improvements, we sense that the very foundation stones of our society – the most fundamental values which form the basis of its order – are being loosened and are shaking. With the threat of a nuclear holocaust hanging over our many social dilemmas and over a world already in the throes of massive and savage disruption, the warning cries of an Isaiah do not seem too wild or too remote:

> The foundations of the earth do shake ...
> Earth shakes to pieces,
> Earth reels like a drunken man,
> Earth rocks like a hammock,
> Under the weight of its transgressions earth falls down
> To rise no more.
>
> Lift up your eyes to heaven and look upon the earth beneath,
> For the heavens shall vanish away like smoke,
> And the earth shall grow old like a robe.
> The world itself shall crumble.[1]

And certainly many modern thinkers, among them theologians, find them realistic rather than exaggerated. Here is Paul Tillich:

> There was a time when we could listen to such words without much feeling and without understanding. There were decades and even centuries when we did not take them seriously. Those days are gone. Today we must take them seriously. They describe what the majority of human beings in our period have experienced, and what, perhaps, in a not too distant future, all mankind will experience abundantly: 'The Foundations of the Earth do shake.' The visions of the prophets have become an actual, physical possibility, and might become an historical reality.... That is the religious meaning of the age into which we have entered.[2]

We need to take our dilemmas and our sense of crisis seriously. How can we explain the fact that – with so much of good achieved, with so many reforms accomplished – we are so deeply apprehensive?

We have seen, too, that the grounds for concern are both old and new. Some, having the sense of some continuing deterioration in the values of society throughout their life-time – through the whole of our century, from the very end of the Victorian era to now – believe that it is the family which has declined; that it is this most basic group in society which has lost its character; that this most important salt, essential in the nature of society, has lost its savour. Some believe that it is the very tenacity and continued existence of the nuclear family with its unbearable intensities which is to blame – in a society which could otherwise be changed for the better. The family, for them, is the obstacle. Others hold the mixed position – recognizing substantial improvements and substantial problems alike. The arguments and facts we have reviewed have undoubtedly demonstrated the strength and durability of the family – even when the indispensability of marriage itself has come to be questioned. Of this we can be sure. But unresolved problems still exist for some.

The improved and enlightened attitudes towards sexuality and the position of women are made questionable by an apparently widely spread casualness and irresponsibility in attitudes and behaviour in both sexual relationships and marriage alike. No matter how interpreted, no matter how much they may point to a woman's increased degree of control over her own life and destiny, the facts and trends of abortion, illegitimacy, and the more calculated attitudes towards indulgence in sexual intercourse, conception, and the termination of pregnancies, seem somehow distasteful, seem somehow demeaning to the very nature of womanhood. Technical skills and expediency seem to have replaced committed affection, sensitivity, and discriminating personal feeling. They leave something lacking – as against a considered approach to committed personal relationships, marriage and parenthood. And though the materially improved lot of most families, the new level of relative affluence they now enjoy, is welcomed – even this affluence, directed, dominated, fuelled by a flagrantly aggressive 'consumerism', has, for some, its questionable morally enervating side. Getting and spending, perhaps we *do* lay waste our powers. Within this same context of an improved society, too, we have noted the existence of a widespread concern over the fact that families – for a variety of reasons – now seem to suffer a qualitatively *new* kind of social isolation: not merely in the sense of living somewhere up the concrete staircase of a block of high-rise flats, or being separated in the crowded housing conditions of impersonal conurbations or congested inner cities, but in some sense of an underlying absence and lack of both the conditions and the experience of *community* within an increasingly complex and large-scale *society*; a society, too, which becomes increasingly characterized and motivated by uncaring self-interest and self-seeking. The 'Free Economy', the 'Laissez-Faire Society', is one riddled with greed and sharp practice, with the quest for power in the service of commercial gain and success, having come to lack all elements of a deeper worth and of humane social or personal purpose. With all the benefits of our new affluence we have only slipped back, to use Edward Heath's phrase, to the 'unacceptable face of the unrestrained capitalism' of the early nineteenth century, to an unprincipled, exploitative competitiveness. Any profound sense of a 'Conservative' concern for the preservation of customs, values, traditions for the whole of our community, has given way to the crass profiteering of the businessman. 'Hard Times' – once radically criticized and lampooned by Charles Dickens – has returned under the guise of 'economic efficiency' and the insistence on 'making things pay'. The milk of human kindness can be entertained ... if it makes a profit! Something has gone wrong at the deepest and most intimate level in the relationship between *self* and *society*. Something human has been lost in the relation between persons and social institutions. Something, in the life of our society, has gone from the heart of every person's inner experience. Every family is better off – and every family is poorer. Every person is courted on all sides by groups and societies feverishly clamouring for his or her attention, spending, investment, charity ... and every person stands alone.

At the heart of our society, lavishly catered for in every direction of appetite, there is a real sense of inner, personal, spiritual nonentity.

No credible judgment on these matters today can possibly present a plain black or white picture, one of *either* good *or* bad, *either* progress *or* retrogression. No facile answer can be true. We are increasingly confronted with a complex picture – of a society still containing some values, qualities of character, and social achievements which are among the highest mankind can ever know (in love, marriage, friendship, familial bonds and loyalties, parenthood), and yet also manifesting the worst qualities of brutality, cruelty, personal abuse, misery, and the most casual and insolent kinds of irresponsibility which could possibly be conceived, and which fills up our daily papers and television screens with our daily diet of 'news'. 'News', today, is invariably 'disaster': stories of terrorism, bombings, rape, the sexual assault and battering of 80-year-old women pensioners coupled with the theft of a few pounds, the kidnapping and sexual assaulting and killing of 3-year-old girls. It is the nature of our times that we can be no other than inescapably perplexed. In these concluding pages, therefore, I want to look carefully in all directions: to be as complete as possible.

There is, however, as part of this, one other central consideration I have in mind, and one to which I attach the greatest degree of importance.

So far, in this entire analysis, we have looked in detail at what might be called the *minutiae* of the facts and statistical trends (the rates of marriage, divorce, re-marriage, re-divorce; the changed position of women; the possible implications of the rates of abortion, illegitimacy, etc., etc.); in short, at those specific elements which seem closely and directly involved in matters relating to marriage and the family. In what follows we shall not lose sight of these kinds of detail or leave them behind, but – going far beyond them – I want to paint a much larger picture, with a larger brush on a larger canvas. I believe that a full and satisfactory causal explanation of all that has happened, and is happening, to the family and marriage, lies not only in these directly connected minutiae alone – but in the nature of the far larger context of what is happening throughout the world in our time. Large contexts have small effects. A full understanding of the most intimate elements in our personal experience can only be arrived at in terms of our being placed within the wider human situation which characterizes our time, and in terms of the influences which this situation has upon us. There *is* a collective condition of the age, a *spirit* of the age, which enters into our own personal spirit, and which we cannot avoid. I believe that the relevance of these larger aspects of things is either not usually seen, or tends to be left completely out of account in thinking about very specific problems. I therefore want to include them, dwell upon them, and explore them here.

Bearing in mind all we have argued so far, it seems the best procedure to begin with what we *do* know, with those elements of understanding and causal explanation which *do* seem plausible. This, by way of elimination, can lead us to the identification of what it is we do *not* know, and what we need to explore and explain further. And this, too, can lead us on to the larger issues.

Accepted areas of causation and explanation

(i) 'The marriage of good friends': the British family improved: progress and problems

The first thing of which we can be quite sure is that no general deterioration which may have taken place in our society or its values can be explained by a deterioration in the nature of the British family. Every fact and argument we have considered shows conclusively that over the past hundred and fifty years or so – since mid-Victorian times – the nature and conditions of the British family have in all respects been considerably improved. Those who do not see this simply lack historical knowledge and are still seeing the present out of a false historical perspective. Later, we shall directly face the elements of crisis in our society, but in this first section I want to emphasize quite forcefully this plain fact of the improvement of the family, and indicate what it implies in the realms of causality.

Earlier, I described the British family of our own day as being:

1 of long duration, since it is founded at an early age;
2 small in size, as a consequence of birth control;
3 separately housed in an improved material environment;
4 economically self-providing, and therefore independent of aid from wider kindred;
5 founded and maintained by partners of equal status, enjoying a marital relationship based increasingly upon mutuality of consideration;

6 democratically managed, in that husband, wife, and children are all taken into account in arriving at family decisions;
7 centrally and very responsibly concerned with the care and upbringing of children, and, finally;
8 aided in achieving health and stability by a wide range of public provisions both statutory and voluntary.

These characteristics and all that they entail clearly represent a considerable improvement upon family types of the past, but a few points deserve a good deal of emphasis in this.

First, these improvements are really three-fold. They embody a more considerate relationship between husband and wife, a more sensitive and sympathetic relationship between parents and children, and a better relationship between families and the wider society, or between families and government – which increasingly recognizes the importance of stable, happy family life. At the heart of the modern family is an *improvement in relationships* both within and beyond the family itself.

Second, the grounds of these improvements are not isolated in, or peculiar to, the family; they are attendant upon wider improvements in society at large. They are, in short, the outcome of securing the rights and improving the status of women and children (and improving those of men), together with the more effective movement towards economic security and equality of opportunity. They constitute a general moral improvement in the status of the citizen in our community – irrespective of age or sex – and this is a point of considerable importance to which we must return in more detail in a moment.

But third, it should be noted that these improvements have been made possible by, and in relation to, the rapidly changing circumstances, problems, and demands of an *industrial* and *urban* society. Quite apart from the ethics of the matter, the modern family is that type of family most appropriate to the conditions of a complex industrial society, and the securing of the rights of individuals within it.

Indeed, the whole perspective stemming from this realization of these improvements and the grounds on which they have rested points to the one way in which changes in the family may be said to be causes of problems. Changes in collective conditions, deliberate social reforms – no matter how good in themselves, no matter how well thought-out and designed, no matter how carefully carried into effect – can have unforeseen consequences. In particular: improvements can cause problems. The gist of all we have said so far is that the very changes which have improved the family and provided the basis for improved and more sensitive relationships within it have, at one and the same time, rendered marriage and the family more vulnerable. Changes in both marriage and parenthood clearly illustrate this. Marriage – an increasingly secularized, civil matter; the provisions of a new divorce law making possible its termination by mutual consent – has been freed from sacramental dimensions (if these are not believed), from ecclesiastical authority and power, and from the necessity (if it suffers irremediable breakdown) of demonstrating the committing of some matrimonial offence on the part of one or both parties. It has been changed in many humane directions. But – just because of this – it has become both more demanding and more vulnerable, and at a time when the longevity of both life itself and marriage has been considerably extended. The bond of personal affection and mutual commitment has become paramount. Similarly, with many extensions in the duties required of parenthood (in the economic upkeep of children to a later age, in being made responsible for seeing that they continue their education up to the age of 16, perhaps longer, etc.), but, simultaneously, with the lowering of the age of majority to 18 – the tensions and problems between adolescents and parents have most probably been intensified. The improved opportunities for children have made for more difficult parenthood. Greater intensities of experience, of reciprocal demands, of vulnerability, are there; problems are there; grounds for anxiety are frequently there; but they are directly caused by improvements, and it is worthwhile to note that this apparently curious conjunction of improvement and anxiety is by no means new. In the past, too, it has been widely shared.

Masterman, for example, writing round about 1909 – when the works of Anatole France and H. G. Wells were symptomatic of this anxiety over the possible decline of moral values in the face of materialism, just as the *Brave New World* of Huxley and the *1984* of Orwell became symptomatic of the same anxiety in our own time – said:

I am not pessimistic as to the future of this 'Sceptred Isle'. Who could be pessimistic who had traced the history of a hundred years, and compared the England of 1811 with the England of today! I believe there are possibilities as yet undreamt of, for the enrichment of the common life of our people, and that in another century men and women – and children – may be rejoicing in an experience better than all our dreams.

I am not *pessimistic*, but I am *anxious*, as I believe all the thinking men of today are anxious when they realize the forces which are making for decay.[1]

And he concluded:

> amid a people of such vast prosperity and comfort, the voice of
> anxiety should never be entirely stifled.

Anxiety, then, is to be understood and commended; a perpetual
vigilance for the perpetuation of important values is a necessary and
a laudable thing; but it should not be allowed to distort our
perspectives and falsify our judgments.

Trying, himself, to apply some sort of perspective to the social
changes of over a century, Masterman also wrote of the British
people:

> The Multitude is the People of England; that eighty per cent (say)
> of the present inhabitants of these islands who never express their
> own grievances, who rarely become articulate, who can only be
> observed from outside and very far away. It is a people which, all
> unnoticed and without clamour or protest, has passed through
> the largest secular change of a thousand years: from the life of
> the fields to the life of the city. Nine out of ten families have
> migrated within three generations: they are still only, as it were,
> commencing to settle down in their new quarters, with the paint
> scarcely dry on them, and the little garden still untilled. How has
> the migration affected them? How will they expand or degenerate
> in the new town existence, each in the perpetual presence of all?
> That is a question of as profound interest in answering as it is
> difficult to answer.The nineteenth century – in the life of the
> wage-earning multitudes – was a century of disturbance. The
> twentieth promises to be a century of consolidation. What
> complete product will emerge from its city aggregation, the
> children of the crowd?

Approaching the end of the twentieth century, we ourselves are
now responsible for the answer to that question, but as we do try to
answer it, it deserves the strongest reiteration that our analysis does
clearly demonstrate that it is not the family in contemporary Britain
which has declined in nature or importance as a social institution;
that it is not the characteristics of the family which warrant at all the
charge of 'moral decline'. If we seek causes of decline, we must look
elsewhere. And this judgment, too, has been shared by others. After
having reviewed a century of changes in family law (in R. H.
Graveson and F. R. Crane (eds), *A Century of Family Law*, Sweet &
Maxwell, 1957), Professor Graveson concluded:

If we have cause for shame over the past, we may take pride in the present for the efforts that have been made in our time, inadequate as they may be, to ensure a better future for succeeding generations.

It may be said, of course, that in all this I have described, really, the formal characteristics of the modern British family, and that this is in danger of being a rather ideal picture – of a type of family, rather than of the thousands of actual, problematical families that exist in the real world; that, in spite of the formal improvements to which I have pointed, many families are still in trouble, and cannot cope with the demands made upon them; that there is still much about which we should be anxious, and that the time has not yet come to be unduly optimistic. But it should be clear from what I have said earlier that I agree with this – with some qualification.

I do not believe that the picture I have drawn is only a formal one. I believe that the great majority of British families are of the kind I have described, and that they do in fact cope successfully with all the internal and external demands made upon them; successfully in the way in which families do – with much conflict, difficulty, irritation; with much that is not only trying but positively exasperating; but with firm loyalties, with ties which go deeper than is often known and acknowledged, with abiding attachments, with much happiness, and engendering a core of character which is a strength in all their members.

Some families, however, do not. This is distressing – but is it a matter for surprise, for blame, or for talk of moral deterioration? Is it really difficult to understand why some marriages break down, and why some families are problematical and badly managed? Surely one reason is that marriage is extremely difficult: the most exacting, demanding, problematical of all the relationships we have to work out – though, if it succeeds, the most richly rewarding. Another reason is that some people do not possess the personal qualities required. Some people are ignorant and shiftless, dirty and undisciplined, insensitive and sluttish, small-minded and selfish, just to mention a few things. And before we settle down with a vision of the east end of London or the black proletarian north, let us hastily remind ourselves that such people are not confined to the working classes. There are middle-class slums too, if you go through the door (or even, sometimes, if you look outside the back door). In any society, and especially in a society as complicated as our own, there are bound to be personal insufficiencies and marital and family casualties. The more, too, that we improve our standards and increase our demands, the more difficult we make matters for some people. Good relationships are harder to maintain than bad ones, and we have seen that a relatively high divorce rate may be indicative not of *lower*, but of *higher*, standards of marriage in society.

My point is that it is certainly true, in terms of the formal characteristics of the modern family, that the family of today is a great improvement on anything we have known in the past, and the majority of families live up to these new expectations. We have, in fact, achieved a legally changed, and an administratively, economically and socially supported context for the family in which 'the Marriage of Good Friends' which Geoffrey Gorer described can now be actually realized; in which – as Kathleen Tiernan (quoting Spencer) claims – reciprocal and responsible personal affection, not oppressive law, is the bond holding husband and wife, and parents and children, together. But this is far from saying that we have no difficulties or that this is the end of the matter. The higher our standards, the greater some of our difficulties. We are really at the beginning, not at the end – for we now have to see by the good upbringing and education of our children that generations of the future will be adequately equipped to realize what is involved in family relationships and to live fully and happily within the improved formal structure which has been to some extent secured.

All this has very clear implications for our approach to the formulation of social policies, but these can best be left to our final reflections on the future of the family.

(ii) Marital breakdown: law and statistics

A second substantial area of understanding of which we can be quite sure – without at all believing the explanations within it to be complete – is that very considerable area covered by changes in the law relating to marital breakdown and the statistics recording the facts and trends of such breakdown. Changes in the law cannot, generally, be said to cause marital breakdown; neither can statistical records. Changes in the law themselves stem from social actuality, from the pressures of marital breakdown; from informed criticisms of the law and proposals for its change which reflect the need and desire for a wider availability of divorce on changed grounds; and, indeed, they make divorce more accessible to all. Statistics reveal the collective nature of social facts and tendencies. Neither cause them. Even so, in changing the nature, conditions and qualities of marriage by changing the legal requirements for its termination, reforms of the law may well come to affect public attitudes and expectations, especially as the principles underlying the law and the implications of its practices become – in knowledge and understanding – more widespread in public opinion. They therefore exert some important degree of causal influence. As with improvements in the qualities of the family, so improvements in the availability and practice of the law may lead to changes in thought, evaluations, and behaviour. Improvements, again, may bring problems. Similarly, though statistics cannot be said to cause marital disharmony, they none the less throw up significant indicators pointing to where the causes most probably lie – areas which may have been unforeseen, and, indeed, even unseen hitherto. An understanding of these causal connections may then, itself, exert subsequent causal influences. In both cases, then, it is clear that there must be some clear implications for the directions and content of social policy.

Details of this whole area need not be too much repeated as we have already covered it quite thoroughly in part I (summarised on pp. 99–106), but some consideration is worthwhile in this place for one chief reason. Despite our concern and anxiety over dimensions of our situation we seem *not* to be aware of and do *not* understand (the elements in which our *crisis* of moral and social values may lie), it is by no means certain where this need for additional explanation lies. Some thought in this direction may therefore help towards an identification of it. We have seen, in fact, that much concerning marital breakdown over the past 150 to 200 years *can* be satisfactorily understood and interpreted in terms of legal changes and statistical interconnections and indicators, and that many of these interpretations are generally accepted. Might it not be, after all, that these explanations are enough? And, if not, which is the area they leave uncovered? Do we, in fact, need to look further? And, if so, where?

In part I and all our subsequent arguments, we saw that all the statistically recorded aspects of the increased resort to divorce from the middle of the nineteenth century up to the 1960s (for over a century from the Matrimonial Causes Act of 1857 to the decade just preceding the 1969 Divorce Reform Act) could be satisfactorily explained. A glance at the graph showing the trend of divorce on p. 49 makes it fairly clear that we already do understand and can explain the trends from the early part of this century to the late 1950s: in terms of the fundamental and significant changes in the law, the extended grounds for divorce, the extended grounds for petitioning on the part of wives, the availability and extension of legal aid to the poorer sections of the community, and the disrupting effects of war. No great problem of understanding or explanation seems to remain there. And it is plain that war itself has undoubtedly been the greatest disturbing factor – the largest increases in divorce occurring during and just after the two world wars. Also, after these periods of war, the rate has fallen – but only to a level higher than that which had existed previously; and the higher continuing rate could still be explained by the further extension of the same factors.

Thinking along these lines – and by way of elimination – the chief period apparently requiring further explanation seems to be that from 1960 onwards. After the Second World War the expected fall had again taken place, but why – in a new period of peace marked by a wide spread of an unprecedented degree of affluence – did the rate of marital breakdown rise again throughout ten years? And why, then, did it soar to much higher levels afterwards – from 1970 to the present time?

I emphasize the word apparently because, as we saw earlier (p. 9), the decade of the 1960s was itself a period of considerable legislation, and this, coupled with the very affluence itself and the continuing improvement in the position of women and wives, could still, perhaps, explain the up-turn in the rates. Even so, on the face of it, the earlier factors do not seem to offer a satisfactory explanation of what was most marked change of the century – a new trend out of keeping with the clear pattern observed before. On the face of it, we do seem to be faced with an upward trend during the 1960s which, at first glance, must have reflected some basic changes in sexual and marital values and behaviour. Even then, however, we must be cautious. It is still by no means certain that the earlier explanations are not sufficient for the whole of the period between 1960 and the present time.

One point which must be made at once is that our analysis suggested that the period from 1960 onwards could, and should, be split – for purposes of explanation – into two periods. We saw that the large increase since 1970 can, still, to a very considerable extent, be explained in terms of the coming into force of the 1969 Divorce Reform Act; the terminating, then, of marriages long-broken in fact (so that no significant change in rates was involved here); the subsequent increase in re-marriages; and the following increase in re-divorce. All this was no more than a legal actualization of what had existed in social fact before (but which could not be formalized and regularized earlier under the old law) and the 'carry-on' effect of the continued popularity of marriage, the extended availability of divorce (on changed grounds), and the higher rates of re-marriage and re-divorce. We have seen, too, added to this, the great significance of the changed position of women, and, indeed, the many aspects of this which we itemized. No great difference or difficulty lies in this latter period, then. Indeed, these considerations seem to suggest that when all the facts of cohabitation, illegitimacy, abortion, the decline in legitimating births conceived outside marriage, are taken into account, coupled with the new up-turn in the rate of marriage (including first marriages – but, in general, at a later age), we may well have passed through a decade of re-adjustment and settling down into the new conditions prevailing after the very considerable reforms of 1969. It does seem, therefore, that the critical and unexplained period of the increased rate of marital breakdown was that between 1960 and the early 1970s – the period, in short, of the 1960s. The increasing and much higher rate seems to have been established then, and may have been continued and statistically enhanced after 1970 by the curious 'carry-on' effect of marriage, divorce, re-marriage and re-divorce, following the new changes in the law.

Let us establish first of all, then, that – leaving the 1960s out of account for the time being – much explanation is already available and seems satisfactory.

Setting aside the impossibility of fully knowing the actual extent of marital breakdown before the mid-nineteenth century, the entire pattern of marital breakdown – and the petitioning for divorce, in particular, as an indication of this – seems quite clear from 1857 onwards. And, crucially from that date – in terms of both legal change and financial provisions – it has been one of the ever-increasing extension of the means of ending broken marriages to all sections of society: what Rowntree and Carrier called 'the democratization of the divorce process'.

That marital disharmony, broken marriages, and irregular unions existed in Britain before the 1850s – and for long after – for those people who had no recourse to the law was clearly evidenced in many early writings. Henry Mayhew, especially in *London Labour and the London Poor*, Charles Booth in the several editions of *Life and Labour of the People in London*, described irregular relationships among many kinds of labourers, and Charles Dickens in *Hard Times* had his eye focused as sharply on the matter of injustice in the field of marriage and divorce as on injustice in any other, describing particularly the enslavement and misery of Stephen Blackpool. Only those who could afford a private Act of Parliament could end their marriages, or so arrange their lives and affairs that marital disharmony and degrees of separation did not much matter. There was nothing new from 1850 onwards, and is nothing new now, about the existence of marital disharmony. The period from 1857 to now, however, has been one of highly significant legal changes.

In 1857, the new Matrimonial Causes Act was the first step in this extension – making civil divorce available, simplifying and changing its procedures, and so making divorce available to the new middle classes. Even so – still based upon the matrimonial offence – divorce remained a disreputable business, in both fact and legal manipulation, and it is worthwhile (to make sure of a sound perspective) to see how small a method of ending marriages it was even at the beginning of our own century; but then how – quite rapidly from this time onwards (with the changes in the law and legal aid) – it grew in comparison with 'legal separation'.

Rowntree and Carrier comment:

> The table makes it clear why the phenomenal increase in the number of divorces cannot be taken on its own as an index of increasing total marital disruption. At least some of the fifty-fold increase in divorce petitions since 1900 was due to changes in the law and its administration which enabled discordant couples of the kind previously resorting only to the magistrates' court, to petition in the High Court for complete legal divorce. Over the same period total applications for matrimonial proceedings increased by much less, i.e. only five-fold, and it is impossible to say how much of this was due to double-counting or to an increasing desire for legal recognition of *de facto* breakdown. While husband-wife relationships have greatly changed in the past hundred years, and in the twentieth century have been subjected to the exceptional strains of two world wars, the increase in divorce petitions implies no more than an increasing desire on the part of estranged couples to seek a complete legal termination to marriage, instead of separating on a partial or informal basis, or 'keeping up appearances' in an uneasy matrimonial truce. It is impossible in the present state of knowledge to invest the increase with a greater significance than this.[3]

Overt termination had simply replaced covert endurance or pretension.

Between 1857 and now, however, the divorce law has been

38 Matrimonial proceedings in England and Wales, 1900–54.[2]

Period	High Court Petitions for		Annual averages of Magistrates' Court Applications†	Total Proceedings	Divorces as per cent of Total
	Divorce	Other lesser Reliefs*			
1900–04 ...	783	126	10,736	11,645	6.7
1905–09 ...	809	139	11,067	12,015	6.7
1910–13 ...	919	182	10,765	11,866	7.7
1920–24 ...	3,150	451	13,603	17,204	18.3
1925–29 ...	3,805	152	14,475	18,432	20.6
1930–34 ...	4,578	169	14,382	19,129	23.9
1950–54 ...	32,451	160	26,835	59,446	54.6

*i.e. petition for judicial separation or for restitution of conjugal rights. The latter were in some cases before 1923 filed as preliminary actions to provide evidence of desertion for subsequent divorce proceedings.

†These averages are based on totals of applications by wives for maintenance orders, which are published only for the peace-time years listed here.

Sources: 1956 Commission Report, Appendix II, Table I and Criminal and Judicial Statistics, published annually.

amended in many ways, and the extension to people in all social classes has continued. Following the recommendations of a 1912 Commission, the 1923 Matrimonial Causes Act introduced equality of the sexes with regard to the grounds on which divorce could be granted, allowing wives (like their husbands) to petition on grounds of adultery. The 1937 Act extended the grounds for divorce to include cruelty, desertion, incurable insanity, and certain vicious practices. The 1950 Act consolidated these changes, but divorce still rested essentially on the matrimonial offence, and it was only the 1969 Act which changed that, making the 'irretrievable breakdown of marriage' the essential ground for divorce, and amounting – in the implications of some of its provisions – to divorce by mutual consent. If this seems 'libertarian' to an extreme degree, it must be remembered that it had long been realized, and after much prolonged debate, that marriages could become intolerable and irretrievably broken in fact quite apart from the committing of any matrimonial offence, and that, in many cases, the 'adversarial' levelling of blame was quite wide of the mark of any genuine understanding. Furthermore, the allegations and public proving of such offences themselves brought marital breakdown and the process of ending it into disrepute. Both marriage, and the ending of marriage, have been changed and tempered by more humane considerations, and we will come back to this.

Despite this extension of legal availability, however, the costs of divorce were still too high for many sections of society, and the gradual extension to all of the use of divorce was only made possible by the provision of financial aid, of free legal services for those with property values and income below a certain level. Initially, this took the form of 'Poor Persons' Rules' (in 1926 Poor Persons' Committees were set up to examine the circumstances of those making application and a Poor Persons' Procedure was established) and this became Legal Aid with the Legal Aid and Advice Act of 1949, coming into effect late in 1950. This, too, has since been extended, so that now wives and husbands in the lowest wage-earning groups can end their marriages, and, if they so wish, enter into new ones.

All these changes – it needs to be emphasized – were *reforms*. They were made in the service of justice. Justice was increasingly done. They were improvements, though, equally clearly, they brought a larger scale of social problems in their train. It is difficult to see how there could be any remaining disagreement about this whole trend of social, legal, and political policy – excepting, perhaps, on what might be called remaining questions on the technicalities of divorce. It is now said, for example, that the adversarial element in divorce is being still kept alive by the lawyers themselves, who, claiming to be acting in the best interests of their clients, keep up a lengthy pressure of claims and counter-claims. One is reminded of Thomas Hardy:

> When lawyers strive to heal a breach
> And Parsons practice what they preach;
> Then Boney, he'll come pouncing down
> And march his men on London Town![4]

Similarly, it is said that some wives want a meal-ticket for life from their ex-husbands, never allowing a divorce to become a final divorce. Like the many-sided aspects of taxation which sometimes make it more financially expedient for couples to cohabit than to marry, such technicalities continue to raise questions. But the intentions underlying the 1969 Act were quite plain, including, for example, the provision for possible reconciliation within the law, rather than any prolongation of conflict, and – these things aside – it is difficult to see on what grounds anyone would want to go back on this century of reform.

Our own concern in all this, however, is quite limited and simple. What is clear is that these explanations – in terms of the legal and financial changes which have made divorce available for all – do explain the rates of overt breakdown which the statistics record. They can be, and are, largely accepted – as far as they go – as being satisfactory. They do *not*, however (a) enter in any detail into what has been the one most evident major cause of the actual increases in the quantity of marital breakdown during the first half of our century – that of war, or (b) explain the one increase in the rate of breakdown which seems out of keeping with the earlier pattern of decline after the periods of war – i.e. that of the 1960s. To these two questions we must now turn, but first, let us very briefly note that – within this one category of acceptable explanation – statistical analysis has uncovered some more specific causal explanations than these.

(iii) Specific and identifiable explanations

These – quite fully set out in part I – can, simply for purposes of clarity and completeness, be very quickly summed up here.

There is little doubt that by far the most clearly identifiable and significant cause of the greater incidence of marital breakdown during the past 25 years – from 1960 to now – has been the continual increase in petitioning for divorce on the part of wives; which, itself, must also rest on the many aspects of the changed position of women. The equality of status achieved by women, the extended opportunities for their employment (full-time and part-time), the support received in child allowances (now paid direct to the mother) and other claims which can be made on 'Social Security' (including favourable consideration for accommodation if a girl becomes pregnant), the possibility of resort to abortion, the passing of contraceptive control into their own hands, the increased efficiency of contraceptives and accuracy in their use, the avoidance of unwanted pregnancy or of unwanted marriage simply to legitimate a birth, the ability to keep and maintain illegitimate children in one-parent families rather than offer them for adoption ... all these have given women a new degree of control over their personal lives and their sexual, marital and parental destinies. All the facts we outlined suggested, too, the existence of much higher expectations of independent life among women – in single life before marriage, in their life within marriage or in relationships of cohabitation, and resulting therefore in higher demands upon their husbands or partners and a lower level of tolerance of a domestic life they find unsatisfactory. These must be coupled, too, with the lowered age of majority (for both men and women), an earlier age of independence, the new grounds which can be given for divorce, and the fact that petitions can now be filed after only one year of marriage.

A wide range of quite definite facts has therefore been reliably identified, all of which, taken together, quite clearly and fully illuminate this one very specific and substantial element of causation: the transformed position of women in society. The liberation of women and their progress towards equality has been, without doubt, the most marked feature in the changing nature of marriage, the family, the household, the domestic group, and the having and caring for children. It is the one factor most radically changing the nature of familial relationships, and may yet prove to be the most significant of all revolutions in the modern world. Again – it is an improvement. And again – it brings new problems in its train. But there seems little doubt that it can be firmly emphasized as a central causal explanation of much recent change.

(iv) Identified problem areas

Within the entire field of statistical analysis, it seems also clear that substantial and reliable evidence points to certain specific areas of collective conditions, social contexts, qualities of cultural background, deprivation, and behaviour, where the worst of our problems most probably lie. These, too, we outlined in part I, and need mention only briefly here again.

Coupled with the extended availability of divorce to all social classes, and the availability of financial support and other provisions of social security to one-parent families and to couples cohabiting or maintaining some relationship of joint care for their children, we have seen that a number of facts are quite clear.

First, the largest incidence of divorce and separation is to be found among the lower social classes and the unskilled manual occupational groups. This is where 'broken homes' chiefly lie. It seems reasonable to suppose that this is the level at which other kinds of poverty and social deprivation exist: the poorest accommodation in the most limited and congested urban conditions (especially in the inner cities); the worst environments in which the worst kinds of behaviour are manifested (the mugging, the casual violence, the burglaries with violence, the street and gang conflicts, the attacks on the elderly, the sexual abuse of young children, the baby-battering, the wife-beating). It is here, too, that educational backgrounds are likely to be of the lowest level, where the cultural equipment of the people suffering from broken families is such as to render them least capable of resolving their own problems and achieving some adequacy and fulfilment in their lives. This is where the 'Cycle of Deprivation' is most probably to be found. In terms of social policy, this, clearly is the area in which the resources and activities of social work and the social services should be most concentrated, and it deserves reiteration that the higher the standards expected in society in general, the larger the number of people at the lower end of the scale of resources and ability who are unable to achieve them, and the larger the army of social workers required to support them. Strangely, a large contingent of social workers seems to be a corollary of a society with high standards.

Second, there is little doubt that the growth in the number of single-parent families constitutes another specific problem area. Some single-parent families may well be deliberately founded as a matter of choice by highly intelligent, well-qualified women with adequate material and cultural resources. Some highly educated and highly skilled professional women choose to have children and run a home without a husband. Similarly, some single-parent families may be left well supported after divorce settlements. It is impossible to generalize. Despite all this, however, it is a clear fact that most single-parent families do *not* exist from choice. Resulting from broken marriages, a large proportion of them face a continual struggle against poverty, and within conditions in which the satisfactory combination of child-care *and* part-time employment is difficult if not impossible. A recent letter to *The Times* put this whole matter very forcefully, and – surely – sensibly. Commenting on a journalist's insistence that though there were now (1 November 1985) 930,000 single-parent families, it was not the role of government 'to impose a moral view upon its citizens. ... Our citizens are clearly exercising their choices as to how they construct their family lives'. Lady Scott wrote:

> No need to talk of moral views, but it surely is the role of government to support such established institutions as are clearly good and useful and to discourage activities that are harmful....
>
> A vast majority of the population would still agree, I think, that the normal family is an influence for good in society and that one-parent families are bad news. Since not many single parents can both earn a living and give children the love and care they need, society has to support them; the children suffer through lacking one parent; the deprived teenager who becomes a single mother is under enormous strain, and the fathers who miss out on the humanising responsibility and satisfactions of parenting are reduced to mere biological adjuncts.
>
> The family as a human institution has evolved over a very long time; it needs to go on evolving, but not to be abolished or to lose its traditionally transmitted human values.
>
> Can we really believe that young teenagers who cannot possibly understand the likely consequences of their actions for themselves, their children and society are exercising their choices as citizens in any meaningful way when they embark on a single-parent life style, or that the State should make it in any way attractive for them to do so?[5]

There is little doubt, too, that it is at this level (though by no means only here!) that the 'half-baked' notions about marriage ('only a piece of paper!') and its rejection, women's rights, women's independence, etc., to which we referred earlier, are chiefly held and influential. Officials in the Department of Health and Social Security, for example, are disturbed to find that numbers of young women deliberately become pregnant as the one clear way in which they can escape from their parental home with some certainty of being able to establish a home of their own under the favourable consideration of 'Social Security'. But in *all* such cases – whatever the rights of women – the rights of children to be given the best possible context for a well provided childhood, for the kind of security, attention, and supported opportunities they need for their growth and fulfilment, seem to be sadly and disastrously overlooked. Indeed, one large question hanging over *all* single-parent families – whether deliberately founded or not – is how far the rights of the child are being properly considered; how far the children in them can possibly enjoy the kind of affection, care, and continuing many-sided support which the joint commitment and partnership of a mother and a father can give. Lady Scott's letter raises one other important aspect of the single-parent family, too, which is scarcely ever considered, namely: the rights of the father, and the dimensions of experience needed for *his* fulfilment. But all of this leads to the third quite plainly identified problem.

This is, undoubtedly, the sheer number of children now involved in the breaking of marriages, homes, and personal destinies, and – at least in many of these cases and situations – the insufficiencies of parental concern and child-care. In general, we have seen that there is by no means an abandonment of the care of children in modern British society. Indeed, exactly on the contrary, there has never been a time when greater emphasis was placed upon the rights and welfare of children. But again, with higher standards in general, the situation is all the worse for those whose conditions and prospects of life – through no fault of their own, and often with a destructive dissolution of the world of their parents – fall far below them. Again, it is doubtless true that *some* step-parenthood following divorce and re-marriage, *some* subsequent cohabitation without marriage, *some* single-parent homes with less durable relationships entered into by a mother or a father, can manifest as high a degree of responsible care as that existing in some normal families. But it seems clear, none the less, that it is in these same areas of less formally regulated relationships that the worst intensities of familial abuse and cruelty take place.

The lowest levels of social class, of unskilled manual occupations, of impoverished environments, of one-parent families, of the care of children who are victims of broken homes ... these, at least, are clearly identified problem areas which can be investigated further, and in which – with deeper knowledge, understanding, and supportive social assistance – some of our worst social and personal problems might be most effectively alleviated.

These, then – though only briefly re-stated here – seem to be the causal factors chiefly at the heart of our worst social problems, the areas in which the grounds for our anxiety chiefly lie, and the implications for social policy seem perfectly plain. But I turn now to a consideration of larger issues.

3

Larger issues
Crisis: the shaking of the foundations

All the causes and explanations touched upon so far have stemmed directly from our earlier statistical analysis. They are quite clear, and it is difficult to see that there need be any continuing argument or controversy about them. As far as they go, they are accepted. They have not included, however, the two areas I deliberately set aside: the major disturbances of war, and that new increase in the rate of marital breakdown, continuing through the 1960s, which was not expected in terms of the trends (following periods of war) earlier in the century. We can turn to these two questions now, but, in doing so, I want to set our discussion of them within the context of larger issues – issues which face us inescapably in the world and society of our time, and which, I believe, lie at the heart of any full understanding and explanation of what is happening to marriage and the family during the second half of our century. We must now come directly to terms with what is deeply felt to be the *crisis* of our time.

Again, we can begin by repeating the problem. How can we explain the fact that – with so much of good achieved, with so many reforms accomplished – we are so deeply apprehensive? Why does progress seem to be correlated with crisis?

There most certainly is a widespread feeling – not merely a superficial sense, impression, or occasional emotional reaction, but a deeply rooted persuasion, impossible to shake off – that our society is becoming, if it has not already become, demoralised at its very roots; that it is falling apart; that, having lost touch with any basically agreed beliefs or values, it moves on without any direction other than that of the momentum of world events. Furthermore, we seem helpless in the sea of troubles that seethes within our own society, and all around us. The list of social evils we can neither understand nor, apparently, deal with, could be very long: the widespread increase of both petty and serious crime; the insolent ignoring of the most ordinary expectations of decency; the mindless and destructive hooliganism – even in sport; the pointless vandalism – extending now even to the smashing of gravestones; the seemingly unstoppable tide of the most destructive kinds of drug-addiction ... but the central fact is that these, and many others, force us to believe, with the deepest misgiving, that something is decidedly wrong at the very basis of our society; that something is wrong at the very heart of our social and personal condition. Yeats's much-quoted poem rings all too true in our contemporary ears:

> Turning and turning in the widening gyre
> The falcon cannot hear the falconer:
> Things fall apart; the centre cannot hold;
> Mere anarchy is loosed upon the world,
> The blood-dimmed tide is loosed, and everywhere
> The ceremony of innocence is drowned;
> The best lack all conviction, while the worst
> Are full of passionate intensity.[1]

And, indeed, the wide sway of public fanaticism does seem to be the corollary of the loss of customary social order, and the loss of inwardly regulated personal conduct. We know, too, as part of this overall malaise, that in addition to the social and moral anarchy in our streets, corruption is at work in the highest places. Dostoevsky's disquieting question has become very pertinent; his vision disturbingly true. Who are the criminals? Those who crack the skull of an old woman in her flat to steal five pounds from her? Or those who, authoritatively manipulating affairs under the sway of all the pressures and interests behind the political scenes, engineer the conflicts between nations and unleash the disgusting business of war upon hundreds of thousands? Dictators, generals, presidents, prime ministers – flags and ideological slogans at the ready ... we know them now only too well, and in all countries, to have any confidence in what they reveal to us about what they do. The list of these kinds of known corruption, too, could be very long. When all this is coupled with the prevailing disorder among the nations of the world, the manifestations of fanaticism in the struggles for power within them, and all under the shadow and real threat of nuclear extinction, no other word than 'crisis' can be used. How are we to explain this profound contradiction in the affairs of our age? – that so much has been for the better, and so much is for the worse?

Let us begin by focusing our attention directly upon what many people clearly take to be the crisis of the family. If the family has been so much improved, how can a crisis of the family even be said to exist? We can begin by recalling Kathleen Tiernan's comment on Westermarck, and the conclusion of Westermarck himself who, in his own questioning only 50 years ago, went, in fact, to the heart of the matter. Miss Tiernan's own conclusion agreed with Westermarck's own judgment that (as she put it): 'the family, founded upon some form of marriage, which is based on deep-rooted sentiments both conjugal and parental, will last as long as these sentiments last.' But it is this last qualification – *'as long as these sentiments last'* – which puts its finger exactly on the problem.

Westermarck's views on the family and marriage were rooted not only in his large-scale comparative study of *The History of Human Marriage*, but also in his even wider study of *The Origin and Development of Moral Ideas*. Like Elaine Morgan, but with an infinitely more detailed background of supporting scholarship, he believed that the family, as the most basic primary group in society, had been long-established in the history of mankind, that marriage was the institution rooted in it – established as the procedure for its foundation in all societies, and that it was the birth-place of the primary moral sentiments and ideals in the growing experience of the child. In particular, it rested on, and perpetuated, the *conjugal* and *parental* sentiments, and established, among its members, all those other primary values, underlying the customs of society, which carried those basic feelings of shared 'approval and disapproval' indicating which conduct was right and which wrong. Sentiments lay at the core of society's regulations and the individual's character alike. It was these, too, that Cooley in particular came to emphasize in stressing the importance of the family and other primary groups in society. These were the groups which established and perpetuated the primary values, the primary ideals, which were the distinctive qualities, the distinguishing marks, of our 'human nature', and Cooley's insistence upon this and his formulation of this fundamental emphasis is especially important. Established earlier in our experience than critical reason and articulated knowledge, the sentiments went deeper than reason, had a deeper claim upon us than pure reason alone, and it was out of them that reflective reason grew. Furthermore, sentiments came to have a historical growth, were of a historically cumulative nature – passing from generation to

generation as the essential elements in the fabric of social tradition.
The following are selected elements of Cooley's own formulation:

> By *sentiment* I mean socialized feeling, feeling which has been
> raised by thought and intercourse out of its merely instinctive
> state and become properly human. It implies imagination, and
> the medium in which it chiefly lives is sympathetic contact with
> the minds of others. Thus love is a sentiment, while lust is not;
> resentment is, but not rage; the fear of disgrace or ridicule, but
> not animal terror, and so on. Sentiment is the *chief motive-power
> of life*, and as a rule lies deeper in our minds and is less subject to
> essential change than thought, from which, however, it is not to
> be too sharply separated.
>
> ... *sentiment is nearer to the core of life than definable
> thought*. As the rim of a wheel whirls about its centre, *so ideas
> and institutions whirl about the pivotal sentiments of human
> nature....*
>
> Where do we get our notions of love, freedom, justice and the
> like, which we are ever applying to social institutions? Not from
> abstract philosophy, surely, but from the actual life of simple and
> widespread forms of society, like the family or the play-group....
>
> A congenial family life is the immemorial type of moral unity,
> and source of many of the terms – such as brotherhood,
> kindness, and the like – which describe it....
>
> The ideal of moral unity I take to be the mother, as it were, of
> all social ideals.
>
> The family and neighbourhood life is essential to its genesis
> *and nothing more is*. (my italics)

One or two more quotations will make it clear how Cooley
conceived the sentiments as coming to form essential ingredients in
the social tradition.

> Sentiment is cumulative in human history in the same manner as
> thought, though less definitely and surely ... So, Greek sculpture,
> from the time of the humanists ... through Goethe to the present
> day, has been a channel by which Greek sentiment has flowed
> into modern life.

And this, too, was true of language and literature:

> A word is a vehicle, a boat floating down from the past, laden
> with the thought of men we never saw; and in coming to
> understand it we enter not only into the minds of our

contemporaries, but into the general mind of humanity continuous through time. The popular notion of learning to speak is that the child first has the idea and then gets from others a sound to use in communicating it; but a closer study shows this is hardly true even of the simplest ideas, and is nearly the reverse of truth as regards developed thought. In that the word usually goes before, leading and kindling the idea – we should not have the latter if we did not have the word first. 'This way,' says the word, 'is an interesting thought: come and find it.' And so we are led to rediscover old knowledge. Such words for instance, as *good, right, truth, love, home, justice, beauty, freedom*; are powerful makers of what they stand for. (my italics)[2]

On this same kind of basis, Westermarck's evaluation of the family in society – which we have already noted (p. 32) – was very fundamental, simple and clear:

it is originally for the benefit of the young that male and female continue to live together. We may therefore say that marriage is rooted in the family rather than the family in marriage. Indeed, among many peoples true married life does not begin for persons who are formally married or betrothed, or a marriage does not become definite, until a child is born or there are signs of pregnancy; whilst in other cases sexual relations which happen to lead to pregnancy or the birth of a child are, as a rule, followed by marriage or make marriage compulsory.

It may be noted in passing (a point deserving much consideration) that Westermarck's findings suggested that the conjugal and parental sentiments were not by any means separate sentiments, but were perhaps more closely connected (indeed intertwined) with each other than is commonly thought; suggesting that the former was only really and fully established and became more deeply developed with the experience of the latter; that, in fact, they were conjoint. But, for now, let us remind ourselves further that he himself was strongly convinced of the permanence and durability of the familial sentiments:

There is every reason to believe that the unity of sensual and spiritual elements in sexual love, leading to a more or less durable community of life in a common home, and the desire for and love of offspring, are factors that will remain lasting obstacles to the extinction of marriage and the collapse of the family, because they are too deeply rooted in human nature to fade away, and can find adequate satisfaction only in some form of marriage and the family founded upon it.

This is a very decided statement, and yet, at the same time, Westermarck realized very well that the continued existence of these sentiments rested upon the continued existence of reciprocally responsible relationships within shared collective conditions; with the continued implanting in each generation of the feelings of 'approval and disapproval' experienced by people in experiencing the pressures upon them and the claims they made upon each other and which they recognized as being right and good (this is very close to Durkheim's insistence that social institutions arise within the experience of a people who, as a whole, are placed within certain collective conditions which they are compelled to share in meeting their needs and working out their way of life); and – in the last analysis – that there was nothing in the nature of things which could be said to guarantee this (again, this is astonishingly and interestingly like the emphasis of Elaine Morgan (see *The Abolitionists*, p. 191–3)). It was at least possible that the sentiments which had been so basic in human nature throughout the whole history of human society hitherto could be eroded and lost. It was in his final pronouncement at the end of his book *The Future of Marriage in Western Civilization* that he put his finger on the crucial question at the root of our crisis. Believing still that 'knowledge and intellectual discernment' were likely to increase, 'destroying much that is due to ignorance, superstition and thoughtlessness'; believing still that there were grounds for some confidence in the continuity of human progress; he none the less thought that:

> At the same time, certain deep-rooted feelings are assumed to endure and continue to influence human behaviour, as they have done hitherto. But although such assumptions possess a very considerable degree of certainty so far as the near future is concerned, they cannot lay claim to everlasting infallibility. And – to speak only of the most essential thesis of this book – *if there will be a time when conjugal and parental sentiments have vanished, I think that nothing in the world can save marriage and the family from destruction.* (my italics)[5]

His doubt, clearly, was that the collective conditions of human society *might* become such as to be in danger of weakening conjugal and parental sentiments, and that if this was to happen then marriage and the family were doomed. The fundamental sentiments of our human nature, the foundations of both social order and individual character alike, would be destroyed.

The question we now have to ask ourselves is simply this:

Is what Westermarck feared exactly 50 years ago now actually happening? Is this where our crisis lies? Given all the improvements which increased knowledge, intellectual discernment, and social reforms have brought about, are we none the less witnessing the strange result, the strange dénouement, that it is these very cumulative changes with their unforeseen consequences in the nature of our societies and the experience of individuals which are actually undermining our basic human sentiments and bringing marriage and the family to destruction? Are these improvements such as to be loosening the very foundation stones they were brought into being to support and refine? *This* is the question I want to explore, bearing in mind again that our crisis, most sharply pointed here, is by no means a simple matter of decline and deterioration. Our great dilemma in arriving at reliable judgment lies, in large part, in this simple fact: that so much has been improved in the world – and yet these improvements appear to carry such fateful unforeseen consequences.

I turn now to what is surely the greatest evil of our century, but one which, in terms of causal explanation, most analysts have seemed to pass by: the preponderance and the increasingly extended domination, in our time, of war.

(i) The long tentacles of war

It is interesting to note that – quite early in this century – the significant effects of war on the incidence of marital breakdown were both noticed and voiced, sometimes in articles and reports, sometimes in the evidence presented to commissions. In the evidence given to the 1912 Commission enquiring into matrimonial causes and grounds for divorce, a Scottish judge spoke of the effects of the Boer War in increasing divorce (Minutes of Evidence, Q6779). In a 1934 article, David Glass wrote of the increase in divorce brought about by the 'long absences ... sexual recklessness, ... and hasty marriages' of the First World War ('Divorce in England and Wales', *Sociological Review*, vol. XXVI, no. 3, July, 1934). The same causes were mentioned during and following the Second World War (*Studies in Social Services*, S. M. Ferguson and H. Fitzgerald, 1954). In their 1958 article on 'The Resort to Divorce in England and Wales', Rowntree and Carrier did at least give some weight to the effects of war, though cautiously. They spoke of 'the abnormal stresses imposed on marriages by the circumstances of war'; of 'two generations of married couples being subjected to these stresses'; and the 'exceptional numbers' eventually emerging 'with new prospective spouses, requiring a legal termination of previous marriages':

> The impact of war is therefore reflected in an upsurge in petitions during the later stages of the war and immediately after its end, and, as attitudes are modified by divorce becoming more familiar, by the stabilisation of post-war rates at a new and higher level. Wars also have the effect of increasing the proportion of petitions filed by husbands, and of correspondingly reducing that of the wives ... this is presumably due to the fact that, where divorce is contemplated, husbands who have been away from home, possibly serving abroad, are on their return in a stronger position than wives to collect evidence of wartime infidelity which the English Divorce Court will accept. Wives cannot so easily substantiate rumours of husbands' 'indiscretions' abroad, nor are they entitled to divorce on grounds of desertion when husbands are called away from home by military duties.

(This, of course, was written (and referred to a time) before the 1969 Divorce Reform Act, and when a 'matrimonial offence' had to be proved. This difference between husbands and wives would not exist in the event of a future war.)

They spoke, too, of the 'flood of war divorces': 'the spate of divorces in the first war raised the divorce rate for 8 years by 53%, whilst in the second war the rise was one of 370% over 10 years'.

Bearing in mind the implications of this last extremely high figure for the generation of people who experienced the war, and the generation which immediately followed it, does it not seem very strange that the many-sided disruption of war, the radical disordering of social life brought about by it, the complete uprooting of the families, communities, and individuals who had settled into a pattern of social life before each war, and their return to a world which, after the duration of the war, was no longer there – has not been given more attention? Surely, on the face of it, it must be regarded as the most savage destroyer of all, extending its grasp over nation after nation and all the details of social life as our century has proceeded – like that of some malevolent giant whose stature has continually grown as his dominion and evil influence has spread. Certainly the story of war has increasingly dominated the literatures of every civilized country in the world, and continues to do so. I want, here, to explore four aspects of it which seem – though they are not separate in fact – to call for separate consideration.

The first stems from what David Glass no more than touched upon when he referred to the 'long absences ... the sexual recklessness ... the hasty marriages', but I want to press these hints a good deal further. Surely it is the case that the mass upheavals of the total war which modern war has become have brought about an unleashing of sexual appetite and of ungoverned sexual behaviour far more deep-rooted than this? Sexual appetite, as such, is no respecter of persons. It is always in readiness for stimulation and gratification (as Plato's picture of the 'hydra-headed beast' of the desiring element in our nature graphically suggests, as do many of Plato's other observations, which are remarkably like those of Freud – pointing, for example, to the excesses of sexual appetite experienced in dreams when the normal constraints of reason and the spiritual defence of reason in waking life are removed). It is always 'active in our members' (as certain theologians from St Paul and St Augustine onwards have not only pointed out but amply confessed), and at worst it can become an undiscriminating and rapacious appetite. Sensuality, it may be remembered, was once thought of as one of the deadly sins. And war, it may be remembered, brings rape and a general abandonment of human decencies as well as slaughter. Within the constraining bounds of normal social intercourse, moral regulation, and the wider dimensions of personal affection and consideration (other than sex) sexual appetite is governed. Removed from that context, it is very readily ungoverned. And war does precisely this: removing the regulatory influences of custom and civilization, and opening the gates to killing and the abandonment of all human niceties. One is reminded of the last lines of the Yeats poem quoted above:

> And what rough beast, its hour come round at last,
> Slouches towards Bethlehem to be born?

It may be, out of the darkness of Yeats's picture of anarchy, the detestable monster of war, its 'gaze blank and pitiless ... moving its slow thighs ...', respecting no society's values and the sanctity of no person, despoiling all. With 'long absences' and in the turmoil of war certainly partners can be easily forgotten. Men and women alike find themselves easily involved in sexual hunger and liaisons having no significance beyond gratification. And as Glass suggests, within this 'sexual recklessness' (the submission to the reign of appetite) old relationships can be despoiled and destroyed. Even youthful relationships only just begun can be destructively interrupted before they have even had the opportunity to come to fulfilment. They are still-born. And some couples are grappled together under the pressure of pregnancies which would never – except for the eruption of war – have occurred. Those who know the chaos of war – whether in campaigns overseas, or in the shift-working organization of factories of working women with camps of allied troops or prisoners-of-war nearby – know much better than I can describe it the true nature of the picture. War is, in many respects, a Bacchanalia – but one in detestable and miserable dress. But I want to press this even deeper.

Might there not be a curious link – on the level of the most basic biological urges (which are, again, no respecters of persons) – between the close presence and threat of killing and death on the one hand and an abandonment to sexual licence on the other? I can only say that I believe that this is so, and, for me, it has been most vividly suggested (indeed asserted) by Axel Munthe in his book *The Story of San Michele*. A doctor, Munthe had worked in the thick of the large-scale carnage of death in both warfare and in epidemic situations of fatal diseases (of cholera, for example) of enormous proportions. A certain conclusion was driven upon him:

> I have not been watching during all these years the battle between Life and Death without getting to know something of the two combatants. When I first saw Death at work in the hospital wards it was a mere wrestling match between the two, a mere child's play compared with what I saw later. I saw him at Naples killing more than a thousand people a day before my very eyes. I saw him at Messina burying over one hundred thousand men, women and children under the falling houses in a single minute. Later on I saw him at Verdun, his arms red with blood to the elbows, slaughtering four hundred thousand men, and mowing down the flower of a whole army on the plains of Flanders and of the Somme. It is only since I have seen him operating on a large scale that I have begun to understand something of the tactics of the warfare. It is a fascinating study, full of mystery and contradictions. It all seems at first a bewildering chaos, a blind meaningless slaughter full of confusion and blunders. At one moment Life, brandishing a new weapon in its hand, advances victoriously, only to retire the next moment, defeated by triumphant Death.
>
> It is not so. The battle is regulated in its minutest details by an immutable law of equilibrium between Life and Death. Wherever this equilibrium is upset by some accidental cause, be it pestilence, earthquake or war, vigilant nature sets to work at once to readjust

the balance, to call forth new beings to take the place of the fallen. Compelled by the irresistible force of a Natural Law, men and women fall in each other's arms, blindfolded by lust, unaware that it is Death who presides over their mating, his aphrodisiac in one hand, his narcotic in the other. Death, the giver of Life, the slayer of Life, the beginning and the end.[6]

I do not want it to be thought that I agree with every part of this. I doubt whether any meticulously exact 'Natural Law' is at work; any 'immutable law of equilibrium between Life and Death'. Even so, I believe the essential point Munthe is making to be true. War – the great destroyer, denuding all individuals of insignificance, the repudiator of all civilized values, the inciter to destruction, the inflamer of hatred, the commander to kill – is also the releaser of moral control, the remover of boundaries for the restraining of appetite, the creator of grossly inhumane situations, prompting to an abandonment of all constraints. To move back again to Plato's imagery, the 'hydra-headed beast' of the desiring element usurps the elements of spirit and reason in us. And why not? – when anarchy prevails? Recalling Cooley's terms, too, it is a situation in which *appetite* (lust) displaces *sentiment* (love). War is one large-scale transformation of collective conditions in which *sentiments* are temporarily abandoned, perhaps destroyed, and are replaced by *appetites* unqualified by reason and wider feelings. No wonder that the foundation stones of social order are loosened and that the whole customary fabric of society is shaken to the foundation.

But this is not all.

A second fact about the preponderance of war during our century – certainly in Britain and generally throughout Europe – is very marked. From the beginning of the century up to the end of the Second World War it had radically disturbed the experience of *each successive generation*. No generation during the first half of our century escaped. The children born towards the end of the Victorian era, who could just remember the Boer War, were that generation of adults caught up in the idealism of the 1914–18 war, and, under its sway, were swept across the channel to the experience, in Flanders, of what was probably the most destructive of all wars. The children of those who survived that war – those who, during the 1920s and 1930s were trying to salvage what they found possible in a society 'for heroes to live in' – came to adulthood exactly in time to be caught up in the Second World War. And involvement in this war was without choice. Idealism could no longer be relied on. This time, the armed forces were recruited on the compulsory basis of conscription. In the experience of this generation too, the family and community life they had known throughout their childhood and youth, and had taken to be permanent, was disrupted before they had even begun to establish a life of their own, or were in a position to found families of their own. All was suddenly, radically, substantially, changed. It could never be the same again. The Second World War was longer than the First. The same 'long absences' were there, the same 'sexual recklessness', the same marital breakdowns, the same unintended pregnancies, leading to the same 'hasty marriages'. But the Second World War was also *total* war. Conscription extended its grasp over the entire population. The activities of war itself – those of actual military experience (the bombings, the blitzes) – were extended into civilian experience. Conscription directed people not only into the armed forces but also into civil defence, war-production, 'work of national importance'. The entire nation was under compulsory control for war. Putting this point in stark fashion: no settled social and community life extending from childhood and youth into full adulthood was experienced by any generation throughout the first half of this century.

Gradually, too, the scale of warfare and the whole ethos of war was extended far beyond Europe to embrace the rest of the world. The destiny of the world's nations, of communities within nations, of families within communities, of persons within families, was changed for ever, and could never – in this changed situation – be made whole in the same way again. Generals and their armies may be said to 'win battles'; the leaders of governments may be said to 'win wars'; but societies, communities and individuals never win modern wars – they lose tragically by them. They themselves are maimed, and perhaps in some of their essential inner dimensions, destroyed. They are changed for ever.

We shall refer again to this global nature of war, but a third consideration brings us directly to the matter of the increase in marital breakdown during the 1960s. Is this, when one stops to reflect on the effects of war – so massive as to have produced an increase in the rate of divorce of 370 per cent over 10 years – really so difficult to understand and explain? After the usual rise and fall of the rate during and after the Second World War – why did it begin, again, to increase? It could not possibly – so the argument tends to go – be war itself in *this* case. But ... is this so? Might it not be that the disruptive effects of war were still active, even if hidden under the energetic surface of new events, activities, and fashions? In my judgment one cannot suppose otherwise. War does not simply happen, then end. It has long tentacles which, long after the cessation of hostilities, continue to coil through the lives of persons throughout subsequent time; invisibly, but none the less certainly, from generation to generation. It is not only the sins of the fathers which are visited upon their children, and their children's children, through many generations. It is true, too, of their wars. *This* time, the children of Britain born during and immediately after the Second World War did *not* face involvement in a new national war themselves. But some things remained true none the less. First, many were children of those new liaisons and 'hasty marriages' formed within the temporary circumstances and conditions of war, of those re-marriages following wartime and post-war divorces, of those husbands and wives whose own homes, marriages, and domestic lives, may well have been vexed by difficulties of adjustment they had never foreseen. These degrees of maladjustment must have been true of many wartime and immediately post-war marriages – though not, obviously, of all. The children of these marriages may well, themselves, have been born into an experience of unsettled and conflictful family and home conditions – perhaps even, in many cases, in the changed post-war world, born into 'nuclear' families (in the very restricted sense of that term) which were isolated in places and situations quite different from those with which their parents themselves had been familiar. In the context of such social changes, a generation is not long. But in addition to such considerations, was there not one other obvious fact?

The Second World War, as we have said, was a *total* war. Among the many 'directives' made necessary by the state of 'national emergency' was that of the evacuation of children from areas of great danger. Not all the children of Britain were affected by this disruption of their home, family, and community life during their most impressionable years, but a large number were. Some of the 'delinquencies' and crime of the 1960s was explained in terms of the young offenders having been evacuees. Could this same element of disturbed personal experience underlie the larger degree of marital unrest during this same decade? It is a plausible conjecture. In any event, it must have been at least one factor contributing to the unsettled experience of many of the post-war homes and families we have mentioned – those perhaps having to live in communities and even geographical locations other than those they had left when war broke out. Not all individuals or families 'went back home'. In an important sense home, for many, was no longer there. One thing seems certain: the tentacles of war must surely have extended from the experience of those who had themselves been unsettled by the war to that of their children born of them and brought up by them during the post-war period when they were seeking to make their own way. Is it too much to say that the many-sided wounds of war had not healed? – that they cannot be healed? – that the long tentacles of war were still there, coiled round lives in ways which could not be seen? The causes of social and personal stability, or instability, are not all such as to be *seen*, and the lasting effects of war may be of this nature: invisible, but deeply there in the nature of social and personal reality.

The fourth consideration is simply that, in at least three important senses, war, since that time, has never ceased. First, the stories, campaigns, heroes and villains of the Second World War (whether of fact or fiction) have been by far the most conspicuous subject-matter of films, novels, and television plays from that time to this; sometimes, indeed, seeming never-ending to the point of satiation. One sometimes wonders what the several branches of entertainment would do if they did not have the events of the Second World War on which to draw. The stereotypes of 'Japs', 'Nazis', 'British fighter-pilots', 'Yanks', people our screens perpetually. Every year is marked by memorial services, recollections of the holocaust, commemorations of the ultimate atom-bomb explosions, and the like. The two World Wars have become a never-forgotten preoccupation. The ancient Greeks (Gilbert Murray tells us) marked the site of a victory in war by a trophy which was a plain wooden cross with a suit of captured armour on it. By Greek law it had to be made of wood only (never of stone or metal), could never be repaired by the conqueror or pulled down by the conquered, and was simply to be allowed to fall to pieces and disappear. They had definite reasons for this. 'It is well', said one writer, 'to preserve for ever the goodwill we feel towards our friends, but to let our hatred of our opponents die.' And Plutarch was equally clear: It would be invidious and malignant that we men should ourselves repair and renew the monuments of hatred towards our enemies when time is making them dim.' The conflicts, enmities, and hatreds of one generation were not to be passed on to the next. But we burden the surface of the earth heavily with massive concrete monuments of war which are well-nigh everlasting, and which, accompanied by impressive rituals, stamp the judgments of our time into the hearts and minds of every generation to come. No one shall be allowed to forget. Second, subsequent wars – arising in the aftermath of the Second World War, and often revolutions following in its train – have never ceased. In several parts of the world warfare has been the unceasing rule; somewhere in almost every quarter of the globe, it has continued. Peace, decidedly, has not come. The scene of international politics – the Berlin Wall, the Cuban missile threat, the massacres in Africa and the Middle East (the list could be long) – has been, and remains, a scene of military activity: of actual war, of threats of war, of making and supplying arms for war; of continual preparation for larger-scale and more threatening kinds of war. And third, within this whole context of a continual preoccupation with war, has come the one centrally distinguishing feature of our time: following rapidly upon the atom-bomb explosions which brought the Second World War to an end, the world-encompassing threat of nuclear destruction, and the world-encompassing actuality – continually worsening with the continual spread of the knowledge, availability, and build-up of nuclear arsenals – of preparation for nuclear war.

Looked at from this one all too realistic perspective, our twentieth century has been especially notable as the century witnessing the achievement (utilizing all our accumulated knowledge and technological skills) of the greatest slaughter of man by man in the entire history of our species. In terms of the deepest kind of personal and social disruption, in terms of the disorder and moral incoherence visited on all its successive generations, in terms of the passing on of its destructive details to the youngest generations alive in the world today, in terms of its culmination in the most terrible threat of human destruction the world has ever known – surely it must be that *war*, more than all else, has been shaking the foundations of human society – frequently and irrevocably wrecking them – and the underlying conditions of the family within it. How could this be otherwise?

All the aspects of this entire point can perhaps be drawn together in a simple way. Our twentieth century has experienced and witnessed that culminating conflict between the world-wide empires of the European nations which has led to their own downfall and dissolution. But in the wake of this world-encompassing warfare, and with the downfall of these empires, all the peoples who had hitherto been subjected under colonial rule have shaken themselves into a struggle for their own independent nationhood. After the spread of commercial and industrial empires, the decline of these empires, and the coming to independence of subjected peoples, the world – through world-encompassing war – is being made one, but one whose nations are linked together in a welter of disputes. And so ... war and revolutions have spread – and will continue.

This, at any rate, is the first of the larger issues – the first large-scale cause of increased marital and familial disruption – that seems to me to warrant the very greatest emphasis. The wars of our time, and the long tentacles of these wars which pass from generation to generation, are now sending their influences, like poisoned tendrils stemming from broken lives, into all the nations and all the individuals throughout the world.

War, however, though often endured as being necessary, would almost universally be considered a complex set of evils, but I turn now to something quite different; something which, on the face of it, would be considered good; a second large-scale constellation of elements of social causation in modern society which is the context out of which have come all the positive improvements we have mentioned – in society, citizenship, and the family alike – but one which also has its problematical side, and which, curiously, can be linked to some of the unforeseen aspects of the aftermath of war which we have just considered.

(ii) New family – new society: a world in transformation

In short compass, I want, now, to throw a very large perspective over those deliberate changes which have been brought about in society since the onset of industrialization, and which amounts – no less – to a cumulative and increasingly rapid transformation of human society throughout the world in our time. It amounts – again, no less – to an indication of the crucial significance of the twentieth century as that which is witnessing and experiencing the culminating crisis of the whole previous history of mankind. It is an enormous perspective, and, like many of the elements we have considered so far, one simultaneously containing great promise and great threat, one of improvements purposefully brought about but also of unforeseen consequences which have brought problems in their train. No matter how large, however, it has the supreme advantage of being true, and an understanding of it is essential for any full explanation of our own immediate condition of crisis. We cannot understand the situation of the family by looking at the family alone. The family is an integral part of society and the world at large, and is affected by them.

We may begin by recalling Anderson's guarded conclusion, resting on his study of what we have called the minutiae of historical facts and trends, that:

a more stable economic position (and, in general, a more predictable environment) plus a rising emphasis on individual rights at a societal level do seem to have been associated, especially perhaps in the years after the Second World War, with some shift of emphasis towards a family system providing a context for the pursuit of the personal happiness and achievement of its members as a prime goal.

It is on his mention of the 'rising emphasis on individual rights at a societal level' and 'especially perhaps in the years after the Second World War' that I want to place emphasis, and my concern is little more than to fill in the entire context within which these achievements which have improved the nature of the family have come to be what they are. The perspective is large, but it very specifically focuses upon the condition and crisis of our own time.

The deliberate making and re-making of political constitutions in Europe has gone on, of course, from the time of the early City States of Greece. Though the many details of this long process cannot be entered into here, their value must certainly not be underestimated. (An excellent, and nowadays unread, account of this entire history is Henry Sidgwick's *The Development of European Polity*.[7]) At the same time as the onset and rapid development of the Industrial Revolution, however, came those political revolutions – the American and the French Revolutions – which were to transform the constitutions of Europe (of France and Britain in particular) and lead directly to the making of the United States of America. Fundamentally, these were rebellions against the entrenched powers of kings and priests; against the hierarchies of both secular and ecclesiastical authority. Monarchical and ecclesiastical powers were in large part overthrown, certainly diminished, in the service of the extension of democracy and the effective recognition (in re-made political constitutions) of the *rights* of *all* members of the political community. 'Liberty, Equality, Fraternity!' 'The Rights of Man.' These were the kinds of slogans and titles of books which indicated the new political principles. At that time (not more than *three* human lifetimes ago!) a vast, radical, and rapid transformation of human society was set afoot, beginning in Europe and the offshoots of Europe overseas, but since sweeping over the entire world.

The fundamental nature of this transition has been that from a condition of relatively simple traditional agrarian societies (though, sometimes, with wide trading and cultural interconnections) to one of highly complex rational industrial societies of much larger scale (with their empires, too, founded upon a different kind and scale of economic and colonial exploitation.) Enormous, profound, and subtle differences at every level of human experience – in mythology, religion, art, literature, morality, etc. – have been attendant upon this transformation. Within the first condition of society, the over-all 'ethos' was one of 'Man in Nature' – with imponderables larger than man, and going far beyond him, held responsible for his destiny. Within the second condition, the over-all 'ethos' is that of man himself dominating and exploiting his natural resources by knowledge and control. And though revolutionary at that particular time and in a political sense, this transformation was not so in any sense of historical discontinuity. On the contrary it was, and is, the culmination of mankind's long and entire history on the earth of his accumulation of knowledge and its ever more effective application stemming from his distinctive (natural) powers of transformation. Man was always distinguishable from other animal species in that he was not bound, like them, to a process of biological *adaptation* to his environment, but possessed qualities and potentialities of mind enabling him, with the cumulative historical development of his culture, creatively to *transform* his environment. The distinguishing feature of the modern situation is that this power of transformation has grown and accumulated to the point of assuming an extensiveness and degree amounting to a difference of kind.

At the heart of this lies the long, slow accumulation of established and tested knowledge which has finally culminated in critical science: the greater accuracy of its methods and powers of prediction; its provision of the means of greater control over nature and society by a mechanized technology; and all the largenesses of scale – in economic productivity, size of populations, spread and density of urban settlement, etc.; which all this has brought about. The many radical changes which have taken place in the social order cumulatively became a *total* change. What we might generally call 'the Ancien Régime' (i.e. as referring to traditional orders of society other than that of France) – the traditional order of institutions with all its founded authorities – collapsed, and a new society resting on a constitution rationally devised in accordance with the new moral and political ideals, had to be created and established in its place. A reconstitution of institutions in their totality had to be attempted, but underlying the *political* changes proper, the even more radical and more all-pervasive transformation of *society* was taking place. Over the past 200 years, this has been the turmoil at the heart of Europe, but as the nations of Europe have built their empires, spread their influences throughout the world, involved the greater part of the world in war in the conflict between their empires, and as their empires have fallen in and after war and the ex-colonial peoples have come to seek the same independent nationhood with the same ideals, this transformation has become a transformation of the world. And so this same critical condition of radical transformation – of the collapse of long-established orders of authority and power and the struggle towards a reconstituted order of institutions in keeping with the aspirations which are now voiced for all men throughout the modern world – is now occurring, and will occur, wherever critical science and industrialization make their many-sided impact upon traditional communities and continue to exert their many-sided and cumulative influences.

The significance of our own age is that on a scale now encompassing the whole world mankind is now compelled to take upon himself the responsibility for re-making his own society, and, in doing this, for shaping his own future destiny. Mankind now – not any of the old Gods – is responsible for shaping the ways of the world. The transformation in which we find ourselves involved is the greatest watershed in the whole of human history in that, for the very first time, it is drawing together literally *all* human societies in the world. It has assumed *global* proportions. We stand, now, in the throes of the revolution which is now racking those many traditional societies in the world (from the level of *tribal* organization to that of the largest *civilizations*) which have been drawn into the range of its influences a little later than ourselves, and are now in the midst of grappling with its dilemmas. It is therefore of the most fundamental importance for all our judgments, theories, social and political policies and actions, that we should recognise our position as such.

Within this same condensed period of time, too, an extensive literature of moral and political philosophy has grown up, and, intimately related to it, a profound making and development of the many interrelated social sciences. (It is only 200 years since the Hume/Kant juncture in philosophy, and all the modern social sciences have been created since then.) The most striking and significant character of all this thought – 'normative' and 'positive' alike – is that it has itself been an urgent engagement in this task of extending human freedom and re-making the institutions of society. *The making of the human sciences has been part of this task of the re-making of society. This* is the perspective of social actuality – including social thought and social science – within which, alone, we can properly assess and judge any specific institutional changes within it – including that of *the making of the modern family*, and strong emphasis has to be placed upon certain features of it.

First, it rests upon a certain over-all picture of social evolution about which we have to be clear. Thinking of the *entire* evolution of mankind in the world, from his origins to now, this view maintains that a very long period of 'genetic' development – in which the many traditional orders of societies had very gradually taken shape in terms of the 'unintended consequences' of their adaptive responses to their environmental and historical circumstances – had been gradually, cumulatively, and then with increasing rapidity, replaced by a condition of increasing rationality and purposive control. Increasing knowledge, increasing control, the necessity of re-assessing and re-making institutions, meant that modern society was marked by increasing *rationality* and *responsibility*; rationality and responsibility, too, applied *both* to the investigation of facts *and* to the critical clarification of values; and that this was an outcome of the insufficiency of the earlier traditional institutions. A rational critique of institutions, and responsible social action in re-making them, was forced upon men by the dilemmas of social disorder.

Second, this new condition of rationality and responsibility carried with it both promise *and* threat. Man's new degrees of knowledge and control, his deliberate attempts at social reconstruction, could bring great improvements but also great disaster. Responsibility was inescapable, but it by no means guaranteed success. Also, increasing rationality and the increasingly calculated and contractual basis of human relationships led not only to possible improvements but also to various dimensions of malaise. Two sources of this, at least, were clearly distinguished.

One was the spread and increasing dominance of a rationally calculated *contractual* basis for human relationships. Primarily, this was the nature and basis of *commercial* commitments, but its character then spread into all fields of human relationships and had at least three deficiencies. (1) It lacked and tended to supplant all those deeper dimensions of 'belonging' which accompanied and sustained the associations of people in simpler communities. (2) It was limited *solely* to the terms of the contract, and had no grounds of commitment beyond this. At best it carried the convention requiring that contracts should be kept, but, at worst, a smooth appearance of mutual interest veiled the realistic intention and expectation of sharp practice. Under its face of conventional politeness – it was ruthless. And (3) it brought the danger of contractual manipulation and inhumane exploitation. It was, in short, the 'bourgeois' ethic, or the ethic of capitalistic exploitation, against which so many came to rebel. Calculated interest was put before a full humanity, or, indeed, before anything which stood in one's way. Association resting on

173

contractual definitions replaced the relationships of whole persons in community. *Calculated interests displaced sentiments.*

One corollary of this was that science – itself an analytical, specialized, supposedly 'value-free' activity – could itself be utilized in the service of effective human manipulation. Why not? If science was a matter of 'truth' independent of other human values, why should it not be used in the pursuit of self-interest and power – even if the ends of these were evil? Rational and responsible men can be evil. Science itself, which some had hailed as the great liberator of mankind, could become one more servant – and an enormously powerful servant – of *de-humanization.* A moving statement of his realization of this is to be found in the *Private Papers of Henry Ryecroft* by George Gissing. As early as 1903, he wrote:

> I hate and fear 'science' because of my conviction that, for long
> to come if not for ever, it will be the remorseless enemy of
> mankind. I see it destroying all simplicity and gentleness of life,
> all the beauty of the world; I see it restoring barbarism under a
> mask of civilization; I see it darkening men's minds and
> hardening their hearts; I see it bringing a time of vast conflicts,
> which will pale into insignificance the thousand wars of old, and,
> as likely as not, will whelm all the laborious advances of mankind
> in blood-drenched chaos.
>   ... Oh, the generous hopes and aspirations of forty years ago!
> Science, then, was seen as the deliverer; only a few could
> prophesy its tyranny, could foresee that it would revive old evils
> and trample on the promises of its beginning.

A sombre and telling warning, indeed – of what, in fact, was soon to come.

The second source of malaise was simply one attendant upon rational choice and responsibility itself. To take traditional values, beliefs, and social procedures for granted on the basis of unquestioned authority was easy. To be *responsible* as a personal citizen for knowing, evaluating, choosing and acting, and accepting the consequences of all this, was far from easy. It necessarily entailed continual alertness and anxiety. But the anxiety attendant upon responsibility was, by many, held to be good. Recognizing modern man's dilemmas, some thinkers urged the desirability of an 'ethics of responsibility' in place of an 'ethics of inspiration'. The latter could no longer be enough.

Following closely upon this is the third emphasis (already mentioned) that many social theorists shared a moral commitment to the making of the social sciences for the making of society. It was not only Marx who forthrightly advocated political action or reform in terms of revolutionary change or 'realistic humanitarianism'. Others too – trying to study social facts without moral evaluation (to establish the truth about them) – none the less formulated their ideas (on the basis of this knowledge) for the reconstruction of the economic and social order of society, but now on the basis of ethical considerations worked out in the thick of the knowledge drawn from empirical investigations, no longer in the philosopher's armchair alone. In the modern world – in science and political action alike – an ethic of responsibility alone was defensible. (This very brief statement entails references to a very wide range of social theorists indeed, including, for example, Tönnies, Durkheim, Weber, Hobhouse, and many others. A schematic indication of the nature and range of their agreement can be seen in note 8, p. 273).

In Britain, from the end of the eighteenth century, and especially throughout the nineteenth century, social reconstruction was very gradually achieved through the making of social reforms, and in our own century, social reform – much more radical and extensive – has been built on the solid foundations the Victorians laid. All this is so well known as to call for no further detail here. But it is here that we come to Anderson's other qualification: *'perhaps especially in the years after the Second World War.'*

The period after 1918 up to the beginning of the Second World War was one of very considerable disillusionment. The high idealism of the First World War, savagely dashed down in the protracted realities of trench warfare, was replaced by cynicism during the depression of the 1920s and 1930s which followed. The 'Land Fit for Heroes to Live In' was found to be characterized by reduced wages, dole queues, and national assistance. After the Second World War no such grandiose offer was made, but, more seriously now, the people of Britain wanted the making of a Welfare State in which the inhumanities of unrestrained commercial exploitation would be eliminated and corrected by policies of public ownership and government intervention in economic affairs which would secure, and protect, the effective recognition of the equal rights of all, minimum standards of living, decent standards of health, housing, employment, education, and, in general, wider opportunities for all – whatever the wealth and status of their forebears. Social justice, at last, was to be done and seen to be done.

All this, so far, may have seemed very remote from our central concern to arrive at a sound appreciation of the nature of the family

175

in society, but, in fact, it is absolutely vital for the perspective I want to uphold. The fact is that *the making of the modern family has been an essential part of this making of a new society*. The making of the modern family by social reforms of many kinds has been a necessary part of this larger process of approximating as closely as possible to the central ideals of social justice in the entire reconstitution of society. Let us recall a few of the examples we have mentioned earlier.

During the constitution of modern nation states on the basis of rationally clarified principle, political citizenship for *men* was established not much more than a hundred years ago. The rights and duties of individuals as responsible members of political society have been clarified and effected in government, law, and social and economic relationships. The same citizenship was extended to women hardly more than *fifty* years ago. With this step has come the effort to obtain equal status for men and women. Sexual differences (like differences in colour) have been seen to be irrelevant to many of the basic rights and duties of citizenship. In this context the status of women, like that of men, in relation to securing rights and opportunities in the ownership and management of property, in education, in the range of effective occupational choice, and in the entering into and termination of marriage, has been much improved. The status of children and young people has similarly been improved. For women and children alike this was not a deliberate aiming at some ultimate form of the family, but an alleviation of intolerable evils, removing them from the harsh conditions of over-work, ignorance, exploitation and an almost total lack of education which had made life – in conditions of peasant community and domestic industry – a brutal and miserable story. Also, inequalities of income have been reduced by more equitable taxation, minimum standards of income have been established, and many social services have been provided, to approximate as far as possible to the ethical ideal of citizenship in which all are fittingly rewarded for the contribution which they make, and in which civilized standards are maintained for the less fortunate.

The modern family as we now know it – defined by government and law, upheld by morality, and aided by the social services – is the outcome. It is founded on the basis of free personal choice by partners of equal status, and the expected basis of it is that of personal affection (not legal constraint). Responsible, planned parenthood is firmly expected of it: casual and irresponsible parenthood is condemned. Within it children enjoy a high status and much parental and social concern. Dogmatic parental (chiefly

176

paternal) authority has been superseded by reciprocal discussion and sensitivity to the needs of all the members of the family, when decisions are made. We have all come to speak of the 'democratic' family. Physical conditions and neighbourhood services alike have been greatly improved when compared with the distressing nature of earlier industrial and urban growth – which persisted to a chronic extent (as did unemployment) up to 1939. There is a much-improved basis of economic security, and the social and welfare services sympathetically aid families in sustaining the best possible qualities of life. Finally, a *chosen* degree of involvement between the family and its wider kindred has replaced the earlier *necessitous* dependence and constraint.

These, in short, constitute the 'rising emphasis on individual rights at a societal level' which Anderson mentions, and which have been effected 'especially perhaps in the years after the Second World War'. The essential point is that the *form* of the British family as we now know it and as we have described it *is no accident*. Neither has it been conceived or created in isolation. It has been shaped within the entire context of securing, for individuals, the full rights of citizenship within a society seeking to maximize freedom, and the opportunities for personal fulfilment which this can give. *The making of the modern family has been part of the making of a new society*. It is the outcome of efforts to approximate to humane ideals, as well as of some process of adjustment to industrial and urban conditions. On all counts it embodies great improvements. It is not just a convenient arrangement or compromise, but that form of the family which is integrally bound up with (i.e., is an 'institutional entailment' of) the achievement of a new, principled, democratic, industrialized society. It is in itself a great achievement; part of the larger achievement of moving more closely than men have ever been before to a just society. Let it be noted, too, however, that there is nothing in all this to imply that the modern family (as an 'institutional entailment' of the changes we have considered) is in a *final* form. As in Lady Scott's letter, it is wise to bear in mind the fact that the family 'has evolved over a very long time' and 'needs to go on evolving'. We cannot know what is *final* here.

This seems a fitting place, however, to suggest and emphasize an 'alternative story' of the making of family in modern Britain to that stridently declared by some Women's Lib writers. The more extreme among these, it may be remembered, described the making of the family during the nineteenth century in terms of the *subjection* of women to men, the *enslavement* of women to the combined role of

177

wife-and-mother, the *imprisonment* of women in the home. But what is the truth about this story of the making of the British family? By removing children from the labour market, social reform created a period of childhood protected from the exploitation of employers and parents (in domestic industry) alike. This period of childhood, and the provisions for it and opportunities presented within it, have been extended and improved ever since by the many improvements in health, education, housing, and other areas of reform. By removing women from certain areas of the labour market, social reform protected women from the appalling and exploitative conditions of industrial labour in both large-scale factories and mines and in small-scale domestic industries. A woman's role as wife and mother has been extended, protected, and improved from that time to this. A man became responsible as husband and father for the support of his wife, his children, his home, and since that time the shared partnership in marriage and the shared responsibilities in parenthood have been improved by the improvements in the status of wives, and children, and in relation to the ever-extended demands upon both parents – in the statutory requirements of economic maintenance, responsibility for ensuring attendance at full-time education, etc., etc. – to maintain higher standards of care and up-bringing for their children. The home and home-life of the family, too, has been improved in terms of material standards and facilities, and supportive social provisions. The modern British family, a hundred and fifty years in the making, is by no means merely an accidental accompaniment of exploitative capitalism, by no means a 'nuclear' prison for under-privileged wives, and characterized by destructive intensities which none of its members want. It is the outcome of long efforts to create a basic domestic group characterized by a form and period of protected childhood, of married and parental partnership, of a shared and protected privacy of the home and of home-life, which have been thought most fitting for the most secure happiness and the best satisfaction of the needs of people in both child and adult life – and in a society deliberately concerned, on the basis of well-thought-out principles of personal and public well-being, to sustain these high standards. The choice facing men, women and children now is whether to defend, sustain, and further improve this form of the family, or whether, by the insistence of some rights and claims without reference to others, to despoil it.

All this, however, may be said to be only a further buttressing of my earlier picture of the making of the British family of today as one of society's 'success stories'. How does it link with the sense of crisis? How does it link with the upturn in the rate of marital breakdown during the 1960s? – or with what I have said about the long tentacles of war still at work in the generation coming to adulthood during those years? What is there in this making of a new form of the family within a new society which even remotely suggests any 'shaking of the foundations'? There are at least two answers which lie, again, in the realm of unforeseen consequences.

The first is the fact (more true than we realize) that a generation is not only not long, but does not have either a long experience or a long memory. The Welfare State was not seen by the younger generation who grew up within it in the same way that it was seen by those who had lived before and during the war, and had been involved in the making of it. Those who had known British society before the war – who had seen or lived in its slums, suffered or witnessed its unemployment, stood in its dole-queues, applied for its 'National Assistance' – knew very well why they wanted the Welfare State the Attlee government was trying to create. The humane promise at the heart of the struggles of the Labour Party over almost half a century was now becoming an actuality. 'From each according to his ability, to each according to his need' was the ethic now actually beginning to qualify the too-long-established principle of 'to him who owns the property, makes the profit, and holds the power'. They knew very well why they wanted some public ownership, some public enterprise, to exert some degree of economic control. They knew very well why they wanted departments of state and social services to remedy gross social inequalities; to achieve some re-distribution of the wealth which the co-operative enterprise and work of all created in society. Their vision was quite clear. It had grown out of the plain hardships, indignities and injustices they had known. There was, for them, never to be a return to the unregulated condition of disillusionment and depression they had known during the 1920s and 1930s. Or ... so they thought.

The young, however, did not see the world and society into which they were growing like this. They did not have this rationale in terms of felt experience. They saw the Welfare State as a large and growing fabric of regulations and requirements which, together with the pressures of their parents, were imposing ever more intense expectations upon them. For them, the society about them was, in fact, a vast House of Administration within whose rules they had to live, whose regulations they had to know, whose forms they had to fill in, whose procedures they had to use, in order to find their way

But there was no sense of personally belonging to it. How could one 'belong' to a world of departments, offices and faceless bureaucrats whose regulations grew ever more complicated if its provisions were to be gained? The probable restlessness and instability of their own post-war families, within which their parents were themselves working hard to find their own way, the intense pressures of a newly competitive education which seemed to be distinguishing them as 'failures' or 'successes', 'sheep' or 'goats', at the age of 11 for the rest of their lives, the playing upon them of the new advertisements of the new media, the continual presentation of the new degrees of affluence and good fortune which others enjoyed ... all these contributed to a new kind of social isolation which individuals experienced: an alienation within which – as individuals within their own limited families – they were for ever comparing their lot with the fortunes and social status of others. Instead of feeling themselves significant members within the organic unity of a new purposive political community, they were competitors, continually stirred to social emulation, within the demands of a large-scale impersonal society.

The second answer, also in the realm of unforeseen consequences, lies in the fact that – coupled with these differing perceptions and different attitudes of the young, but also involving members of the adult generation themselves – there came to be an *abuse* of the Welfare State. Those who reform a human condition, who work to bring about an improved situation for their fellows and their children, and who do so on the basis of the highest ideals, cannot believe, and do not foresee, that – when the improvements are achieved – people will not only not appreciate them, and what has been done for them, but will calculatedly make use of them, exploit them, and abuse them out of sheer self-interest; that they will betray them, and will not care about their betrayal. But this, in fact, is so. Gradually, for some, the Welfare State changed from some humane achievement to which they owed continuing obligations and duties, to something existing for their own use, and from which they had a right to demand their rights. The *rights* came to over-take and over-turn the *duties* side of the equation. The Welfare State began to be seen, by some, as a gigantic milch cow from whose flowing udder they should squeeze the maximal benefits they could. The list of abuses and deficiencies could be long – but we have all known and seen many examples of them. Landlords cashed in on the provisions of 'Social Security'. Busy officials took easy ways out of administering complex and ever-changing rules – paying rents, for example, direct to landlords rather than to their individual clients. Profits were made by the exploiting property-owners of sub-standard houses out of the provisions society made for the needy. The list of abuses could be very long. All this was in the period, too (throughout the 1960s – though it has continued and worsened up to the present time) when a new affluence was orientating the young and adult members of society alike to a new *consumerism*. Every group in society – large-scale property-developers in league with public officials, employers in their manipulation of prices and products, trade union leaders insisting on maintaining differentials (whilst believing in equality), maximizing annual increases in pay, and turning a blind eye to practices of over-manning and under-working – jumped on the bandwagon of new social and economic well-being with new motives of gain and greed. The making of the new society – the Welfare State – took on a new complexion, came to have a new 'image'. No longer the embodiment of humane ideals, it came to be regarded as just the reverse: the embodiment of relaxed efforts and lax morals, of the slacker and the slick clever exploiter. Instead of representing a scene of humane provision for those in need and a collective maintaining of standards, it came, in itself, to be a scene of corruption and of the expedient pursuit of self-interest. The phrases in common currency plainly indicated the attitudes of the time: 'I'm all right Jack!' – which was a puerile abbreviation of 'Fuck you, Jack – I'm all right!', and 'I couldn't care less.' The good things achieved in human society by a number of generations can be quickly derided and abused by others which follow.

The working of the long tentacles of war, the changes in attitudes towards the Welfare State – even towards the provisions within this for the improvement of the family, came together to create a different ethos in society. So evident and powerful was this as to give rise to what came to be called 'the generation gap'. People of the older generation who could never have brought themselves to apply for state assistance – as being a shameful reflection on their own self-reliance – had no understanding of those among the young who would shamelessly take from 'the State' all they could lay their hands on. Old trade unionists looked down in disgust on the new trade unionists whose attitudes and self-seeking claims were a flat denial of the moral ideals and humane aims of socialism and a sabotaging of all it had managed to achieve. The new society had brought about a character – in social affairs and in individuals – which had not only been unforeseen, but which no one would have believed possible. 'They don't know how well off they are,' said the elderly, disillusioned to a point beyond their comprehension. 'It makes you wonder what we're coming to.' The young ... 'couldn't care less.' And within this over-all context of a change in values, certain quite specific features were noticeable, pointing in a much more telling way to the underlying condition of *crisis*.

(iii) Secularization: a changed condition of knowledge and behaviour

One of these already noted (p. 85–6) was the marked secularization of thought, attitudes, and behaviour. There is no doubt whatever about the considerable growth in the number of civil marriages and the parallel decline of marriages solemnized within the rituals of all the religious organizations. Clearly, this trend could not, in itself, be taken to signify any decline in responsibility in marriage or in subsequent family commitments, but the changed behaviour with regard to marriage could not possibly have existed alone. It must have rested upon a change in underlying convictions, or, at least, an acknowledgment of the absence of certain convictions, and this has very far-reaching implications.

In the first and most limited sense (relating to marriage alone), and coupled with the changing attitudes to divorce which culminated in the Reform Act of 1969, there is no doubt that the conception of marriage was changed for a growing number of people in one quite fundamental sense. Though, in civil marriage, couples still committed themselves to a shared partnership for life, marriage, for them – having lost its sacramental nature – was no longer (of its essential nature) *indissoluble*. Of a civil, contractual nature, it was now terminable. Under the new law at the end of the 1960s, it could be ended by 'mutual consent', and, if so desired, very quickly. To use Barbara Wootton's language, the basic considerations on which its continuity or termination rested were now those of 'happiness' rather than 'holiness'. Together with the 'sacramental nature' of marriage, 'holiness' had gone. For many, one large range of obstacles to the termination of marriages – religious considerations which had made the ending of marriage seem, necessarily, a wrong and evil thing – had gone.

But more deeply than this, two other implications seem bound to be true. First, with the increasingly widespread acceptance of the *authority of science* in establishing our knowledge about the nature of the world, and of its application through technology to the solution of human problems and the bringing of greater degrees of comfort and well-being in every area of human life (the combating of diseases, poverty, etc.), came a definite decline in religion and the authority of its doctrines. This seems arguable because some intelligent people still belong to religious organizations. But the deep and wide decline in the holding of religious beliefs is not arguable; it is an indisputable fact. The demonstration lies in the answer to a simple question: in what area of knowledge about the natural, human, and social world do we now turn to the church, or to any religion, for authoritative answers? The answer is: none. The great majority of people no longer look to any of the churches for authoritative knowledge of any kind. It is not, necessarily, that they have thought matters through deeply and carefully and have come to reject religious doctrines. They simply find these doctrines irrelevant in their experience and out of keeping with such knowledge as they now possess or can readily acquire. Judging, too, by the stances of bishops and priests who patently and fundamentally disagree with the wording of the very doctrines whose words they repeat (and require of others) whilst officiating in the sacraments, and which it is their sworn duty to uphold, religious doctrines are reduced to a babble of unresolved notions of no consequence.

It is not long ago that the minister of religion, especially within the eccelesiastical hierarchy of the Church of England, carried great weight in British society – exercising an authority and power which ranked high in the affairs of state, and one which could be crushingly exerted over individuals in every parish. Now, he goes unregarded. Indeed, in the conflictful transformation of societies in the world, in countries where priests *do* continue to hold authority, religions are coming to be seen, more often than not, as the grounds of fanaticism resisting change and rendering the problematical situations in which they exist incapable of solution. Northern Ireland, South Africa, the Middle East, the Arab world itself, all provide good examples. Religions are commonly assumed to be forces for good in the world, but even this assumption now calls for critical reflection.

But the second, deepest, and most serious matter for concern in this whole area of undermined and rejected beliefs is that the majority of people – deeply affected by the long tentacles of past wars, continually apprehensive under the threat of new and more destructive wars, bewildered and at a loss (sometimes amounting to despair and apathy) within the changing complexities of attitudes and values within the 'House of Administration', the Welfare State, continually subjected to an inundation of 'news' about the conflictful changes in societies throughout the world – *no longer have any firm beliefs whatever*. They live and die within institutions and rituals impregnated with religious symbols (like the burying of their dead) which no longer hold any truth or meaning for them. A general decency is enough to guide most people in regulating the day-to-day expedience of their living – but no view about the nature of the world, the nature and purposes of human destiny, the significance of their own personal lives, is available for them. No clear and firm articulation of beliefs and values lies at the basis of society any more, unifying the minds and feelings of its people, linking together in a meaningful way their feeling, thought, and action. And perhaps in ways more deeply influential than we realize this goes beyond *belief* alone. It is by no means certain that a large proportion of the labouring classes in Britain ever seriously held or knew or understood the doctrines of the church. But, by and large, they had a *respect* for religion. And, more particularly, whatever the beliefs of their parents, children in Sunday Schools, children in their daily school assemblies, sang hymns collectively and took part in shared occasions of public worship (whether the elements of doctrine in them were known or believed or not). Rituals and seasonally recurring festivals embodied religious symbols, and *sentiments* were established within them. But now these actual situations providing shared experience and behaviour, as well as indications of the grounds of belief, are largely gone, or, at the very least, are greatly diminished. There is an anarchy of doctrines now, and an anarchy in values, and therefore a directionlessness and incoherence of behaviour. We no longer know in any ultimate or satisfying sense where we are going, or why, and know that within the gigantic scale and complexity of things which knowledge presents, and with the continually extending range of knowledge which lies further and further beyond our scope and comprehension, we cannot possibly establish such a satisfactory over-view for ourselves. In the 1920s and 1930s, T. S. Eliot voiced the dilemmas and agony of this situation as he saw it:

> The endless cycle of idea and action,
> Endless invention, endless experiment,
> Brings knowledge of motion, but not of stillness;
> Knowledge of speech, but not of silence;
> Knowledge of words, and ignorance of the Word.
> All our knowledge brings us nearer to our ignorance,
> All our ignorance brings us nearer to death,
> But nearness to death no nearer to God.
> Where is the Life we have lost in living?

Where is the wisdom we have lost in knowledge?
Where is the knowledge we have lost in information?
The cycles of Heaven in twenty centuries
Bring us farther from God and nearer to the Dust.[9]

Finding no consolation, no position of doctrine to meet our spiritual
need, he bemoaned our condition:

... our lot crawls between dry ribs
To keep our metaphysics warm.[10]

But now ... we do not even have a metaphysic!

All this has two clear corollaries which are important for the
development of our analysis. First, with the decline of religion, one
large ground for the *establishment of sentiments* in society and
individuals alike has largely gone, and, so far, has been replaced only
by radical and continuing doubt. Under all the continuing panoply of
State and Church in our new society, within the enormously
complicated architecture of our House of Administration, (our
Welfare State) there is, in fact, a void. At the heart of our personal
nature, where a core of deeply established sentiments should give
some meaning and direction to our life, our courses of conduct, and
our death, there is only a vacuum.

And second, within this vacuum, lacking any touchstone of truth
and value, what I have called the 'half-baked' notions of personal
relationships and their reciprocal obligations – especially with regard
to marriage, cohabitation, and the like – have a wide ground for their
display and for their assertive claims to be as authoritative a basis for
life in society as any other. When it is generally thought that there are
no demonstrable grounds supporting some beliefs as against others,
some values as against others, the emphasis upon equality within
democracy becomes a sufficient criterion for believing and doing
anything. Libertarianism becomes licence; tolerance becomes an
uncaring disregard of others; any opinion is as good as any other.
But, says Plato, the extreme 'democratic man' is only one step away
from the dogmatic 'tyrannical man'. Later, when considering the
ways in which *appetite* has displaced *sentiment* within the new
society, we will come again to Plato's warning: that, in a condition of
extreme democratic anarchy, when the 'hydra-headed beast' of the
desiring element in our nature usurps and supplants the elements of
spirit and reason, the 'hydra-headed beast' – promising to serve all
our appetites – can quickly become the worst of dictators. In a

vacuum – a star, a demagogue, a leader, is easily noticed, and just as readily worshipped.

(iv) The de-moralization of society

We come now to what I believe lies at the very heart of our crisis. Troubled within the social and personal disorders of a century of recurring and still threatening war, troubled within the unforeseen and changed character of the House of Administration we have built, troubled within a growing complexity of *societal* regulations and requirements which increasingly denude us of a natural environment and the conditions of *community*, troubled within unresolved and many-sided disagreements about beliefs and values – we have also created a *crisis of communications*; and this it is which I believe to be fundamental.

It is here that we can usefully turn back to the diagrams in the introduction (p. 34) and the ideas of Cooley and Mead (briefly mentioned there) about the basic nature of communications in human experience. Communications, they claimed, were not only something taking place *between* people, but, more fundamentally and within primary groups, were involved in the actual *making* of the human person. Gradually moving through the process of growth and maturation from childhood and adolescence to adulthood, and, during this, moving out from the home and family to the ever-widening awareness of society beyond, *sentiments* were inwardly established as part of the very nature of the 'self' as the regulations and values which constituted the forms of social institutions were observed, encountered, and experienced. In the two diagrams, the *subjective course* of this process can be traced within the *objective nature* of society. In a relatively simple society, the process will, itself, be relatively simple; in a highly specialized, large-scale, and complicated society – not so. But in *all* cases, the growth from birth to maturity of the *human person* is essentially a *social-psychological* process. At the origin and heart of it, as the essential condition for it, lies the nature of *primary group communications*. And these, initially, lie in *the family*. As Cooley very firmly puts it: 'The family and neighbourhood life is essential to its genesis, *and nothing more is.*'

THE NATURAL-SOCIAL SEQUENCE: SELF AND SOCIETY: INSTITUTIONS AND SENTIMENTS

Let us now think of the family in Britain not narrowly – in terms of marriage, cohabitation, or sexual morals alone (of who sleeps with who and the many ramifications of all this) – but more fundamentally as the primary *domestic group* in society: essentially involved in the stable satisfaction of the whole range of our needs, and involving all the dimensions of our human nature and personal fulfilment. Let us do this thoroughly, too, in such a way as to see the broader context but also make clear the *uniqueness* of our own situation and experience in the second half of the twentieth century.

The first clear point is that in *all* human societies hitherto, the domestic group of the family has been *universal*. In all societies *domestic groups* have existed as the smallest formally defined *primary* groups in their societies: long-abiding, face-to-face groups of parents and children tied to each other by the most intimate bonds of blood, upbringing, and the continual sharing of circumstances, conditions, family tasks, joys, problems, pleasures, and couched within the context of wider kinship relationships which constitute a special set of relationships within the wider community. Such primary groups have been essentially the same in many respects – have possessed the same kinds of relationships and characteristics – no matter what the kind of society or civilization in which they have existed, no matter by what religion, political authority, etc., they have been regulated. And *everywhere* it is in them that primary group values – 'primary group ideals' – have been established. It is here that those basic conceptions and sentiments – of motherhood, fatherhood, brotherhood, filial loyalty and duty, natural justice, concern for dependent young and dependent aged, etc., etc. – which have been found everywhere in the world's folklore and literature, and which enable human beings everywhere in the world to understand each other, have been established. When we speak of our 'basic human nature', we speak not only of anatomical, physiological, and psychological elements genetically established, but also of those basic sentiments and social relationships which everywhere distinguish human character. Domestic groups, everywhere, have formed the primary group context for the establishment of those primary ideals and values which we know as our 'human nature', and by which most of our conduct is inwardly as well as externally governed.

187

The second important point is that, hitherto, in all societies, it has been through this primary group experience of domestic groups that individuals have grown from infancy to adolescence, and then into their adult commitments in the secondary groups of society – economic, religious, political, professional, military, etc. The domestic group in every society has been the universal *avenue* of growth from birth to adulthood. There has always been, in short, a *natural-social sequence* of growth through which the natural world and society have been gradually experienced, and during which *sentiments* have been gradually established as a ground for *personal character* and for the regulation of behaviour within *social institutions* alike. Just to be meticulously clear about all this, let us stop to trace it as being true in the most ordinary and familiar experience of every one of us.

In times past, a child has first known, during its earliest years, its own hearth and home, its own parents, brothers and sisters. Only gradually has he or she then explored the world beyond his own doorway: only gradually explored the back-yard, the fields, the lanes, the streets, the countryside and neighbourhood round about – and then chiefly in small play-groups appropriate to his age. Only gradually has he then moved beyond the neighbourhood and immediate community to the larger and more distant organizations of society. Through his own experience at school, through his own teachers, he has gradually become aware of the entire educational system in society beyond. Seeing the policeman on the street-corner, he has gradually become aware that there exists beyond a whole system of law and order – of magistrates, judges, courts. Through attending his own local chapel or church, through the minister or vicar or local preachers, he has gradually learned that larger churches lie beyond them, and, indeed, other religions beyond the shores of his own nation. Through witnessing local elections and the occasional ceremonials of councillors, he has gradually become aware of the wider political system as a whole with its central government seated in the capital city. There has been a clear measured path from his home-conditions and experience in infancy within the domestic group, to his adult membership in some of the many secondary groups and larger organizations in society – his place of work and occupation, his trade union or professional organization, his political party. This has not, by any means, been a matter of simple 'determinism', of having his character 'moulded' to fit society, without conflict or disagreement (no doubt in every group and at every stage), but it has been a clear avenue for the process of growth and a clear basis for establishing stability and ensuring continuity. In particular, through the general awareness of the values which lay at the core of the customs, conventions and institutions of society, *sentiments* have been established as a core of values within the very self-consciousness and character of the individual's own nature (as part of the 'self'): a clear set of *feelings* of approval and disapproval, right and wrong, but also accompanied by *reasons* for the inner self-regulation of conduct.

All this leads to a further point. In relatively simple societies (from those of the pre-literate peoples to those of our own agrarian societies before the onset of industrialization) this pattern had a measured degree of *continuity*. Sons and daughters followed their mothers and fathers into the same kinds of homes, crafts, trades, professions, levels of education, conditions of life, within the same areas and communities. By and large, where they were born, there they lived and died. Even with the degree of mobility mentioned by Anderson during the nineteenth century (when, of course, rural life was being – in many areas – supplanted) there was no sudden 'cutting off' of children from the *general way and level of life* of their parents. The sentiments of one generation informed the next. There was a substantial degree of continuity through life of those kinds of relationships and values which had been established within the domestic groups of their childhood experience. The *natural-social sequence* of personal growth, of the growth of character, was the basis of a total way of life, and for the whole of life.

In traditional societies experiencing relatively little change, the *natural-social sequence* of human growth led to the establishment of *sentiments* which were the firm foundation for the continuity of 'self' and 'society' alike. The core-values of customs, conventions and institutions were closely related to the core-values of personal character and conduct. And it was the *domestic group, the family*, which was at the heart of the process of establishing these living elements of the social tradition.

But we come, now, much more directly and forcefully to Westermarck's basic question.

Are the collective conditions of our modern society such as to be eroding the very basis of the domestic group and community life which have so far been the most fundamental foundations of our social order and personal character alike? Are they such as to be preventing the very establishment of such sentiments? Are they preventing the very coming into existence of such sentiments – either in the 'self' (as the basis for the inner regulation of character and

189

personal conduct), or in 'society' (as the core of institutional regulations and the necessary basis for the continued observance and maintenance of these regulations) –therefore undermining both the personal and the social order we have long taken for granted? Has the very society we have created by our 'improvements' come to be destructive of the very roots of morality we had hoped more deeply to have established, and more richly and more discriminatingly to have refined? Are we witnessing, literally, a de-moralization of society – in 'self' and 'society' alike?

In what follows, I want to try to answer this large question by pointing to some considerations which do at least seem plausible. The crucial fact on which I want to concentrate is the radical disturbance, if not the destruction, of the *natural-social sequence* (this, I believe, is where our crisis really lies), but, before this, one other widely voiced ground for concern which we noted earlier must at least be mentioned.

SOCIAL ISOLATION

Time and time again we have seen – though perceived and emphasized very differently from different approaches – that one very widespread suspicion, mounting in some to full conviction, is that families in modern society suffer (in some way or other) social isolation. It is in this sense that the nuclear family has been sharply distinguished from the extended family and adversely criticized. There is clearly a many-sided persuasion that in the complex and large-scale collective conditions of our present-day society domestic groups may be so driven into situations of social isolation, into so confined an inward-looking and intense privacy, that they never experience any conditions or sense of familiar and supportive community at all. This has many aspects. On one hand, urbanization itself – the endless growth of conurbations spreading outwards in shapeless congestion from our towns and cities – seems such as to confront families with almost completely impersonal conditions of life. Studies of families moved out to the 'New Towns' have described this.

One other deeply important (but often neglected) corollary of this *total* urban environment – of buildings, streets, traffic, and its night sky of electric lights – and one going beyond social considerations alone, is that it is such as to blot out the *natural world* and any experience of it entirely. Of the nature of the created world beyond its street-frontages – there is nothing. Society is all. There can be no experience here of a Wordsworthian appreciation of the 'powers in the great and permanent objects' of the world so closely linked with the 'indestructible qualities of the human mind'; no sense of glory in the apprehension of the forms of the natural world experienced by Traherne; nothing of the almost mystical sense of some spiritual relationship with nature experienced by a Richard Jefferies or a W. H. Hudson. Social experience aside, *some* sentiments – with all their profound implications for some of the most important dimensions of our nature, and our awareness and cultivation of them – *are never experienced at all*, and *can* never be experienced within such an environment. But the sheer material aspects of urbanization are not all.

Besides the streets and squares of brick-and-mortar, glass-and-concrete, there is also the 'House of Administration' we have made: the modern 'social system'. Each family is placed, too, within a vast fabric of regulations it can never possibly fully know. It can never have time enough to read through all the 'small print'; to keep abreast with all the ever-changing formulations. Even officials themselves are defeated by the rapidity of change. The scale and complexity of our governmental and administrative apparatus – with its departments of state, council offices, channels of application, hierarchy of bureaucrats – is such as to make the relationship of the family to society a matter of endless, detailed requirements, statutory obligations, entitlements and calculations and regulations as to how to make claims. Each family, each household, each home, is one 'cell' defined and regulated within the administrative 'system'. For many, any sense of community or of personal significance in society of their individual membership has been sorely diminished if not completely destroyed. It used to be said that a man was a 'number on a clock-card'; now he is a name and number on a thousand forms. Our many well-intentioned social reforms, all actually making many important welfare provisions, have constructed a vast over-arching system of rules, offices, and officials within which families and individuals have lost any sense of a life of personal significance beyond their place within the system itself. Clearly, in terms of social policy, this points to the desirability of finding some way of *building community back into society*; of making the House of Administration habitable.

But I come back, now, to what I believe to be the most crucial consideration of all.

THE NATURAL-SOCIAL SEQUENCE DESTROYED: MASS-COMMUNICATIONS AND THE INVASION OF THE HOME

There is one obvious and quite unique way in which the families in modern society, these 'cells' in the 'social system', are linked more intimately than they have ever been before, and it is here that we come to the *crisis of communications*. Boxed into urban privacy, largely stripped of a context of wider community, the domestic group – the most important primary group in society – is now continually invaded by all the secondary-group influences of society through the mass-media: especially by television. The entire world is brought into each living room. The television set in the corner is now the window in every home through which the members of every family look *out* on to the world, and through which society pours its influences *in*. It is more than a little significant that the *hearth* is no longer the focus of the home, domestic gatherings, and family conversations. The flame of the domestic fire which was once the *sacred* flame for home and society alike, binding together all the families and ancestors of the whole people – the significant symbol at the heart of some religions – has gone out! Now central heating pipes run inconspicuously round the edges of our rooms, and the focus of attention is ... the television set.

The point of central importance here is that the earlier *natural-social sequence* of the growth of the human person has been, and continues to be, disturbed in the most fundamental way, and perhaps destroyed. Literally from the point of birth onwards, the window of television is an integral and perhaps the most dominating part of the child's environment. Long before a child has crawled out of the door of his home down the path to the gate (if there *is* a path and a gate), kicked a tin over the nearby rubbish tip, played in the park down the street – perhaps before he has even seen, let alone played with, the children in the houses round the corner – he will have seen hundreds of instances of the worst human catastrophes in Latin America or Africa, floods in Bangladesh, bomb atrocities in Northern Ireland (the cameras dwelling for some moments on the blood-stained pavement), the hijacking of planes over the Mediterranean and the Middle East; thousands of advertisements for every product on the market – brands of petrol, breakfast cereal, deodorants, soap-powders, alcoholic drinks, cruise holidays; as well as plays, films, and 'comedy series' exhibiting every diversity and extremity of adult behaviour – including the most brutal violence on the street or in warfare, nudity, copulation, and the advertisement, display, and dramatic presentation of all kinds of abnormality and perversion – from homosexuality to drug-addiction. In a way completely new in the history of mankind, the many-faceted outside world has invaded the home. Society has invaded the domestic group. The natural-social sequence has been radically changed. In the form (and of the nature) in which it once existed, it has been destroyed.

What does this mean for what was once a process of learning gradually about the institutions of society in terms of gradually widening personal behaviour and experience? What does it mean for the inner establishment of sentiments as this gradual accommodation to the institutions of society took place? What does it mean for the shaping of human character? – for the making of 'selves' in society? We must probe further into these questions, but it is worthwhile to note that this same point, this same concern, has been voiced in another way.

In America (as in Britain) the effects of television on children has been the subject of much research. One such researcher, Professor Neil Postman of New York University, has concluded not only that these effects are in many ways 'disastrous', but also, and more fundamentally, that they are 'robbing children of their childhood' – of the childhood which used to be taken for granted as 'normal'. He goes so far as to write of the 'Disappearance of Childhood', and some of the facts he has assembled go a very long way towards demonstrating 'the destruction of the natural-social sequence'. The average American child between the ages of 6 and 18 spends 13,000 hours at school, but 15,000 to 16,000 hours in front of the television set. Furthermore, television is deeply influential in the home long before school is encountered at all, and continues to be powerfully influential throughout the whole of school life and after. It is, in fact, the *normal* ever-present background and accompaniment of communications into which 'education' can be said to break. It is a myth, too, that there is any effective distinction between 'children's' and 'adult' programming. Between midnight and 2.00 a.m. in America, 750,000 children are still 'viewing'. Childhood and adulthood are being brought together in the same range of experience and influences. A process of 'homogenization' has taken place. The following are just a few of his comments:

> The language of adults and children tends to merge, as do their
> interests, their dress, their amusements. There are fewer and
> fewer distinguishing characteristics in children's clothing or in

children's games. Television communicates the same information to everyone simultaneously, regardless of age, sex, level of education or life experience. Therefore television eliminates many of the important ways that we distinguish between children and adults. . . .

For example one of the main differences between an adult and a child is that the adult knows about certain facets of life – its mysteries, its contradictions, its violence, its tragedies – that are not considered suitable for children to know, or even accessible to children. What television does is to bring the whole culture out of the closet, because programmes need a constant supply of novel information.

In its quest for new and sensational ventures to hold its audience, television must tap every existing taboo in the culture: homosexuality, incest, divorce, promiscuity, corruption, adultery, and terrible displays of violence and sadism. As a consequence, these become as familiar to the young as they are to adults.

Some of the highest-paid models in America are now 12- and 13-year-old girls who are presented to us in the guise of sexually enticing adults, so much so that old-timers might yearn for the innocence of Lolita compared to these. If you look at the children as they are depicted on situation comedies, you find that they're really little adults. Their language is the same as adults, their interests the same, their sexuality the same. It's getting harder to find children who are portrayed as children in many prime-time shows.[11]

Surely it is not too much to say that the natural-social sequence of times past has been *destroyed*? But, radical though this is in itself, and of itself, other changes in social facts have accompanied it and reinforced its effects.

PLAY

Within this entire context of relative social isolation, the increasingly contained privacy of the family, and the dominant intrusion of mass-communications into the home, it seems likely, too, that the natural-social sequence has been further affected by changes in the nature and significance of *play*. Play-groups, of course, are the other primary groups within the neighbourhood outside the family, and Cooley emphasizes their importance too (as, incidentally, does Jean

Piaget). To a considerable extent, children no longer *go out to play*. The Newsons, in particular, have shown how far it is true that parents tend to prevent their children from playing in the streets and neighbourhood because of their fear of the new collective conditions of the environment, and the kinds of influence their children will encounter there (see 'Four Years Old in an Urban Community', note 12, p. 272). This *was* especially true of middle-class families. But conditions have worsened since the Newsons wrote. In general, and now for the children of *all* social classes, to go out to play is not *safe*. The fact, and the increasing consequence, is that the only street-playing, street-marauding children or young people of both sexes are likely to be those whose parents lack persuasive influences or disciplined control. The streets, after school and in the evenings, are the places for the gatherings of the louts, the vandals, the hooligans. Instead of being allowed to run off into the woods (if there are any woods), dam up and paddle in streams, slide down rubbish-tips or grassy banks on old tin trays or lengths of cardboard, children are now kept indoors to play on the floor at home with the latest mechanical and electronic toys advertised on television – which tend to go wrong within a few days of purchase. It is probably not too strong to say that it is the least intelligent parents who are attracted (by advertising) to the worst kinds of toys. Here again, families – domestic groups – in ways additional to those mentioned before, have become inwardly contained 'cells' of the great society, more and more prone to the extensive influences and titillations of a 'consumerism' more and more bolstered by all the arts of modern advertising and marketing.

EDUCATION: THE PEER GROUP: THE 'CUT-OFF POINT'

One other result of our deliberate reforms lies in the changes brought about in education itself. This has many aspects but we may begin, again, by recalling Anderson's description of the *protracted* nature of the passing of an individual from childhood and youth to an adulthood in which he, or she, was head (or partnered the head) of an independent household. During the past 25 years a very considerable difference has been brought about by *three* reforms.

First, education has now become *universally systematized*. Until the Second World War, the vast majority of children left school at the end of their 'elementary education', and, at the age of 14, became employed in the neighbourhood in which their parents were living.

Only a small minority went on to secondary education, and very few indeed to higher education. Since the Second World War (with the coming into force of the 1944 Education Act), two fundamental changes have been made. First, secondary education (and therefore greater opportunities for moving on to some form of the further and higher education) has been extended and made compulsory for all, and second, under the influence of political pressures, has come to be organized in the one form which is now almost universal throughout the country: the form of comprehensive education.

The results of this are extremely complex, but a few points seem clear. First, the demands and pressures in education upon all children, the expectations that they should try 'to do well' and 'better than their parents', have been increased and intensified. The range of opportunities and choices before them has been extended. Children no longer expect, and can no longer be expected, to do what their parents did, to be satisfied with what satisfied their parents, to stay, live, and work in or near the same neighbourhood, and follow the same occupations. The old ground for a continuity of ways of life shared by generations has gone. The natural-social sequence has been disturbed even here. But there has been one much more clear result. Now, every new generation of children passes through the same educational system (through primary school and then through comprehensive school) in the same way and through the same sequence of age-groups and stages. Having experienced the same pattern and pace of education, each generation of children leaves the educational system to enter adult society in the same way and at the same time. This has created a qualitatively new element in British society: *the peer group*, and this, in itself, has come to have many implications.

With the new levels of affluence, and from the earliest years (within the primary school, for example), children have generous allowances of pocket money and are exposed to all the fashions continually exhibited on television in their homes. Manufacturers and entrepreneurs – of toys, clothes, musical instruments, pop records, hair-styles, make-up – direct their marketing activities in this direction. Children and teenagers are identifiable markets; distinct commercial bands of the population. And this – at the most sinister level – seems now to include a massive commercial exploitation of the market for drugs, down to 'pushers' in the streets and the school playgrounds. Part of the 'exploitation' of a market, too, is the actual creation of such a market. Fashions are changed so deliberately and frequently that each peer group (each generation) will come through their own particular period of childhood and youth having experienced one range of such fashions, consumer goods, clothes, songs, kinds of dancing. So powerful have all their combined influences become that the peer group has become a powerful repository of *sentiments* in its own right. The vast implanting of values and attitudes in one such generational clientele is powerfully resistant to the influences or efforts at discipline of both parents and teachers alike. The television screen at home carries its own continual basis of comparison between the possessions, styles of life, and characteristics of celebrities and those of parents and teachers – and parents and teachers frequently come off worse, seeming very drab, 'wet', 'square', by contrast. The peer group is a new social entity in our new society – a new clientele, a new quasi-group, with its own 'culture', tastes, attitudes, and demands. It is significant too – a point to which we shall come later – that this entire development became more marked during 'the Swinging Sixties', having become even more marked and more systematically exploited ever since.

But the power of the peer group has been reinforced (perhaps in part created) by two other quite precise changes. On the one hand, the age of majority was lowered from 21 to 18 at the end of the 1960s (from 1 January 1970, following the Family Law Reform Act). On the other, the school-leaving age was raised from 15 to 16 in 1972. Far from being protracted in the ways Anderson described, the transition from dependent childhood and adolescence to that of independent adulthood was now very precisely marked indeed. We have now, in short, actually created a sharp cut-off point between childhood and adulthood: a point between two statutorily determined ages with only a very brief period between. The great majority of children find the education of their last two years in school of little intrinsic interest, of no use, and, particularly, of no relevance to what they will have to face when school is over. With all the 'cultural' influences playing upon their peer group, they will have been militating against school, chafing against the authority of teachers – even deriding it, and beginning to rebel against the attempted advice and control of parents at home. At the same time, the income-earning (even if it is only from 'Social Security') and responsibility of adulthood – with its new realm of freedom – has been brought very close. They know that two years after the (in their minds) pointless and artificial extension of their supposed childhood, they will be adult members of society: able to marry (or cohabit) without consent, own property, enter into hire purchase agreements, claim social security ... and that they will be surrounded by banks,

197

stores, and financial organizations, all ready to provide and extend credit-facilities for them. Within two years of an education which, in trying to widen their orientations may well have disorientated them, they have to face the actuality of a specific scope of employment within their area, perhaps the prospect of long-term unemployment, and must enter the world of adulthood towards which they have long been tempted by deliberately directed advertising and the desire for an early income. The cut-off point is now sharp and clear.

Is there any wonder that all the families in Britain (parents and children alike) now experience tensions and difficulties as the age of 16 is approached and the age of 18 is reached? Is there any wonder that teachers are faced with indiscipline, disregard, and an insolent and disobedient rejection of their efforts as the age of 16 approaches? The peer group in British society has come into its own: possessing a power and exerting an influence stronger than those of both parents and teachers, home and school. We are now faced not so much with a single 'generation gap' as with a continuing succession of generational peer groups each of whose experience (of particular fashions in clothes, pop music, and the like) has been similar throughout their journey through the schools.

But the most central and important point here – deserving the strongest reiteration – is that the conjunction of all these elements has created a built-in 'cut-off point' in family experience – general, now, throughout society – in what was once a continuity in the natural-social sequence. Parents in every family are now faced with some form of rebellious insistence on independence on the part of their children between the ages of 16 and 18, and it is a structured corollary of the new social system we have made. All family continuities are disturbed and disrupted then – and few of us (as parents) know how to deal with the situation. To help – is wrong. Not to help – is wrong. Everything – is wrong.

Clearly, not *all* children, parents, and teachers find this period and constellation of experience and behaviour as conflictful as my description of it. But the probability is that it is under the conjoined pressures and influences of all these factors that the 'half-baked' conceptions of morality, including those relating to marriage and the family, find their most fertile breeding ground. *This* is the context for the rejection of authority, leaving home, experimenting with drugs – including smoking and alcohol, becoming pregnant as a way to gain independence, etc., etc.

But this is not the end of the story. There is a question which goes deeper.

THE EROSION OF SENTIMENTS?

Might it not be that the conjunction of the radical disturbance of the natural-social sequence, the continual play upon the young of the mass-media, and the power of the peer group, etc, have become such as to be actually destroying some of our most deeply-rooted sentiments of the past? – indeed, preventing the very establishment of them in our nature? Is 'human nature', the human 'self', no longer being formed in the same way, and with the same core of values, in our new society?

Let us, in this, recall Cooley's distinction between an *appetite* and a *sentiment* – that *lust*, for example, is an appetite, whereas *love* is a sentiment – and consider one example: the ideal of 'love' between a man and a woman. It is a commonplace, nowadays, to hear the notion of 'romantic love' being brushed aside as a historically recent and silly aberration of the 1930s. It is more adult, now, to put such nonsense aside and think more realistically about the business of sex. Here, for example, is just one recent publisher's advertisement of a 'new guide to sexuality in the 1980s':

> a guide which is original, unconventional, and fun! Its message is about pleasure and the responsibility of pleasure – physical, emotional, and spiritual. Its conclusions dispel the myths and syndromes that have built up over the last two decades.
> ... The suggestions in '... *Sex*' are all challenging and exciting, and include video fantasy material as the stimulus to enhanced erotic enjoyment; subtle, new erogenous zones, both male and female; how sexual fright can be harnessed for longer, more arousing love-making and why taking intimate risks is the most powerful bridge to higher levels of sensual reward.
> ... What makes '... *Sex*' particularly special is that woven throughout the book you will find a special true-life love story, one which incorporates some of the most erotic and sensual scenes that you have ever dreamed of. These will help to give you even more original and unusual ideas.

The new guide, it is said, 'could alter your private life for ever'.

One is tempted to drop straight down to the vernacular and say that it is enough to make a cat laugh! – but ... let us maintain our serious composure and simply ask: is this really the way of human love? Is there not an ideal of love between a man and a woman, a sentiment which has been deepened and elaborated by poets and others over countless years, which goes much deeper than either 'romantic love' in any superficial sense, or a detailed skill in producing multiple orgasms (to the point of physical exhaustion!)? – which has far deeper roots in the history of mankind than either the cinema-films of the 1930s or the sex guide-books of our own day? Shakespeare's well known sonnet will stand repetition here:

> Let me not to the marriage of true minds
> Admit impediments; love is not love
> Which alters when it alteration finds,
> Or bends with the remover to remove:
> O, no! It is an ever-fixed mark,
> That looks on tempests and is never shaken;
> It is the star to every wandering bark,
> Whose worth's unknown, although his height be taken.
> Love's not Time's fool, though rosy lips and cheeks
> Within his bending sickle's compass come;
> Love alters not with his brief hours and weeks,
> But bears it out even to the edge of doom.
> If this be error and upon me proved,
> I never writ, nor no man ever loved.

– and in the concluding chapter (p. 256) I will come to other statements about the same ideal which may well be surprising. But a thousand other comments of Shakespeare's are equally relevant and revealing. 'The expense of spirit in a waste of shame is lust in action'. 'Love is too young to know what conscience is, yet who knows not conscience is born of love?' His conviction, clearly, is that some moral feeling and commitment stems from a sheer ideality of experience which would be despoiled, betrayed, belittled, by any falling short of it in spirit, or by any conduct which fell below its own high qualities. Moral ideals, in short, are not ephemeral, but part of the *actualities* of our experience. They are *real* in our experience, and exercise a sovereignty over us – even if, sometimes, we are little and fallible enough to fall short of their truth, demeaning both them and ourselves in decidedly ignoble behaviour. And Shakespeare is clear here again: 'The fault, dear Brutus, lies not in our stars, but in ourselves – that we are underlings.' If such ideals do not exist within us, exercising such sovereignty over us, we can have no inner touchstone of values. 'If this be error and upon me proved, I never writ, nor no man ever loved.' *Was* Shakespeare in error in writing about the nature of love in this way?

And Shakespeare, of course, was not alone in probing the nature of moral ideals in us. Dante, Elizabeth Barrett Browning, and hundreds of other poets have clarified the nature of the same sentiments. Some, too, have tried to speak clearly about the consciousness of moral sentiments in our earliest experience, and the peculiarly telling and lasting power of them. Wordsworth, in his 'Ode on the Intimations of Immortality from Recollections of Early Childhood', speaks of:

> ... those *first affections*,
> Those shadowy recollections,
> Which, be they what they may,
> Are yet *the fountain light of all our day*,
> Are yet *a master light in all our seeing*.

And Emily Brontë (in her poem 'Stanzas') from the limited context of her home and family on the edge of the Yorkshire moors:

> Often rebuked, yet always back returning
> *To those first feelings that were born with me*,
> And leaving busy chase of wealth and learning
> For idle dreams of things which cannot be....
>
> I'll walk, but not in old heroic traces,
> And not in paths of high morality,
> And not among the half-distinguished faces,
> The clouded forms of long-past history.
>
> I'll walk *where my own nature would be leading*:
> *It vexes me to choose another guide....*

But in the past, and a long way short of this high level, there were also matters of sheer need which compelled responsible and reciprocal consideration. We must think again at the most practical level of *collective conditions*. Sexual intimacy between young people, between people not joined in marriage, carried the danger and fear of pregnancy, of illegitimacy, of the discovery and disclosure of illicit relationships, and – given the social standards then prevailing – of guilt and shame. Part of the ideality of love was sexual fidelity in ideal terms (as described above) but love also clearly entailed a consideration of a person in ways going far beyond casual sexual gratification alone. And certainly marriage – entailing the lifelong

201

sharing of an undivided way of life, a community of goods, and, within this, a commitment to the having and upbringing of children, should not be entered into lightly, but only when based upon genuine affection and after much consideration. *Now*, however, our new knowledge of contraceptive techniques and the ready availability of them makes it possible to indulge in sexual intercourse without fear and purely for gratificatory pleasure – as we would enjoy any other excitation, or indulge in the satisfaction of any other appetite. Indeed, we now speak of it exactly in these terms as *'having sex'*, and are supplied with guide-books to equip us with the skills required both to extend and intensify our appetite and to gain more intense pleasure in its satisfaction. *Appetite* has displaced *sentiment*. But the question arises: what kinds of personal character and personal relationships can stem from such indulgence alone?

Thinking still of collective conditions, there are also – in addition to these aspects of sexuality itself – the many new complications in the law (e.g. of divorce: the liability of a second wife to have her own income and property estimated as part of her husband's in maintaining his ex-wife, etc.) or in tax regulations which make it, in some circumstances, calculatedly advantageous not to marry. Matters and considerations of this kind, which now surround the relationships of cohabitation or marriage, are extremely complicated. All these factors combined seem to suggest that sexual fidelity is no longer considered an essential element in love, and love is certainly no necessary part of sexual enjoyment. Sexual fidelity does not seem an expectation within marriage either, or marriage any longer a corollary of love. Within these same complexities, too, shared parenthood seems to have become a diminishing element in the bond between a wife and a husband. With some couples, at least, Westermack's notion of the full establishment and deepening of the *conjugal* sentiment with the shared experience of *parenthood* does not seem, very powerfully, to occur. A quickly felt incompatibility following a pre-marital pregnancy and early marriage can lead to a quick divorce against which shared parental responsibility does not stand in the way.

We have thought here only about the sentiment of love and the appetite of sexual desire, but in many other ways one could show, similarly, that the new collective conditions of our society are changing the very basis on which our sentiments are formed – and within which, therefore, the *same* sentiments are no longer being formed at all. But the crux of this entire matter comes with the invasion of the primary group in the home by the mass media, and the radical disturbance, if not the destruction, of the natural-social sequence.

Might it not be that the collective conditions of our present-day society are such as to be eroding the most basic sentiments on which our personal conduct and social institutions have hitherto rested? – that we have made for ourselves a condition in which the problems of largeness of scale and rapidity of change are *defeating* us; in which our basic values, our basic conceptions – though we go on talking about them at a high public level – may, in fact, be in process of being lost, of being insufficiently *realized* in the actuality of individual experience, appreciation, and conscience, within too inflamed a scene of activity – in which *appetite*, and even *contrived appetite*, have displaced *sentiment*. Might it not be a danger that basic sentiments – *conjugal* and *parental* sentiments among them – are failing to become established in the young at all, resulting in a situation in which individual character no longer possesses any firm core of established and binding sentiments, and therefore no ground at all for the *inward self-regulation* of conduct? – and hence our apparent situation (as a society and as individuals) of having no firm inwardly grounded basis of *social control*. Under the clever, technically skilled façade of our society, might it not be that a moral malaise is at work at its very foundations? – that a moral vacuum, a moral anarchy, is being created? – that our problems of social control go down to the very roots of a basic insufficiency of conscience? Does our consciousness of crisis lie here?

Before trying to answer this question in a way which is fully satisfying and convincing to us, one final consideration must be voiced and weighed. It adds a necessary dimension to our analysis, but also bears particularly on the increase in the rate of marital breakdown which took place during the 1960s, which seemed unusual, and for which we need some kind of additional explanation.

APPETITE – NOT SENTIMENT: THE INFLAMED SOCIETY

Following Cooley, we have touched from time to time on the distinction between appetite and sentiment and the displacement of the one by the other. We have seen, too, that war disturbed settled sentiments under the pressure of more immediate appetites; that the change from the use to the abuse of the Welfare State marked a movement away from an attachment to governing principles towards appetite, self-gain and self-interest; that the decline of religion meant the removal of one many-dimensioned ground for the establishing of sentiments – leaving an emptiness of doctrines and a lack of coherence in some thinking, feeling, and behaviour; and we have seen that the crisis of communications, the breaking of the natural-social sequence, led to conditions making for an erosion of sentiments – even to a failure in establishing them in personal character – and therefore to a possible condition of radical de-moralization. The displacement and replacement of sentiment by appetite is therefore a fact, and a theme, of obvious importance. Following Plato, too, we have mentioned the usurping of reason in the government of our whole nature by the 'hydra-headed beast' of the desires – especially when these are inflamed and overrun all bounds of constraint in unfettered freedom. These two ideas, essentially the same, now require further elaboration, and it is best to begin with Plato.

Writing some two and a half thousand years ago, Plato believed that the kind of human situation we are discussing would always arise (i.e. not *only* in modern industrial society) whenever appetites were allowed to displace more deeply founded sentiments, whenever desires were allowed to brush aside values and ideals. In analysing this danger to which mankind was perennially prone, he drew the distinction between 'the Simple Society' and 'the Inflamed Society'.[13]

The Simple Society was that in which man, possessing his own distinctive nature (that distinguishing him from other animal species), fulfilled this nature in the satisfaction of all his needs (not simply some to the exclusion of others) in reciprocal relationships and commitments with his fellows, and on the basis of clear moral ideals and principles which regulated his individual character and the order of his community alike; which governed both the individual 'self' and 'society'. These moral ideals rested upon the long experience and customs of generations of people, well considered by reason, and were abiding verities because they were rooted in the permanent elements of man's nature, the permanent interconnections between them, and the socially necessary kinds of relationship which they entailed, with their standards of reciprocal conduct. By clearly recognizing the *several* pressing elements of his nature (needs, appetites, rational and spiritual elements alike), and governing these in accordance with reason and the recognition and clarification of the ideals they and the relationships between them entailed, man could enjoy a fulfilment of character and an achievement of excellence in all his activities within the context of a clearly known life of community and through the whole natural course of his life – from birth, through growth and maturity, to death. A recognition of needs and ideals, of the fact that limits were a necessary condition both for regulation and for growth and fulfilment, of the related conditions of both discipline and cultivation, were the grounds for excellence in all directions of human effort and achievement, and of spiritual growth in the making of character. The character of the good individual and of the good society were all of a piece.

By contrast, the *Inflamed Society* was that where unrestrained and extravagantly extended appetite became dominant; in which limits, constraining ideals, discipline, and, indeed, the very government of human nature and society *as* a whole (taking into account and regulating *all* the elements of it in relation to each other) were abandoned if they conflicted with desire and self-interest; in which men calculatedly used and (when expedient) denied all ideals and principles in the ambitious pursuit of wealth and power to gain those ends of gratification and exhibitionism which had become fashionable. With the endless excitation and contrived multiplication of competing wants, the division of labour in society itself became highly specialized, inflated and extreme. Men were no longer related to each other in terms of face-to-face reciprocal co-operation with immediately seen obligations and responsibilities, but – in a highly organized, complex, crowded, confused society – manipulated and exploited each other, treating others only as means to the securing of their own ends. The Inflamed Society lacked statesmen of principle who sought to clarify the ideals of the good society and worked in government to approximate to them as closely as possible for the well-being of all the people, but was plagued, instead, by 'politicians' and 'negotiators' – who used any chicanery, any trick of demagogy, which could win people in the direction of their own interests.

It is necessary to add to this, that, in speaking of the 'desires' and their demand for gratification, Plato did not believe that these were simply of the nature of (say) hunger, thirst, sexual propensities, or those other straightforward appetites at the core of our needs. They were not simply plain and relatively innocent promptings. He believed that, ungoverned, they readily led to excess, endless excitation, a kind of cumulative intensity of hunger, and to viciousness. Like the 'hydra-headed beast' (and hence the image), when one head was cut off (one appetite gratified), several more reared up to take its place – all more ravenous than the last. Plato believed, in short, that the appetitive dimension of human nature had a dark and potentially evil side, and that the unrestrained unfettering of the desires, the allowing of full freedom to the appetites and the unlimited excitation of them, could quickly lead to a condition of *inflammation*, and then to an erupting of the *worst* desires. 'What we want to be sure of', he writes:

> ... is this: that a terrible, fierce, and lawless class of desires exists in every man, even in those of us who have every appearance of being decent people. Its existence is revealed in dreams.... The worst of men is surely the man who expresses in waking reality the character we attributed to a man in his dreams ... he will ever be dragged about by a madness of desire, and be full of confusion and remorse ... every day and every night will produce a thick crop of terrible desires whose wants are many.[14]

The usurping of reason and spirit in the service of appetite can quickly lead to the tyranny of appetite in the whole constitution of the individual and society, and it is in this sense that the extreme democratic man – allowing equal reign to all elements of human nature, without discrimination, government, or control; allowing all things and all opinions to all men and giving equal weight to them whatever the level of their nature and cultivation – is only a very short step away from the tyrannical man: the man dominated, ruled over, by his desires and all that will seem to serve them. The picture brings us back to the lines of Yeats, speaking of our modern condition:

> Things fall apart; the centre cannot hold;
> Mere anarchy is loosed upon the world,
> The blood-dimmed tide is loosed, and everywhere
> The ceremony of innocence is drowned;
> The best lack all conviction, while the worst
> Are full of passionate intensity.

The point I wish to make is that it is this – the change from a Simple Society to an Inflamed Society – which is exactly the kind of change which overcame Britain during the years following the Second World War, and which, coupled with all the factors we have already mentioned, especially characterized the 1960s.

The beginning of the 1960s was just the time when the 'war-children' and the children born into the families established in the immediate aftermath of the war were reaching adolescence and early adulthood. It was just the time when the established apparatus of the Welfare State, having succeeded in bringing about a more widely shared affluence, was beginning to be taken for granted, found irksome by the young, abused rather than supported and used by a growing number. It was just the time when the pressures of the new education – competitive at the point of secondary school selection, vexed and

206

intruded upon by a politically contrived picture of class inequalities and injustices – were being felt more and more intensely; when status consciousness and status emulation were becoming more intense; when education was coming to be looked upon *not* as education but increasingly as a set of avenues and badges-of-qualifications leading to something else. It was just the time of the conjunction of all these (and other related) elements, when a climate of libertarianism, of rebellion against both austerities and authorities began to develop. Rapidly, this became all-pervasive. In particular, closely related to the newly acquired degree of affluence, it led, too, to an enhanced and widespread focus upon the deliberate multiplication and inflammation of appetite, a growing focus upon 'consumerism'.

Already, during the 1950s, the commercial cultivation of youth fashions had been at work. Teddy Boys stood about, exhibiting their splendid Edwardian clothes and distinctive hair-styles. But at the beginning of the 1960s, 'pop culture' and the ethos of 'the Consumer Society' erupted suddenly, became a new social phenomenon, infecting and coming to characterize the whole of society. The whole decade – marked by its wide and wild liberation from constraints, by a social satire which sneered at respectability – became known as 'the Swinging Sixties'. 'Beatle Mania' swept over the entire country; became, indeed, almost the image of post-war Britain overseas. Strangely, the career of the Beatles exactly spanned the 1960s – beginning at the very beginning of the decade and ending in 1970. But this was not just another popular 'craze' – a new music, a new proliferation of guitar-playing 'groups'. The accent was on the word 'mania'. A qualitatively new mass phenomenon, a kind of mass fever, had emerged; something closely connected with (made possible, and then enhanced by) the new mass media and its degree of availability which was being rapidly widened. Pop stars became idols worshipped in a new climate of mass hysteria. Teenage girls screamed, wept, swooned in concert halls and at airports. And the newly young found a distinctive life of their own presented to them in other, but related, ways. Leather jackets, slicked-back hair-styles, miniskirts, motor-scooters ... new fashions followed on the heels of new fashions. Group-patterned stereotypes of behaviour were rapidly established and as rapidly spread. Different fashions distinguished different gangs (Mods and Rockers, for example), different kinds of holiday gatherings, and sometimes gang conflicts and gang fights sometimes ending in an uncaring, mindless, frenzied smashing of property. At the same time gaily coloured vans, brightly painted with large-spreading petals, toured the roads of Britain symbolizing the peace-loving (and sometimes drug-enhanced) life-style of the Hippies and their Flower Power. Later, carrying on through the 1970s and into the 1980s, came Punks with safety pins through the skin of their foreheads, ears and noses, and Hell's Angels, the full blast of their motor-bike exhausts roaring up and down the promenades of seaside resorts and needing deployments of police as large as those called out for conferences of the National Front. Part-bald, shaved to the scalp, part stuck-up into spear-like points or like the brush of the Last of the Mohicans, and now multi-coloured (red, white, green, yellow, blue, shocking pink), new hair-styles for men replaced the staid and universal 'short back and sides' of the pre-war world. It seems true, too, that the trends in most of these fashions was markedly and deliberately, in fact, opposed to any kind of social formality and respectability, a rejection of all the gradations of civil society, levelling, a rejecting of all social distinctions, even to a rejection of cleanliness. If cleanliness was next to Godliness – than they would go to the Devil! As denim jackets came into being, they had to be patched. As jeans came into being, they had to be too long, dragging along the paving-stones, ragged round the bottoms. You had, too, to look perpetually unshaven, and, it seemed, go unwashed. The old and respectable were no longer able to understand the young *at all*; they could feel nothing but impatience, distaste, disgust – and also despair. So outrageous, so extreme, so pointless in its frequent outbursts of aggression and destructiveness, so lacking in the most minimal consideration of others ... the behaviour of the young was such as to widen the 'generation gap' into a gulf beyond all possibility of bridging. What values motivated young people like these? How had post-war society – which had done so much for them – given rise to them?

It would, of course, be churlish, absurd, and false to link all high-spirited activities of young people with immorality, or think that the entire younger generation was enslaved by these fashions or devoid of moral values – despite the fact that the anti-social behaviour of some was plainly reprehensible. Obviously, too, the very focus of the mass media may well have exaggerated the extent of it. In any event, it was by no means only a creation of the young themselves. Commercial exploiters – agents, manufacturers, record companies, clothes designers, were already cultivating the new market. The contrivance and engendering of appetite was now 'big business'. But the nature and scale of this mass behaviour was something new in British society, a unique corollary of all the social changes, changes in technology, changes in mass communications, which were afoot.

Even in itself, this seemed a rebellion against authority, a rejection of the respectable order of society, and perhaps most of the young involved in the more public demonstrations of behaviour were those who could not see a way ahead through the newly established but conventional avenues of social opportunity to satisfactory ends of education, occupation, status, and wealth. They were (perhaps?) finding other ways of calling attention to themselves, registering their presence, making a gesture to indicate their existence and their own need for feelings of personal significance. But deeper elements of libertarianism – also, under the same influences, becoming ever more extreme – were parallel with this, and again had both their good sides and their bad. Improvements ... they provided society with new problems.

With the new openness of attitudes towards sex and contraception, the ready availability of contraceptives and the falling away of any sense of social disapproval over buying and using them, came a new libertarianism in sexual behaviour itself – extending now to the very young. Here, too, appetite seemed uppermost. 'Having sex' – like smoking and drinking – was a partaking in adult appetites; a tasting and enjoyment of what was withheld. School children now talked of their 'right' to 'have sex'. The very word 'morality', just one other aspect of 'respectability', brought smirks to lips or outright guffaws. It was 'square' – a thing of the past. 'Ah, yes ... well ... things have changed.' On televised discussion programmes young men would ridicule chastity and boast of how many women they had taken to bed. They knew the exact number (not 83 or 85, but exactly 84), almost as though, like outlaws of the Wild West, they took pride in notching up each killing on the butt of their revolver. But the libertarian climate spread to kinds of sexual appetite and behaviour previously considered abnormal and perverted. The law relating to homosexuality was changed. Between consenting adults, homosexual behaviour was no longer a criminal offence. On the face of it, this was a change to be approved. Like the many reforms of the Divorce Law, it seemed an extension of social justice. But it unleashed a spate of behaviour which was not merely a more open practice of homosexual behaviour but an ostentatious proclamation and advertisement of it. Again, in televised discussion programmes teenagers talked about 'coming out': describing how, having 'tried it' with members of both sexes to discover their true sexual nature, they then, realizing that they were 'gay', made open confession of it, 'came out', and practised it. It sounded like a new institutional procedure debouching an entirely new kind of debutantes into the ranks of society. The Libertarian became the libertine. An extension of humane freedom became a flaunting of indulgence. Terms taken to be offensive – 'queer', 'pervert', 'poofter', 'Nancy boy' – were replaced by the term 'gay' – a plain perversion of language, as though the qualities of vivacity and joy were only for the abnormal (for homosexuality *is*, of course, by definition, an abnormality). 'Gays' then insisted on their right to open recognition everywhere – even in the Church. An association of gay vicars was founded, with the suggestion, from some of them, that they needed, and had the 'right' to, separate worship. The removal of a criminal category and a social stigma opened the door not only to libertarian display, but also to a curious enhancing of the status and even exclusiveness of minorities – as though to be abnormal was also to be superior. In the 1980s, this has even entered seriously into official educational policies. In Haringey (as I write) it is proposed by the local council that children from nursery school onwards are to be taught about homosexuality and lesbianism to combat any false emphasis upon 'heterosexism'. In our condition of extended 'democracy', lunatic fringes (I mean councillors, not homosexuals) are able to dominate committees and determine official policies.

But liberty stretched out in other, though parallel, directions. The period of the 1960s was the period of the publication of the 'banned books'; the issue having been tested by trial in the courts. The kinds of obscenity Kate Millet was to write about (of Miller, Lawrence, Mailer, Genet) became not only available, but – by the very publicity of court procedures and the new publications – *marked out* for wider consumption. There was a sudden vogue of 'good old-fashioned Anglo-Saxon words' (as they were affectionately called by those who wanted to appear smart and shock by using them). A little earlier, George Bernard Shaw (who made a career out of audacity, of transferring platform oratory to the theatre, and beginning the since-then-much-copied practice of blowing one's own trumpet) shocked society – but ever so slightly – with the word 'bloody' in Pygmalion. Now, people of decidedly smaller intellects followed his example. One of the most unmentionable four-letter words of all – 'fuck' – was uttered in a broadcast by an avant-garde theatre critic. We were all now able, quite comfortably, to use such four-letter words in drawing-room conversations (if we still had drawing-room conversations). But it was not only books. Now, glossy magazines coloured every station bookstall throughout the country with provocatively nude women (rarely, if ever, men) presenting their large round buttocks to prospective readers like female chimpanzees on heat. Newspapers, too, developed 'Page 3': selecting girls with the most blossoming breasts and filmiest pants. Television programmes leapt to exploit the new freedom from constraint. Censorship well-nigh disappeared. Some 'situation comedies' came to depend almost entirely on the 'double entendre' (not so 'double', either), decorating the scenes about the archly grinning comedian with flimsily clad girls. It has since become commonplace to watch actors and actresses undressing and copulating – sometimes under bedclothes, sometimes with hardly any bedclothes left. Even the kiss has changed. In the cinema of the 1930s, the lips were placed – then tightly pressed – together, the male bending the female over backwards, pulling her close to his chest. This has been replaced by the 'immediate-open-mouth-approach'. The two heads in camera close-up approach each other opening their mouths, tongues at the ready, and then proceed to lick one another's tongue, teeth and tonsils for two or three minutes of peak-viewing time whilst gently unbuttoning and taking off (or wildly tearing off – depending on the nature and intensity of the drama) each other's clothes.

Throughout the period, too, cries of outraged morality were strident on the one hand or held up to ridicule on the other. Mrs Mary Whitehouse and Lord Longford were lampooned as the most reactionary 'squares' of all time. The 'Responsible Society', founded to oppose what it believed to be a headlong slide towards demoralization, was ridiculed and itself driven to extremes. And strange anomalies and ambiguities of attitudes have since appeared in the law. Mrs Victoria Gillick (with, one would think in the light of the above arguments, the right of plain and common reason on her side) has argued that if the age of majority is 18, if the age of consent to sexual behaviour for girls is 15, if it is a criminal offence for a man knowingly to have intercourse with a girl below this age, and if the entire responsibility of parenthood continues up to the age of 18 (for statutory obligations in education and many other matters) – then contraceptives should not be prescribed to girls under the age of consent without the knowledge of their parents, and, preferably, without some consultation between a girl, her parents and her doctor. What seems unexceptionable, clear, sensible, and – above all – in keeping with the law of the land, has, however, become a *cause célèbre* in British justice, the British courts, and the bewilderingly confused position of the British Medical Association and its many individual members. All we need note, however, is that girls under the legally defined age of consent, still attending school, still legally under their parents' control, are, in fact, able to enter into sexual intercourse, consult their doctors, receive prescriptions for contraceptives (e.g. the Pill), without the knowledge of their parents if, in the judgment of the doctor, the needs and circumstances of their 'patients' (the under-age girls) are such as to justify it. Now this, clearly, is an extraordinarily complex issue. The actual situations of young girls must vary enormously, and one cannot possibly expect any simple and totally general solution to the problem. No one ruling can fit all cases. Even so, what is obvious in the most minimal sense is that – whether in the area of intercourse rendered safe by contraception, intercourse resulting in illegitimate births, or intercourse leading to pregnancies terminated by abortion – the facts, grounds and judgments of morality within the ordinary day-to-day realms of professional ethics and practice have become decidedly unclear.

It was as though, in this particular period, the last tight-laced corset of Victorian morality, the last voluminous all-smothering skirt, was finally cast off. The swing of the pendulum was extreme. So far, however, we have thought about the 'inflammation' of appetite and the freeing of behaviour only in matters relating to the new 'youth culture' and sexuality, but the new freedom from a morality thought to be false, bogus and in decay, a distasteful and outmoded stuffiness of cant and hypocrisy, found its expression elsewhere. Throughout the 1960s, and with a mounting sense of ever-increasing pervasiveness through the 1970s and 1980s, moral laxity has come to mark every area and every level of our social life, so much so as to make this question of the *de-moralization* of society a matter relating to the whole of our national life and matter of overall national concern. It is surely significant that in current opinion polls almost 70 per cent of respondents record their conviction that Britain is now in a condition of *irreversible* decline. Our sense of *crisis* is *real*.

From top to bottom of our society a suspicion of corruption, a cynicism about the conduct of public affairs, has come to prevail. At the very highest level, in central and local government alike, so much evidence of corruption has been revealed as to render us cynical about any pretension of probity among men and women in positions of authority. We no longer believe anybody. We know very well the secrecy and chicanery characterizing the behind-the-scenes manipulation of power. Even here, sexual scandals have erupted – from Profumo to Jeremy Thorpe to Parkinson. But these are slight (for society – though not for the individuals concerned) when compared with larger issues. The 'development' of the North-East by Mr Poulson and Mr Dan Smith seemed to involve politicians at the highest level in receiving 'considerations' in the securing of shady property transactions. Reginald Maudling felt bound to resign from a ministerial post because of it. Hospitals in Malta as well as schemes in Newcastle appeared to be involved. What, in truth, were all the ramifications? More recent disclosures by Mr Dalyell about the secrecy and strange cloak-and-dagger affairs apparently surrounding the sinking of the *Belgrano* point to dubious exercises of power which must always remain secret to us. Similarly with Mr Brian Sedgemore's allegations about the dealings of certain banks in the City of London, including officials of the Bank of England itself. In this case, the Fraud Squad of the City of London Police claimed to have found evidence of fraud, but the Director of Public Prosecutions decided that there was no evidence to justify charges, and so an affair which had commanded the uproarious attention of both parliament and press for weeks, and which had followed months of investigation, ended not with a bang, but in the whimper of a short two-column statement on the back page of *The Times*. In the trial involving Lord Ryder and British Leyland (over allegations of bribery and the keeping of a 'slush fund') two executives of British Leyland required as witnesses for the defence were protected by High Court injunctions from having to appear in court. No precedent for such a ruling – whereby the evidence of witnesses which the defence believed vital for the full hearing of the case was excluded from the court proceedings, and denied to the court – has ever (then or since) been stated. On the other hand, a witness visiting Britain from South America to testify *against* Mr Jeremy Thorpe was granted immunity from personal prosecution during his stay. The law has come to have every appearance of being not so much an ass as a much more wily and sinister animal which can be led by the nose in any circumspect direction by those who possess both the knowledge and the power to be able so to lead it. In the recent Westland Affair, a parliamentary committee of inquiry seemed to find all the leading figures of the government involved guilty of improper actions, evasion, and a withholding of information from the House of Commons and from the committee itself. Those charged included the chief adviser to the Prime Minister and the Head of the Civil Service. Suspicion was even cast on the conduct of the Prime Minister herself, and it has since been said that the Attorney General was on the point of sending the police to Number 10, Downing Street. In all such affairs, we know very well that we shall never, and can never, know the truth, but enough reaches us through the press and the courts to make us quite certain that corruption in the whole range of public affairs is rife. The same kind of picture could be painted of every other area of social life – commerce, education, the arts, etc. The day-to-day face of public life in modern Britain resembles nothing more closely than a satirical film (part farcical, part outrageous and sinister in its evil) by Charlie Chaplin. '*Modern Times*' ... indeed!

Within this overall acceptance of the fact of the extensiveness of corruption in public life, our resignation to the fact that this *is* so, one other development seems of central significance. There seems, now, to be a lack of confidence in – even a lack of belief in the existence of – moral motivation proper. No one seems any longer to believe that moral motivation exists *as a distinctive category in its own right*. When a person takes a stand on some principle, judgment, or action as being right, everyone begins to look for his ulterior motives (whether in the play of underlying psychological factors, or suspicious of elements of self-interest or sectional interest at work). No one appears to believe, now, that one should do what is right *because it is right*; that to show that something is right is a sufficient, indeed an imperative, reason for acting in accordance with it, and that if something is shown to be wrong, this is a sufficient and imperative reason for refusing to act in accordance with it. Moral arguments, even when conclusive, are no longer taken to be binding or obligatory. Moral feeling, thinking, reflection and demonstration (i.e. in thought and logic) are not recognized as constituting a distinctive kind and level of human experience. The sovereignty of moral ideals has weakened to the point of having given way to the stronger considerations of appetite, interests, expediency. At this most fundamental level, the proof that something is right and obligatory may now be received with only a shrug of the shoulders, and a 'So what?' Or 'Well ... yes ... I suppose so. ... But what does it matter?' It is not only *apathy*, in the sense of feeling helpless within the complexity of society, of feeling that – whatever is right or wrong – what we can do will have no effect whatever, but, more fundamentally, a sense of *having given up* on morality, a feeling that morality has lost any actuality or force of its own, and, in any event, even if it has, it is no longer any concern of ours. The sense of the inner spiritual significance of these matters has left us.

The conclusion to which one is driven is that the malaise in our society is, at its roots, a moral malaise, and one which encompasses the whole of society – from the highest level of public affairs to the most intimate condition of personal conscience. *Our crisis is a moral crisis*. And we can conclude with three clear points at least.

First, it is the case that appetite has largely displaced sentiment in

214

the consumer society. Appetite, and the contrived creation, extension and excitation of appetites in any direction productive of profit, has come to be the influence dominating over all morality. It is the condition of the Inflamed Society which came to dominate our society with the extended libertarianism of the 1960s, and which has continued to dominate it ever since.

Second, it was within this climate (enveloping all areas of morality) that the most ill-considered and 'half-baked' attitudes towards sexual behaviour, marriage and the family found propitious scope for their spread and development, and most probably were the new and additional features of personal and social behaviour explaining the increased vulnerability and breakdown of marriages, bringing great harm to the children (but not *only* the children) who resulted from, and were the victims of, such casual attitudes and relationships.

And third, it was this wide-ranging world of the cultivation of the appetites in the inflamed society which increasingly, and then continually, passed through the window of the television screen into the primary group of the family within the home. In place of the gradual experience of the natural-social sequence from birth to adulthood, now – from the very point of birth onwards – this was the world brought into the experience of the child long before wider social groups were encountered, before school was experienced, and which, when and whilst these were encountered, continued in conjunction with them throughout the individual's experience. In an enormous and multi-faceted way, it is the television portrayal of the inflamed society which is, nowadays, the child's most all-embracing environment and experience from the earliest days onwards, against which everything else comes to be compared, out of the context and orientation of which all other experience comes to be perceived. Within this context, what values are established in the individual's character for inner moral regulation? – in relation to what customs, conventions, and social institutions? What relation between the 'self' and 'society' have we created here?

It will be appreciated that it is difficult to decribe these kinds of change pointedly, and with sufficient clarity, without seeming also to exaggerate. Clearly, there is another side to the coin of all that I have said. Television's open window can provide much information and transmit many influences which are for good, which make for an enlargement of awareness, an enriching of human experience, in some ways, making for wider ranges of individual opportunity, and, indeed, for a world-wide apprehension of the very moral issues in the now globally extended crisis of our time which I have been concerned to stress. Let me recall, too, all we have noted hitherto about the good which has been achieved by the reforms of our time. But ... be all this as it may, one *has*, in the face of all these considerations, to sharpen the outlines of the picture and to be moralistic. The changes we have witnessed in our time – whether good or ill – may be in danger of destroying the very foundation of morality at its roots, where it most matters, in the grounding of moral values in the awakening 'self' of each individual. The many features making for greater liberty for all have led to a society where the home and family may no longer be a place for the measured upbringing of the child, but one where television's necessarily manufactured picture of the world dominates the experience of all within the range of its influence, and especially that of the impressionable young.

At the end of all our discussion, I leave the essential question as I initially posed it: *Are the conditions of the society we have created in terms of liberty, equality, and all our social reforms, such as to have left a moral vacuum at its heart? – and at the heart of the nature of ourselves as individuals? Has the situation Westermarck envisaged as a remote possibility actually come to pass?*

At this point, I want only to come to this conclusion: that these further considerations of these larger issues do explain why it is that whilst many conditions of the family and the whole of our society have been substantially improved, we have come to feel ourselves in a condition of crisis – a crisis so profound as to seem nothing short of the de-moralization of our society. But my essential point – and my reason for considering these larger issues – is that, when all of this is taken into account, it is surely plain beyond any doubt that our dilemma, our apparent contradiction, can most certainly *not* be laid at the door of the family in society. Not by any stretch of the imagination can the family be blamed for all this – and from any point of view, whether in its supposed intensities, limitations, insufficiencies on the one hand, or in its supposed strength, tenacity, durability on the other. On the contrary, besides being the beneficiary of society's improvements, in the making of a new society, the family is also the victim of their unforeseen consequences and of society's large-scale evils.

What can we justly blame, then, for the disturbances which have racked marriage and the family? We can blame the radical disruption of generations by war. We can blame the changed character of the

Welfare State which began well but went wrong; which began as the making of a new society for human betterment but changed to a society within which – enjoying the new affluence which had been achieved – individuals and groups exploited public provisions in terms of self-interest. We can, in short, and in this respect, blame our own insufficiencies and short-comings of character. Shakespeare again: 'The fault ... lies not in our stars, but in ourselves that we are underlings.' We can blame the calculated creation, contriving, extension, excitation, and exploitation of appetite within the newly achieved affluence to form a new 'consumerism' which has come to dominate almost all other considerations, almost to the point of obliterating them. We can blame the new crisis of communications in which families within their homes have been invaded by all those influences which can destroy the essential nature of family and home life and the natural-social sequence of growth which is necessary for the measured growth of stable character. We can blame the hunger of ambition, the quest for power, the calculated manipulation of others and of large organizations to both acquire and keep power, which – born within the usurping influences of inflamed appetites, and continuing to serve them and to be ruled by them – spill corruption throughout our political, economic, and social life. And, too – large-scale though it seems – we can even blame, now, the conflicts beyond our own shores in which we are inescapably involved.

The truth is that in the throes of the war-ridden transformation of human societies throughout the world, we do now face the many-dimensioned crisis which is the culmination of the long history of mankind. Stemming from the accumulated achievements of all times past, it holds a promise of great fulfilment. But during the course of its transition, it is so deeply dissolving the traditions and values of societies the world over, so creative of conflicts on a scale and range, and with a complexity so altogether unexperienced hitherto, that it also threatens, and, indeed, in particular parts of the world as it proceeds, is actually entailing, great disaster. The mass graves of the twentieth-century world cannot be remedied. Is this time in which we now approach the end of our century one which will whelm the whole of mankind in societal chaos, military destruction, nuclear extinction? – or is it a kind of crucible within which a turmoil of incalculable historical forces is mixing, out of which a new global society might be finally forged? – a society within which the long-articulated ideals of mankind can, at last, be actually realized?

Visualizing this very chaos of modern communications and the problematical making of 'human nature' and the modern 'self' within

217

it, Cooley (in *Social Organization*) was quite clear:

> When we come to the modern era, especially, we can understand nothing rightly unless we perceive the manner in which the revolution in communication has made a new world for us....
>
> The creation of a moral order on an ever-growing scale is the great historical task of mankind.

And it is well to recall the warning of A. N. Whitehead – perhaps the greatest philosopher of our time who (unlike other modern philosophers) was also a well-informed and perceptive sociologist:

> It is the first step in sociological wisdom to recognise that the major advances in civilization are processes which all but wreck the societies in which they occur.[15]

Whether these processes break us or make something more worthy out of us rests at least in large part on our own efforts in establishing the truth about social facts and trends, sound perspectives of understanding and judgment, sound directions of action, and then so acting. What is certain beyond any doubt is that to blame the family in society for all the ills our society is heir to – from any point of view whatever – is a plain and misguided error. It is a strange myopia, without any foundation, and wrong.

If, however, there are at least some grounds for thinking that Westermarck's conditions for the continuity of the family and marriage – the continuity of the conjugal and parental sentiments – are at risk, what are we to think about the future of the family? In answering this question we can come to our final conclusions.

4

The Future of the Family

(i) A changed 'human nature'?

One large question must not be avoided, though, having briefly stated it, I shall for certain reasons set it aside.

If we take seriously the continual play upon each generation of children of all the influences of mass communications, in home environments of which these influences have become a perpetual and dominant part (and there can be little doubt that this situation is here to stay); if, in relation to this, we take seriously all the closely related changes we have considered; then we must take seriously the possibility that those sentiments which have characterized domestic groups and 'human nature' hitherto will suffer erosion and that something else will be established in their place – even if this is only an all-dominating preoccupation with the continual play upon appetites. This poses an immediate question: in the critical transformation of the modern world, are we in a condition within which 'human nature' is being *fundamentally changed*? – and not necessarily (as I have so far supposed) for the *worse*? Bearing in mind the infinity of the future before us, if our race survives the present threat of self-destruction, it has a long way to go. Nothing in the nature of things guarantees the eternity of the human race, and perhaps not even the continuity of 'human nature' – as we have known it to be – throughout the remainder of mankind's history.

It would obviously be possible, and on grounds of reasonably reliable knowledge, to outline the history of the making and changing of the human family in times past. It could be supposed, for example, that in the long history of mankind, certain crucially significant junctures have arisen – coupled with fundamental changes in environmental and evolutionary conditions, shifts in knowledge, technical applications, inventions and new systems of peace and war built upon them, historical circumstances, and, in general, the collective conditions of societies. Suppose that in the very long pre-history of man and the earliest foundation of human communities there was (as Westermarck, Elaine Morgan, and others have believed) some necessitous, 'natural' foundation of small human sexual and parental groupings; and suppose that through many long early millennia, in a condition of extremely limited knowledge, *woman*, with her distinctive nature (menstrual bleeding, the menstrual cycle, the nature of gestation, the nature of child-birth) was initially and conspicuously at the heart of human fertility and all the early symbolizations of it. Suppose, then (as some *have* supposed), that new factors supervened – the knowledge of paternity, the growing importance of property, the related significance of war, the development of structures of political power, law, and religion – and that these led to the dominion of the male in familial relationships (and, indeed, in all the relationships of authority and power in society) and to the systematic subjugation of the female, as seems to be evidenced in the traditional religions of all the earlier large-scale civilizations. Suppose, further, that with our recent industrialization and the reforms undertaken to ameliorate its harsh conditions, there came to be a marked division between male and female at work and at home; a marked distinction of status between them; so that the woman was to a large extent domesticated, and the man became the earner, breadwinner, owner, and authority in familial, social, economic, and political affairs. It is clear that an outline of this kind could make possible an exploration of the relations between the sentiments developed and the various sets of collective conditions and social institutions – to which men and women, throughout particular periods (sometimes, perhaps, of millennia) and in particular societies and civilizations, then became long accustomed. But then ... in relation to the fundamental question we are asking: *what now*? Are we at another such crucial juncture in which the sentiments at the heart of our nature are being profoundly changed?

As our knowledge (especially, but not only, in relation to sex, contraception, and the increasingly artificial ways of managing procreation) becomes greater – removing earlier fears and constraints; as the revolutionary change in the position of women and the related changes in employment, distribution of property, legal and political status, make these earlier factors no longer relevant in male-female, husband-wife, distinctions; as longevity, health in longevity, the duration of 'life-long' marriage within this longevity lengthens, and the changing opportunities for both men and women throughout their lifetime grow; might we not be on the brink of the emergence and establishment of quite *new* sentiments? – which will make the old sentiments of home and family seem like relics of a former, more primitive world? – a world in which men, women and children were still tightly bound (some may come to think) in bonds dictated by their biological nature? Might it not be that new conceptions of 'human nature', new attitudes towards sexual experience and behaviour, new assessments of the degree of importance and indispensability (or lack of importance and dispensability) of domestic groups, and of the degree of importance of community conditions, or the undesirability of them, become very different in the new world of mankind now in the making?

There seems little doubt that during the past twenty-five years (from the beginning of the 1960s) such a change in sentiments and attitudes has taken place among at least a substantial minority of the population, and I have considered these in terms of being grounds for a process of *de-moralization*. But is this too one-sided? Are such changes necessarily all bad? Might some be for good? – and might it simply be that we have not properly understood them yet? I leave the reader to consider this question. All one can say at present is that so far no one has offered an optimistic evaluation of them, and it seems worthwhile to recall that some have already described their visions of this possibility. Aldous Huxley drew his picture of the 'Brave New World'. The kind of genetic engineering he envisaged, and many related developments – in the artificial inducing of fertilization; the growth and cultivation of embryos in the laboratory; the freezing, keeping, choosing and implanting of some of them and continued experimentation on others – already constitutes a large field of scientific work. There already exists, too, in America, a 'bank' of sperm donated by highly intelligent men, from which single women select the originating sperm-cells of the kind of child they want. Alphas and Omegas are on the way. George Orwell offered his picture of a bare, inhuman 1984, and some totalitarian systems fall only a little short (if at all) of his description. E. M. Forster described the 'cells' within the totally man-made 'social system', within which human nature had been denuded of qualitative experience and nature itself had been entirely excluded – alienated – from the condition of mankind. He also described what was likely to happen when 'The Machine Stops'. And Yeats – again – voiced his fear of the uncouth beast slouching towards some modern Bethlehem to be born. Why – one wonders – are these visions all fearful? Why do they depict the state of human society to come as a *lamentable* end which mankind will have brought upon itself? Are we to believe that the radical changes in 'human nature', and in man's control over the making of his own society, which modern society is making possible are bound to be for the worse?

Whatever one's inclination in answering this question, at least three other considerations make our initial question by no means an idle one. First, in a highly centralized and organized society, if only a *small* minority of citizens are able to seize power and maintain it on the basis of sentiments, values, doctrines which are quite different from those shared by the majority (all the agencies and avenues of mass communications then being drawn together at their disposal) – untold evil can be caused. The Nazis in Germany, the Fascists in Italy are immediately called to mind, but the world holds many more examples; and, to think of visions again, Orwell's *Animal Farm* provides a telling and both sad and fearful analysis.

Second, if – even *without* gaining any formal or constitutional power – a *substantial* minority of citizens lacks the sentiments of the majority, demonstrably rebels against them, rejects them, and behaves in ways totally out of keeping with them, life in a highly populous and congested society can be rendered unmanageable, miserable, and intolerable, casting an ethos of disorder, gloom, despair over the whole. Our own society, the United States, and other societies in Europe all bear testimony to this.

And third, in the large-scale kind of societies we know, subjected to all the influences we have described, the *majority* comes to feel itself helpless, and in many respects *is* helpless. Either when the *small* minority has effectively established power over them (whether by dictatorial or democratic means), or when the *substantial* minority has broken through and broken down all the effective safeguards of public control, the members of 'the great majority' can, quite quickly, be drawn into the mass warfare of millions (by the mere decree of conscription – which every government now takes for granted as its constitutional right), or driven into the shelters of their homes by growing fear and intimidation.

Far from being idle, then, our initial question is all too real.

Deliberately, however, I set it aside here – though by no means because I do not think it of the utmost gravity. Partly, I do so because it is clearly far too large an issue to be explored here, so many aspects of it lying in the realm of imponderables. But partly too – and more positive than this – because I think it more constructive to focus on two other considerations.

The first is that there is at least some persuasive evidence suggesting that the long-grounded sentiments of our 'human nature' of the past are *not* being destroyed; that they are withstanding, and not giving way to, the many influences playing upon them which could be destructive; that they are as strong and deeply rooted as (with Westermarck) we supposed them to be; and that, at least as far ahead as we can possibly see, they are likely not only to survive, but perhaps also to enjoy a strong re-affirmation and an increasing dissemination and establishment throughout the world. This persuasion agrees with Plato's belief that 'human nature' *does* have permanent elements, which *do* have permanent interrelationships, and which *do* present perennial dangers if they are allowed to become ungoverned, and that our problems are not so much new in human experience so much as being experienced with a new scale and degree of difficulty in a situation which renders them far more crucial in terms of man's overall fate.

And second, we can, in fact, do much to secure this survival. If we value these long-established sentiments and the qualities of human life (including married and family life) we have built upon them, we can – assembling, understanding, and using such evidence – make *efforts* to support and maintain them, clarify and cultivate them, and make their value known and effective against all the influences making for their destruction. The forces in the modern world making for their erosion and overthrow can be opposed. In the transformation of our world which is occurring, we can – as Cooley insists that we should – make ourselves responsible for 'the great historical task of mankind ... the creation of a moral order on an ever-growing scale.' The defence of the sentiments which are the bedrock of human character and society alike should, in short, be at the very forefront of our attention, and, in this connection, it is both interesting and worthwhile to recall the conviction of one of the greatest statesmen responsible for much in the shaping of the modern world – and in so forming the machinery of power in the modern state that it should be such as to serve the people, not control them. I mean Abraham Lincoln:

> Public sentiment is everything. With public sentiment nothing can fail; without it nothing can succeed. Consequently, he who moulds public sentiment goes deeper than he who enacts statutes or pronounces decisions. He makes statutes and decisions possible or impossible to be executed.[1]

(ii) Conjugal and parental sentiments: strength and continuity

What evidence is it, then, which suggests that the conjugal and parental sentiments, the family as a domestic group, marriage itself, and even the new form of marriage and the family which has been ethically re-formed within the conditions of industrial society, are, in fact, withstanding and surviving the great inundation of modern social change, and – beginning even now, to be re-assessed – may well come to be seen (elsewhere in the world, as well as in Britain) to be founded on important facts and considerations, and to be justifiable, and right?

One kind of evidence comes from the comparative and historical studies of the kind Westermarck himself conducted. One such study was carried out by Ernest Crawley and – published as *The Mystic Rose* – was almost as wide-ranging as Westermarck's own, its value being recognized by Westermarck himself and other leading anthropologists. For Westermarck, for example, it was 'one of the most important books on social anthropology ever published'. Malinowski was of the same opinion. It was, he said, 'a work which appears to me among the best and most important of the psychological studies in primitive custom.' All that is necessary for our purpose is to note that Crawley's study was well-nigh exhaustive, surveying the detailed nature of marriage in societies in every part of the world. In view of this, his conclusion was highly significant, all-embracing, and very definite:

> It may be confidently assumed that individual marriage has been, as far as we can trace it back, the regular type of union of man and woman. The promiscuity theory* really belongs to the mythological stage of human intelligence, and is on a par with many savage myths concerning the origin of marriage, and the like. These are interesting but of no scientific value. They are cases of mental actualisation of apparently potential states which were really impossible except as abnormal occurrences. When men meditated upon marriage ceremonial and system, they would naturally infer a time when there was not only no rite, but no institution of marriage. Hence the common idea of which the promiscuity theory is a result, that marriage was ordained to

---

*i.e. The theory that there was a 'stage' of primitive promiscuity, just as there was a 'stage' of group-marriage, and that other systems of kinship, family, and marriage came later in the process of social evolution.

prevent illicit intercourse; this, of course, it does prevent, but it invents it first. Taboo and law when they sanction a human normal practice produce the possibility of sin. There was a time of course when there was no marriage ceremony, but the ideas of such were latent in the actual union of man and woman.

The survey of marriage and of sexual relations in early races suggests many thoughts. For instance, one is struck by the high morality of primitive man. Not long ago McLennan could assert confidently that the savage woman was utterly depraved; but a study of the facts shows quite the contrary. The religious character of early human relations ... gives a sense of tragedy; man seems to feel that he is treading in slippery places, that he is on the brink of precipices, when really his foot stands right. This sensitive attitude would seem to have assisted the natural development of man. We have also seen the remarkable fact that most of these primitive customs and beliefs are repeated in the average civilized man, not as mere survivals, but springing from functional causes constant in the human organism.... In connection with marriage, this diffidence and desire for security and permanence in a world where only change is permanent, has led to certain conceptions of eternal personalities who control and symbolise the marriage tie. Psychologically, the union of man and woman amounts to identification and combination of the two sexes.... [Many of the simpler peoples] have deities who combine the attributes of both sexes. The Greeks and Romans sometimes included male characteristics in their conception of the Goddess of Love, and lifted marriage to the ideal plane in the conception of the *sacred marriage*. More simply, many peoples have thought of a divine trinity of persons to symbolise the family of husband, wife and child; Christian Europe, for instance, has worshipped the Holy Family for many hundred years. For the male sex an ideal of the eternal feminine* often satisfied such aspirations, and this survey may fittingly close with a reference to the most prominent ideal personality for modern Europe in this connection, the Maiden-Mother, the Mystical Rose, for her figure enshrines many elemental conceptions of man and woman and their relations.[2]

Let us note that this was said about *marriage* itself – in its own right (not about the family as a domestic group and marriage as a part of

*Readers may recall the very end of Goethe's 'Faust' as a good example of this.

this) – but also that it does fully bear out all that we said earlier about the *universality* of the family and of marriage as the institutionalized procedure for founding it. (Germaine Greer (see *The Abolitionists*, p. 152) quoted from Crawley, but seems not to have taken seriously his over-all, and very decided, conclusion.) And the conclusion of Crawley's detailed and scrupulously exact study deserves a good deal of emphasis because the influence of social anthropology since Westermarck's and Malinowski's day – consisting chiefly of isolated monographs, each offering a structural-functional account of the social system of a particular people – has given an impression of the wide *diversity* of cultures and (consequently) of the *relativity* of ethics. The diversity of morals, however, is by no means the same as (and does not at all imply) the relativity of ethics (as has been pointed out but widely ignored), but, in any event, studies like those of Westermarck and Crawley reveal, by contrast, the *common* sentiments of mankind which exist despite great cultural differences.

The evidence of scholarship, however, is far from being all that exists. Is it not the case that – in a world still threatened with over-population, plagued by destructive wars, shaken by natural tragedies which are all the greater in their outcome because of the increased massing of large populations in areas of natural danger (e.g. the earthquake tragedies in Mexico), and radically disturbed in social upheavals of a revolutionary kind (e.g. in China) – evidence for the deep-rooted hold of the family, and conjugal and parental sentiments, is plentifully supplied in the newspapers and television reports of every day? In China, we have seen that the western form of the family, even to the same form of marriage ceremony and the same conception of personal affection and personal choice as a basis for marriage and parenthood, is today increasingly taking hold as the status of women is gradually winning its way from its long traditional roots in the ancient family; as women, that is to say, are effectively freed. Elsewhere, I have noted the nature of the Chinese Marriage Law, and we have seen that the Chinese 'communes' were never 'alternatives' to the family but actually were *communities of families*. A recent letter from the Chinese Embassy in London confirmed this (checking these matters in 1986 this arose in correspondence with the First Secretary (Press)):

> As far as I know, the Chinese Government has not drawn up a new code of marriage law since 1980 (though some amendments might have been made to the law). It is an entire misunderstanding that communes in China set up since 1958 were ever opposed to the family. The People's Commune then served

as the lowest government level in rural areas. Its function combined local authority and production. Since 1980, the *responsibility system*, a new production system, farming on a household basis, has been introduced in the countryside. The 'commune' does not exist in China now.

The emphasis is now quite clearly placed on the individual household and the family, though, even in the earlier communes, their importance was never ignored or denied. Is it not the case, too, that not only in China but wherever women are liberated from their earlier traditional bonds and inferiorities, they choose monogamy? Is there, anywhere in the world, an example where this is not the case? In natural tragedies like that of Mexico, too, is it not the saving of newborn babies pulled out from under the fallen wreckage of hospitals which is most hailed with joy? And are they not then cared for with particular tenderness and concern by the close relatives of the parents who were killed? In the starvation-ridden wastes of Africa – what are the groups television films show us trekking for scores of miles across the drought-dried landscape, from one source of water and food to another? Are they not family groups? Are they not mothers still holding their skeleton-like children to their shrivelled breasts? Are they not fathers placing the wrapped-up bodies of their dead children in the dust-hole graves in the desert? Are they not families who set up their tents and shelters in the vastly over-populated camps? It seems always to be the family, in all the filmed recordings, which is at the centre of the chaos of the world.

But even within our own 'western' societies, is the same kind of evidence not plainly to be seen? We have already mentioned much of this. It is always repeated that one marriage in three now fails, but the self-same fact states that, despite all the forcefulness of the new changes, conditions, and attitudes, *two thirds* (66 per cent) of marriages remain firm. Furthermore, we have seen that the figures of marital breakdown obscure and belie the still predominant practice of living in families. Eighty per cent of the British people – the large majority – do still live, and clearly want to live, in family groups, shared households, homes. Also, the many facts relating to cohabitation, illegitimacy, re-marriage, etc. (see pp. 70–81) do clearly suggest that responsibility for shared parenthood still accompanies much cohabitation. We have seen, too, that the popularity of marriage continues, that its rate is increasing, but that marriage is now taking place at later ages, so that there is a decided possibility that we may be coming to the end of a decade of adjustment to the new conditions of marriage and divorce brought about by the 1969 Act.

Other kinds of evidence are provided every day. Again – in a world still facing the threat of massive over-population, and in which contraception and abortion are so widely practised – infertile couples persist over long years in efforts to have their own children. Artificial insemination, *in vitro* fertilization, surrogate motherhood, and other methods of overcoming infertility are increasingly practised. Many couples clearly need and seek shared parenthood as part of their close personal union. The conjugal and parental sentiments still seem all of a piece here. Newspapers continually carry articles describing how illegitimate children, no matter how old they have become, deeply want to trace their fathers or mothers and persist in their efforts to do so. Adopted children, too, seem to need to discover the identity of their natural parents. Why – one wonders – having been accustomed to life in a particular family for so long, often well cared for, and often with deeply felt and happy relationships with their foster-parents – is this so? Why do they need to feel the link with their true, original parents? Is it not because the child-parent link – the link, actually, with the whole of the created world out of which they have come – is as important for the child as for the parent? Similarly, almost every day brings its story of brothers, sisters, or other relatives – long separated by war-time refugee experience, or torn apart in prison camps – now having been re-united? Why should bonds of this kind persist, despite long separations and absences? Is it not because the parent-child tie, the rooted nature of the child in the love of its parents, the rooted nature of kinsfolk in their common ancestry, is the deepest root in human experience, the deepest root relating individuals to the world? Is it not because, in some way or other, the bond of *love* is a bond of *identity*? Is it not the case, too, that 'Geneaology' has become the bane of Public Record Offices? Everybody, sore-tried officials complain, seems intent on tracing their 'family tree'. People, in a world of chaos, seem to be searching for their spiritual roots in the nature of things, and this lies in and through the family.

There is considerable evidence, then, that, in fact, the conjugal and parental sentiments are by no means dead. Certainly this seems to be true among the majority of people in Britain, and, as it seems, throughout the rest of the world, despite all the forces ranged against them. Westermarck's own deepest persuasion (in *The Future of Marriage in Western Civilization*) seems, in fact, to be confirmed and justified:

There is every reason to believe that the unity of sensual and spiritual elements in sexual love, leading to a more or less durable community of life in a common home, and the desire for and love of offspring, are factors that will remain lasting obstacles to the extinction of marriage and the collapse of the family, because they are too deeply rooted in human nature to fade away, and can find adequate satisfaction only in some form of marriage and the family founded upon it.

Given all this, is there not something positively strange, even inexplicable, about those attitudes which casually reject marriage and the family? Is there not something fundamentally misguided, wrong-headed, superficial, radically to be criticized in those conceptions of human relationships which run so strongly counter to the experience of the large majority, and also to the practice of the members of the apparently substantial minority who hold these views? What can be said now about these, and about the true conception of marriage which most people still hold? Are there deeply founded, true, and worthwhile sentiments which we can support as against other sentiments which are superficial and false?

(iii) The nature of marriage

Let us think first about those attitudes underlying the rejection of marriage which – so much at odds with both the attitudes and the actual practice of the majority – seem not only inconsistent and without firm grounds, but also positively bogus. At least five positions seem distinguishable.

There is, first, the situation where a couple live together – as a family, with their children, in a household – but who dispense with marriage because, they say, for them, to go through the formal procedure of marriage would itself make no difference. The bond between themselves as partners, the shared bond of responsibility for their children, the serious commitment to the reciprocal claims and obligations between them – in maintaining their home, caring for each other, and caring for their children – is enough in itself. These are the actual bonds of affection which hold them together. The mere ceremony of marriage – making vows before witnesses, the Registrar, or a Minister of Religion – would add nothing. Now this sounds morally upright and praiseworthy; there is something to admire in the position where people can say that their affection and their mutually felt obligations constitute the bond between them, and that on the strength of this bond they can rely. But all these people are saying is that the true and actual nature of marriage, the true substance of marriage, is that which, in fact, they are experiencing. This is actually what true marriage is. The public procedure, the institution, is only an extraneous form which they do not require. The question is, however, if they so much agree with the substance of what the formal law of the land regards as the core of the institution of marriage, and if society and the law, through the institution, accords them the recognized status of a married couple so that all their rights, reciprocal claims, and relationships – not only among themselves, but between themselves and all other people, institutions and organizations, and authorities in society – can be clearly regularized and protected, what is their real objection to formal marriage? With so strong an agreement, should they not be joining with the majority of citizens in supporting that institution in society which seeks to uphold the very qualities in personal relationships, in family relationships, which they admire; which requires and encourages a serious and careful approach in entering upon such relationships; and which ensures the regularization of all the relationships within the wider society stemming from such personal unions and committed family groups? Is not their objection to this simply perverse?

Second, there is the position – almost always stemming from this – where such couples, having dispensed with marriage, none the less – and especially when problems, disputes, and broken relationships arise – try to claim exactly the same treatment from the law and society (the social services and 'social security', for example) as if they *were* married. Having rejected the institution of marriage as provided in the law – claiming that this makes no difference to them – they then refer to the law pertaining to marriage as though they were fully entitled to its provisions. They insist on the same recognition by society of their reciprocal claims upon each other and the same obligations of society to them and their own familial group. Having deliberately had illegitimate children, they insist on the same status of *legitimacy* for their children. They insist on the status formally accorded by marriage though having been deliberately unwilling to accept its form; sometimes, indeed, having derided it. In their insistence, they seem to be trying to make the common law what, at present, it is *not*; and the use of the terms 'common law *wife*' and 'common law *husband*' point to the bogus nature of their position. But if the common law was so changed as to provide for a status of cohabitation which was in every respect the same as, and equal to, the existing law pertaining to marriage, *it would, in fact, be legally recognized marriage*, so why deny the law as it exists? It may be recalled that the Romans did, in fact, provide such a kind of marriage – the *usus* – and perhaps this is the kind of provision to which we should return. On the face of it, however, this position seems one of conspicuously throwing the institution of marriage out of the front door – with much protest, exhibitionism, and display – and then smuggling it in, surreptitiously and shame-facedly, by the back. And surely this, again, is perverse?

Third, there is the position where people in the most casual way possible, simply shrug marriage off as being 'just a piece of paper', claiming that what they want to do, and decide to do, is no one else's business, and that they have a right to do just what they like. Now on the one hand, this is simply inane, and on the other plainly mistaken about the most ordinary facts of personal relationships and their implications in the law. To take the second point first, even the new *Cohabitation Handbook* (by the Rights of Women group) makes the matter meticulously clear:

> Whatever your personal reasons may be for the way you live,
> private relationships, especially those between men and women, are
> a public concern. The law has always been concerned with marriage.
> People who 'cohabit' do not avoid this public concern.[3]

One cannot possibly enter into personal relationships entailing the sharing of property, income, the having and upbringing of children, without involving oneself in reciprocal responsibilities and the possibility of claims and counter-claims, with which the law (especially when disputes arise) must be concerned. The casual 'We're going to do what we like – what business is it of anyone else?' is simply unintelligent, brash, lamentably ill-informed about the most elementary nature of social life, and devoid of anything approaching morality.

To turn to the first matter, however, is it not equally clear that anyone who regards the solemnization of marriage as 'just a piece of paper' must possess little more than a vacuum between their ears? The 'piece of paper' received on marriage is, indeed, no more than a certified recording of the fact that, before witnesses, certain vows have been publicly made, certain personal promises have been publicly given, certain contracts and commitments have been entered into. The substance of marriage clearly lies in all these undertakings which – after very precise and careful warning from Minister of Religion or Registrar – have been solemnly entered into in a considered way. The piece of paper certifies the conferring of the status of marriage upon the couple who have so committed themselves. To speak of marriage as 'just a piece of paper' – which can be torn up and tossed into the winds of circumstances as and when it may become expedient – is really to say that one has conformed with a social custom under false pretences, participated in a social form which has had no meaning, and that one has attached no seriousness to one's considered word. When the simple wish arises, every committed undertaking can be discounted and thrown away. When people boast about having this conception, as though being something of an 'avant garde' attitude, they must simply be boasting about being worthless people. If they, too, when disputes arise, then wish to lay claim to the status of 'common law wife' or 'common law husband', their expediency and superficiality is proved to the last degree.

A fourth position, just remotely possible (see p. 83), is that where – when they speak of marriage as being 'just a piece of paper' – people are really confusing the wedding with the substance of marriage, and simply thinking that the paraphernalia of that kind of theatrical performance can itself be shallow, the outcome of family pressures or social expectations, and therefore of little worth. It may be true, of course, that the external dress (so to speak) of a wedding may be of the most superficial kind (a 'white wedding in church', for example, may be entered into when it has no religious significance whatever for the couple concerned). Even so, this attitude rests plainly on a mistake; is one 'half-baked' notion among others. The social ornamentation of the wedding may be whatever it may be, but the fact remains that the substance of marriage is entered into within that form, and this is by no means either superficial or just a piece of theatre.

This is not the place to repeat, word for word, all the elements of the Christian marriage service or the words spoken in the Registrar's office – but all will know that the very solemn nature of the occasion is emphasized, the central reasons for marriage are given, important qualities of married life and parenthood are made clear and upheld, and specific vows are made: concerning sexual fidelity and exclusivity, the physical and spiritual union of the couple, the joining of their property into one, the joint undertaking of responsibility for the care of their children, the commitment to care for each other – in adverse as well as fortunate circumstances of life. Perhaps it is worthwhile, in this place, just to remind ourselves of the solemnity and gravity of marriage emphasized in the *civil* ceremony (no element of *religious* sanctity or belief entering here at all.) At the beginning the couple are reminded of the seriousness of the occasion:

> Before you are joined in matrimony I have to remind you of the
> solemn and binding character of the ceremony of marriage.
> Marriage according to the law of this country is the union of one
> man with one woman, voluntarily entered into for life, to the
> exclusion of all others.
>
> I am now going to ask you each in turn to declare that there is
> no lawful reason why you should not be married to each other.

Having each declared that there is no impediment, the ceremony
proceeds, and comes to an end with these words from the Registrar:

> You have both made the declarations prescribed by law and have
> made a solemn and binding contract with each other in the
> presence of the witnesses here assembled. The law of this country
> now deems you to be man and wife together.

The several religious formulations of the vows taken in the
marriage ceremony are, of course, more detailed – according with
their particular doctrines. The point is clear, however, that anyone
who declares that the witnessed certificate of registration that a
couple have seriously entered into these commitments is 'no more
than a piece of paper' is really announcing that he, or she, is not a
responsible citizen.

By way of completeness, a fifth position must be noted: that in
which – whatever a couple may think about the nature of marriage –
they find that certain tax regulations or post-divorce technicalities
make it materially advantageous for them to live together without it.
It may well be thought a pity that some of the technical provisions in
our 'House of Administration' have become such as to militate
against the observance of the social institution which seeks to uphold
important qualities in personal relationships and reciprocal
commitments, but, however this may be, this position is clearly no
more than a technical one – and one which has become more
common as our administrative machinery has become more
complex. On this basis, a couple, with their children, in their home,
may well live as fully, happily, and responsibly as they would if
formally married, but it is the technicalities which have come to
prevail.

The upshot of all this must surely be, that marriage *is*, in social fact
and in truth, the important institutional procedure for ensuring the
serious entering upon the foundation of a family, for ensuring the
joint responsibility of couples for their mutual care, the making and
upkeep of their home, and the serious task of parenthood, and that
the grounds curiously held for rejecting it are patently inconsistent

and superficial. Let us now face the question, then: how should marriage be truly conceived? What is the true nature of marriage? And, for the present, let us think of this analytically, without at all referring to any high idealities of 'love' and the like – though I shall come back to these at the very end of our discussion.

A SOCIAL INSTITUTION

First, marriage is a social institution: a flat statement which seems to say little, but entails a great deal. In ways hard to articulate, a social institution is something other than and more than all the human individuals who, at any time, make up the total population of a society. Rational considerations and reforms enter into it and can change many aspects of it, but it has not been consciously devised or created by the people who live within its constraints. Nor was it ever consciously devised and created by any one generation. It is a constellation of regulations and values which emerged and took shape over many long successions of generations within the history of society, within certain collective conditions, according to certain values, and rooted in an immemorial past. This leads to a quite specific point deserving separate mention.

ANTECEDENT TO THE STATE, BUT ENFORCED BY IT

Marriage emerged within the long-established custom of *society*, and the State – once having been created with its defined form of government – had to take it into account. A social institution of long growth and long standing, it fulfils functions which may well go beyond conscious device and even conscious understanding. Crawley's analysis shows, for example, that it emerged in relation to deeply rooted and deeply felt considerations of certain aspects of bodily contact between the sexes, which were once the subject of powerful taboos, which forced a certain sharply marked distance between the sexes, a distance requiring to be overcome by ritual and ceremonial. Degrees of consanguinity and affinity still exist at the heart of the regulations of marriage, and, as lawyers might say, marriage – embodying certain feelings of 'approval' and 'disapproval' about certain kinds of relationship and conduct, certain rights in private relations, certain family or household rights, the reciprocal rights and duties of husband and wife, parents and children – was an institution antecedent to the State, but which it has become the office of the State to enforce. Marriage in society, then, is not just a matter of abiding personal love; not just a continuing relationship of sexual intimacy; it is – as an institutional set of commitments – much more, entailing many other dimensions, expectations, orientations towards experience, and obligatory duties.

But what – having said this – is its particular nature in our own law, experience, and social usage? A number of elements need to be separated and made clear.

MORE THAN A CONTRACT

First, though closely resembling a contract and containing elements of a contractual nature, marriage is much more than a contract, differing significantly in the nature of the 'rights' that it secures and protects. It resembles a contract in that the full and free consent of both parties is required before it can be considered valid, and great care is taken to make sure that consent is freely given and that all the grounds which would nullify a marriage are previously known and guarded against (for example, the existence of a previous marriage, insanity, the undue proximity of a relationship – e.g. of consanguinity or affinity, or being below the legally required age). But the distinction between a 'contract' and the agreement entered into on marriage can best be seen in terms of the 'rights' which marriage establishes and seeks to protect.

A right of 'property', for example, is a right (again, as lawyers say) 'against all the world' over a particular thing. A right established by 'contract' is a right with reference to the particular person (or persons) with whom the contract is made – to claim a specified performance (or forbearance) over a thing, or some other prescribed behaviour. The 'rights' established bertween a husband and wife, and between parents and children, are both rights 'against all the world' but also rights with reference to the person (not over a thing) with whom marriage is contracted. They claim certain kinds of behaviour (and forbearance) from all other persons in relation to a specific person, and certain kinds of behaviour from the particular person, whilst excluding all others from claiming them. The essential point, however, is that these rights (though entailing matters of property, material maintenance, material care, etc.) are rights over persons, and – entered into with consent; with knowledge of what impediments are to be avoided, and of what commitments are being entered into – are reciprocal. The rights a husband claims over his wife (and their correlated duties) are rights (and correlated duties) his wife can claim over him. (The same, with slightly different terms, applies to the rights and duties between parents and children.) Every effort is made to see that those entering into marriage know very well both those facts which are impediments to it, and will nullify it, and the nature of the vows which are to be made and the life-long reciprocal commitments these entail. To ensure sufficient time for all such care to be taken, a licence has to be granted, before a religious marriage there is the repeated calling of 'banns', advice is offered before marriage, and in the civil ceremony, a solemn warning is given, as we have seen.

A STATUS

Marriage, then, is much more than a contract. It is, more fully, and properly conceived, a status conferred upon two people who have, knowing of no impediment to prevent it, freely entered into a union for the whole of their lives, involving responsibility for all the kinds of reciprocal conduct they have accepted and have publicly undertaken – both in relation to each other and to any children which may result. From the point of the celebration of the marriage onwards, society and the State recognize a new status on the basis of which the two people will thenceforward be regarded as one united pair: as having entered into a *union*, jointly responsible for their property, their home, their mutual care, and the maintenance, protection, and education of their children.

RIGHTS AND THEIR IMPLICATIONS

A little more must be said about the reciprocal nature of the rights involved in marriage in order fully to appreciate the nature of the union recognized between a husband and wife. First, the union entered into, even in the physical sense alone, involves far more than a purely gratificatory interest in the partner – as an object for the satisfaction of sexual desire. Sexual union, including the full enjoyment of all that this entails, is clearly part of the relationship between a man and woman in marriage, but, going far beyond this, there is the further consideration that a man desires and seeks the well-being of his wife as a person for whom he feels love and concern, a well-being which he feels to be bound up with his own well-being and with the qualities of the home and family life which they are together establishing. The same is true of his wife's regard for him, and of the regard on the part of both of them for the well-being of their children. There is in marriage, in short, an other-regarding concern for the well-being, protection, and care of the person connected with oneself by sexual relations, and those persons and relationships arising out of these. The sexual union is the intimate core, but the core only, of the other-regarding relationships which arise out of it, and which remain continually related to it. The commitment goes far beyond the gratification of sexual appetite alone. If this were not so – if sexual desire and its gratification was the only element involved – the entering into a lifelong commitment of reciprocal care, entailing the establishment and maintenance of a shared household, a family, and the responsible upbringing of children would simply not arise.

THE 'UNION' BETWEEN HUSBAND AND WIFE

The union in marriage, then, is a union of two persons – including sexual union (as a centrally important element) but going far beyond this. It is a union in many other related and important ways. It is the commitment to a union for life – recognizing that the protection of the rights of all the persons involved in such a set of interrelationships requires this total commitment. It is (for the same basic reason) a union committed to the sharing of a community of goods throughout life. And, throughout life, it is a union committed to an undivided manner of living. These are the *consortium omnis vitae* and the *individua vitae consuetudo* which Roman law regarded as the essential elements in marriage. ('Nuptiae sunt conjunctio maris at feminae, consortium omnis vitae, divini et humani juris communicatio' *Digest*, xxiii, 2, 1; 'Matrimonium est viri et mulieris conjunctio individuam viate consuetudinem continens' *Institutes*, i, 9, 2. See Note 4, p. 274.) The meticulous wording of the Christian marriage service makes all these points abundantly clear. Marriage, it declares, should not be 'enterprised, nor taken in hand, unadvisedly, lightly or wantonly to satisfy man's carnal lusts and appetites ... but reverently, discreetly, advisedly, soberly.' In addition to sexual intimacy, it entails, too 'the mutual society, help and comfort that the one ought to have of the other, both in prosperity and adversity.' The parties undertake to 'love, comfort, honour, keep in sickness and in health, and, forsaking all others, keep themselves only – each to the other – for as long as they both shall live.' They undertake to take each other 'to have and to hold from this day forward, for better for worse, for richer for poorer, in sickness and in health, to love and cherish, till death us do part.'

And on all this, they 'plight their troth'. When the ring is given, too, the wording seeks to lift sexual love to a higher plane, and also makes quite clear the union of material possessions: 'with my body I thee worship, and with all my worldly goods I thee endow.' Whether or not one is Christian; whether or not one agrees with all the religious references in the marriage ceremony; what one must agree without doubt is that the full nature of the status being entered into is made perfectly plain.

AN INSTITUTION IN ITS OWN RIGHT

A last point deserves separate mention. Though, according to Crawley, marriage has always been an institution regulating the relationships between a man and a woman, there is no doubt that as an institution in modern society it has been reconstituted, by reforms, to accord with very high standards of personal commitment and reciprocal consideration. In our recent history in Britain, a century of reforms has reconstituted marriage as an institution in its own right, more independent than it has been in the past of family arrangements and the constraints of property, religion, law; and now a long-abiding relationship resting essentially on affection and choice. This is why it has become so demanding and difficult. This is why it has so much to offer. And most people realize this very well – and hence its popularity. They need it, they want it, with all its problems. It gives them more than anything else.

These, then, seem to be the essential elements in the true conception, the true nature, of marriage, and a number of points are very plain in the light of them.

(1) Those who shrug marriage off as being 'just a piece of paper' really do need to go back to school and learn how to read, or, indeed simply listen to the marriage ceremonies they attend. They can never

have had any idea whatever as to what marriage really is, or what it entails, and cannot be taken seriously. (2) Bearing in mind the full nature of the reciprocal rights for husband, wife and children secured and protected by marriage, it must be completely clear (a) that cohabitation without the fullest consideration of these rights can be no other than irresponsible, and (b) that single-parent families cannot possibly ensure their fulfilment – particularly for children, and quite apart from ruling out any consideration of the rights and conditions for the fullness of development of the father (or the mother – if the family is a motherless family). One-parent families resulting from divorce, of course, cannot necessarily be judged in this way. They may well be the victims of unfortunate circumstances. But the deliberate creation of single-parent families falls very far short of the responsible concern for the rights of persons in society that marriage seeks to establish both within the family and beyond it. (3) Bearing in mind the curiously inconsistent and sometimes apparently outright bogus grounds for the rejection of marriage; and also the fact that the new divorce law (in the full knowledge that, no matter how well-intentioned and seriously entered into, a marriage can break down unhappily and irretrievably) makes provision for irretrievable breakdown; there seems absolutely no reason why marriage should not be observed when two people are wishing to enter into an abiding relationship, establish a home and a family, and feel a responsible concern for the other person (or persons) and the protection of his or her (or their) rights. Putting this in another way: given the present reformed nature of the institution of marriage, with the availability of civil marriage and the provisions of the new divorce law, to enter into such abiding relationships without marriage is decidedly an irresponsibility. (4) It should be noted that the securing and protection of these rights in marriage has a very close bearing on (indeed, in part, receives its justification from) the fundamental right of the individual to an unhindered life in the pursuit of his or her own happiness and fulfilment (this most basic right, too, being reciprocal – requiring the same dutiful observance by all who demand it of others.) Marriage, then, is perhaps the most essential institution, and the family the most essential group, for effectively securing the basic right of the liberty of the individual in a free and democratic society. (5) It must be clear, too, that only monogamy can ensure the fullest guarantee of these rights to all the persons involved in familial relationships. It can be shown, for example, that in polygamy or polyandry, the rights of one or other of the parties are insufficiently met and protected, and that the status of some individuals is therefore diminished. Monogamy, then, is not only the form of marriage appropriate to certain social conditions, but is that form which is ethically justified. (6) We have noted that during the past century or so of reforms, the nature of marriage itself, and the more humane considerations attending its ending when breakdown is experienced, has actually improved the possibility of more equal, sensitive, and reciprocal considerations between husband and wife and between parents and children. And finally (7) we need to remember (a) that the large majority of the people of Britain still *do* marry with this seriousness of commitment, and (b) that even those who do *not* to some extent give the lie to their rejection *either* by laying claim to the same treatment in the law and the social services as is provided in the law pertaining to marriage (clearly thinking these provisions necessary, desirable, and socially just) when they themselves have refused the status and commitments of marriage, *or* by living together in family groups (as 80 per cent do) and actually involving themselves in familial relationships without having taken the trouble to secure the rights of those with whom they live which the status of marriage affords.

There is, surely, only one conclusion to which we can come. Marriage in Britain is, in fact, an altogether defensible and justifiable status for the continued maintenance of which there is every good ground, and that it is therefore this constellation of sentiments and values which we should be strongly upholding against all the changes, inconsistencies, and superficialities making for its overthrow. There is no doubt whatever about the sentiments for the future of marriage and the family which we should be encouraging, and the superficial, mistaken, and 'half-baked' attitudes which we should be attacking and discarding.

The future of the family is not an issue, then, which can be analysed, judged, surmised, predicted in terms of *fact* alone. To a crucial extent it will depend on our conscious *efforts*, and the direction these efforts should take has become perfectly clear. What, however, can be said about the facts themselves and some of the problems they actually entail? What trends seem to lie ahead?

(iv) Outlook – and policies

CONTINUING TRENDS – AND PROBLEMS

There is every reason to suppose, first of all, that the trend towards the kind of family we described on p. 2 and 136 – the small, planned, independent, democratic type of family – will continue in Britain and in all societies where the processes of industrialization and political reform take place. Every movement of thought and policy seems to be moving towards in an increasing awareness of what, in terms of human relationships (both conflictful and otherwise), is involved in this kind of family, and an increasing tendency to support it and to improve it still further. The economic and social conditions of our modern industrial and urban society seem to make for it, and every moral persuasion seems to desire it. The freedom and mobility required in our society – geographical movement, and the extended degree of educational opportunity and movement between social class and status groups; the desire on the part of families for economic independence, security, and the personal freedom of their members; the growing sense of the moral rightness of limiting the size of a family to the number who can be adequately cared for, and with regard, too, to the happiness and fulfilment of the parents; all these factors seem to make it clear that the small, planned, democratic family is here to stay. Increasing standards of welfare and greater security may at some time lead to a slight increase in the average size of the family (though, at present, it is slightly diminishing), but, given the ordinary population problems of a large industrial society, and the enormous population problems of the world at large, it does not seem likely that any such increase will ever be considerable In any case, it would be a matter of choice in accordance with family means, and there seems no likelihood of a return to the completely unplanned large family and the situation of the annual pregnancy. Indeed, there are some signs to suggest that those large families which, through ignorance, still suffer frequent and unwanted pregnancies are being relieved by the extension of family planning advice through domiciliary services in addition to clinics, and this is to be welcomed.

It seems, too, that the degree of dependence of each family upon its wider kinship relationships will continue to diminish. Independence seems to be desired by every family This does not mean at all that every relationship beyond the immediate group of parents and children will be cut off, or will cease to be desired. Nor does it mean that, for example, the aged, in particular, will suffer from a lack of continued relationships with their children and grand-children. This could certainly happen. But the benefits of industrial security and prosperity which, in a way, give rise to the problem, may also lead to its solution. Old people themselves – whether still married, alone, or remarried – are increasingly likely to desire their own independence, just as much as their children do. And in the days of telephone and car, there is no reason why the degree of contact desired by everyone should not be maintained. As Anderson argues, the contacts between families have probably increased, not diminished, with modern communications. But such wider relationships will be chosen, not – any longer – imposed by necessity. There is also every reason to suppose that new conditions of security and independence will make for happier – not more miserable – relationships between kindred. But in the broadest sense of the term, the 'extended family' – the large interdependent network of extended kindred (whatever people may believe about its existence or otherwise in the past) – is decidedly outmoded in a modern industrial society. The days of the clan, and of any village network of aunts, uncles, and forty-second cousins, is over. The functional roots of the extended family, if ever they existed in Britain, have gone.

All the other characteristics of this 'modern' family are also likely to continue. The improved status of women is here to stay, and will be carried even further. The economic necessities of employing women; the desire of women to lead a more active personal life in a situation in which they are relieved of child-bearing and child-rearing to the extent that they and their husbands want to be relieved of it; and the moral persuasions concerning the rightness of the equal status of women, will all ensure this. The same is true of the improved status of the child in modern society. Problems may be attendant upon the new degrees of freedom and self-sufficiency young people have – especially when early employment and relative affluence return – but it seems inconceivable that these problems will be resolved by going back to the restrictions upon young people of an earlier age. The problems will be solved by improved education related to the new situation in which young people are placed.

The popularity of marriage is also likely to continue. Nothing suggests its decline. Indeed, in the late 1980s, the rate of marriage seems again to be increasing, and – entered into in general at a slightly later age – may well give rise to more stable marriages. We have seen, too, that the rate of re-marriage has been increasing, parallel with the suddenly increased rate of divorce after 1971, and have noted the curious 'carry on' effect of the statistics. It may well be that we have passed through a decade of settling down to the provisions of the new divorce law and that (failing the outbreak of a new war!) a new period of stability may be reached (though yet with a high divorce rate reflecting the fact that happy marriage is highly valued.) Such a stability could also be made more likely by the new education in the sentiments underlying marriage and the family which we have been suggesting.

The point which (again) deserves emphasis in all this is that marriage seems to be becoming, and is likely to become increasingly in future, a relationship of affection and companionship quite apart from the having and rearing of children. Crawley, of course, claims that it was *always* this, but modern conditions certainly seem to be reinforcing it. It remains true, of course, that for the vast majority of married couples, the founding of a family and the enjoyment of parenthood is a central feature of their happiness. But it is clear first, that if, in the future, a large number of marriages continue to be founded at an early age, and if the present limitation of births continues, this must mean that many couples will have completed the child-rearing period of their family life at a relatively young age, still having a long period of life before them, from their middle years onwards, for whatever activities – whether undertaken jointly, or independently of each other – they wish to pursue. Both during the child-rearing period of their family life, and especially afterwards, marriage has become and will become increasingly a matter of personal companionship. But also, there seems little doubt that those people beyond their middle years who are widowed or divorced will increasingly be able to contemplate remarriage as a new companionable relationship – and a relationship of long duration – without any reference to children.

Though it remains true, as I have maintained in earlier chapters, that marriage is centrally rooted in the founding of the family and in shared parenthood, and that, as such, it can be enjoyed with more freedom and security now than before – it now seems clear that there is a sense in which marriage as a relationship in its own right is being liberated, as it were, from any necessary connection with parenthood. It can now increasingly, and at all ages, be entered into as a relationship of enjoyed intimacy for its own sake. And this tendency is likely to continue. Also, if attitudes towards marriage and divorce continue to change as they are now changing that is

243

away from the sacramental conception of marriage, and away from the conception of divorce as being necessarily blameworthy, resting upon some kind of matrimonial offence – then there will be a far greater opportunity of achieving happy marriages than ever before.

This leaves, of course, the one other important area of changing ideas and values which is bound to have a marked effect upon the future nature of marriage – the area of sexual morality. The issues raised here are so many, complex, and controversial that it would be absurd to attempt an exhaustive discussion of them in a final chapter. But some facts and their implications seem clear.

Firstly, sexual impulses and sexual experience themselves are now fairly thoroughly released from the darker clutches of 'sinfulness' with which some elements in the Christian tradition had long strangled them. In future, sex will be regarded as a natural desire, and the satisfying expression and experience of it a fulfilment of certain aspects of our nature. There will be nothing improper in claiming that sexual experience is enjoyable, and that it is an important aspect of a marital relationship, quite apart from procreation.

Second, techniques of birth control will reach new levels of efficiency, so that sexual intimacy may be enjoyed without any likelihood of conception. Furthermore, as we have seen, they are increasingly passing within the control of the *woman* in sexual relationships.

Now these developments alone must have very far-reaching consequences for sexual ethics. Sexual intimacy and marriage will no longer necessarily be thought synonymous. And, if sexual intimacy is entered into with responsibility and mutual consideration, there is no self-evident reason why this should not be so. We know that the greater part of 'cohabitation' is cohabitation as a prelude to marriage or re-marriage, and the whole question of whether pre-marital sexual experience is permissible, desirable, right or wrong, will have to be examined again. It is true that sex is one of the important bases of a happy marriage, and, consequently, of a happy family life – but, it might be argued, *this is just why* people should be as clear in mind and experience about it as possible before they commit themselves to the serious status and duties of marriage, entailing, centrally, the having and rearing of children. Also, though important, sex is far from being the *only* important thing in marriage. Married love includes sex, but is certainly not to be equated with sex. It is also much more than romanticized sex, and it is of the very greatest importance that young people should not enter into marriage on the grounds of the sudden or mounting pressure of the desire to sleep with each other, or with the belief that marriage is merely legitimized gratification.

When people totally reject the propriety of any experience of sexual intimacy before marriage, it seems usually to be on the grounds (a) that marriage is a sacrament and that sexual intimacy should not precede it, (b) that people may make a disastrous mistake in involving themselves so deeply before marriage, and it is therefore better to avoid sex until the partners are actually committed in marriage, and (c) that sex before marriage entails the possibility of deception and the exploitation of one partner by the other for his or her own gratification. But these points do not seem very firm.

If, because of a belief that marriage is a sacrament in its own right, men and women are forbidden to know each other before marriage, and are then to be bound together throughout their lives no matter what fundamental mistake they may have made, no matter what misery they may be suffering through whatever maladjustment, this is clearly to treat human individuals not as ends in themselves but as means only – in this case a means to the correct observance of religious law, or even the divine law. But if God exists, and is a moral being, he could not possibly want it so. He could not treat a person as a means only, even if it were as a means to the maintenance of his own law, or even to his own greater glory. Such a religious law falls very far short, therefore, of our ordinary human standards. Indeed, one sad feature of social policy during the early 1960s was the vision of the Church standing in the way of the humane reform of the divorce law on unethical grounds. If the Church maintains with such rigour that true marriage can be founded only on mutual love, how can it possibly maintain with equal rigour that marriage should be perpetuated when that same love has ceased – and perhaps for reasons for which no one is to blame? Is this not a curious inconsistency? – a religious insistence upon an immoral situation?

As a matter of fact, however, the Church conceded much, and the successful drafting and passing of the Divorce Reform Act (1969) was in large part a result of considered compromise on its part; the acceptance of the 'irretrievable breakdown' of marriage as the basic ground for divorce, making much more ethical sense than any rigid sticking to the doctrine of the matrimonial offence.

Second, though it is true that people may make mistakes and suffer deception and exploitation in sexual relations before marriage, it is equally true that the same things can happen *within* marriage. The truth is that, in general, people never think about the ethics of sex *within* marriage, only outside it. And their attitude seems to carry the rather appalling implication that, once marriage has occurred, less concern need be felt about these matters. Sex is all right now – it is safely confined, firmly controlled, hedged round with social and legal safeguards. This, too, is surely a treatment of individuals not as ends in themselves but as means to what is thought to be a socially necessitous regulation of sex.

It is difficult not to conclude that the conception of marriage which these objections imply – a kind of social or religious impounding of the sexual impulse, only to be allowed expression on the presentation of a licence – is itself immoral. In the future conception of marriage, the sanctioning of sexual intimacy seems likely to be a factor of diminishing weight, though this is far from meaning that sexual fidelity may not continue to be a desired characteristic of marriage.

In this, as in all human relationships, individual discrimination and responsibility will come to be emphasized as the basis of morality. What people actually do in their own sexual behaviour – whether pre-marital, marital, or extra-marital – must be their own responsibility. Our public duty can only be to make available all relevant knowledge – of sex itself and reproduction, of venereal disease, of contraceptive techniques, *and* of what is involved in the true nature of marriage itself – so that everyone has an adequate basis of knowledge on which to take their decisions, and so that – whatever they decide to do – a minimum of unhappiness will be caused either to themselves or to others.

It is worthwhile to repeat here – with reference to almost all the points mentioned above: the acceptance of sex as an enjoyable part of marriage (without sole reference to procreation); the acceptance of sexual experience as something to be enjoyed equally by both women and men; the acceptance of contraceptive practice and voluntary family limitation; the acceptance of a thorough-going egalitarianism in marriage, with a minimal differentiation of roles, and the desire for a personally worked-out companionship – that Gorer's most recent findings were to the effect that the vast majority of young people had, in fact, come to approach and develop their relationship responsibly, and still with fidelity and family concern at the heart of it. Despite what seems to many like a revolution in attitudes towards sexual relationships, the responsible companionate marriage seems to be becoming a reality.

There seems no doubt that these changed attitudes towards the nature of sex, the use of contraceptive techniques in marriage, etcetera, will spread and become commonplace. The continuing deliberations of the Roman Catholic Church, in particular, constitute clear evidence of how even the most strict religious doctrines must bend and give way before new knowledge, modern techniques, and fundamental changes of behaviour. In 1967, it was reported that *most* of the Pope's 'Birth Control Commission' were in favour of ending the Roman Catholic Church's ban on contraceptives. Some details of the Commission's secret report to the Pope were quoted in a newspaper – the weekly *National Catholic Reporter*:

> The regulation of conception appears necessary for many couples who wish to achieve a responsible, open and reasonable parenthood in today's circumstances.... If they are to observe and cultivate all of the essential values of marriage, married people need decent and human means for regulation of conception.

Views such as these rested on the Commission's persuasion that marriage, the family, and the position of women had undergone a social change, and so had views on the meaning of sexuality and conjugal relations. Much later, in October or November of 1980, even Cardinal Basil Hume told the fifth World Synod of Bishops that many 'good, conscientious and faithful' Roman Catholics could no longer accept the Church's stand against artificial birth control. Catholics, he said:

> cannot accept the total prohibition of the use of artificial means of contraception where circumstances seem to make this necessary or even desirable.... It cannot be just said that these persons have failed to overcome their human frailty and weakness. The problem is more complex than that.... Such persons are often good, conscientious and faithful sons and daughters of the Church.

Such changing conceptions of sex and marriage have led to quite fundamental changes in the law, and it seems certain that, in future, there will be a considerable increase in the social and legal investigation of all aspects of the family and marriage which may lead to further changes in the law, and in attitudes underlying the law, to remove remaining sources of conflict, hardship, and unhappiness.

Those who, in general, stand opposed to such changes and to any further changing of the divorce law do not see that other things have already changed in society and will change with it. All this was clearly foreseen by a much-neglected 19th century sociologist – Herbert Spencer – whom we have (in connection with Kathleen Tiernan) already mentioned. 'Already,' he wrote, towards the end of the nineteenth century:

> increased facilities for divorce point to the probability that whereas, hitherto, the union by law was regarded as the essential part of marriage and the union by affection as non-essential; and whereas at present the union by law is thought the more important and the union by affection the less important; there will come a time when the union by affection will be held of primary moment: whence reprobation of marital relations in which the union by affection has dissolved.

Spencer knew quite well that his prediction, which is now being fulfilled, would be unacceptable to many, but, he said, those who rejected his arguments:

> nearly all err by considering what would result from the supposed change, other things remaining unchanged. But other things also must be assumed to have changed. With higher sentiments accompanying union of the sexes, with an increase in altruism, must go a decrease in domestic dissension. Whence, simultaneously, a strengthening of the moral bond and a weakening of the forces tending to destroy it. So that the changes which may further facilitate divorce under certain conditions, are changes which will make those conditions more and more rare.

The bonds of love, affection, and mutually accepted duties, are the bonds on which marriage should rest, not the bonds of legal compulsion. Individuals should not be sacrificed to some supposed verity of religion and law. Marriage should not be constrained to fit the existing law. The law should be so shaped that marriage is not hindered from becoming a thing of love and happiness.

But other aspects of the law, and of legal and social procedures regarding marital and familial situations, are also likely to be more closely investigated and changed.

A FAMILY COURT AND DOMESTIC LAW?

One clear possibility of development has already arisen very conspicuously within the law itself. Family disputes arising over all such matters as divorce, custody, maintenance, adoption and wardship, have become very complicated, but these complications are made even worse by the fact that they are dealt with by three systems within the law: the High Court, the County Courts, and the Magistrates Courts. The over-lapping jurisdiction is evidently confusing and costly, cases sometimes being moved backwards and forwards from one system to another. During the ongoing debate about this matter, one custody case was reported, for example, which had six hearings at the three levels, took three months to resolve, and cost £20,000. There is now an almost universal demand for radical reform, and one of these proposals – for a single Family Court, first put forward by the Finer Committee in 1974 – has since received much support. In the autumn of 1985 a 'Family Court Campaign' was launched. The Lord Chancellor has since made his own proposals, and the Government, in May 1986, has published a consultative paper – stemming from officials from the Lord Chancellor's Department, the Home Office, and the Treasury – setting out three possible models for a Family Court. The legal implications are complex, and no clear conception or decision has yet been reached, though one principle seems to be generally accepted. This is that any such single Family Court should not be a welfare institution, but one focusing entirely on 'rights' in the law. The Finer Committee's principle was that 'the individual in the family court must in the last resort remain the *subject of rights*, not the *object of welfare*.'

Our own discussion of one of the contributions to the Womens' Liberation Movement and of some of the 'half-baked' notions of marriage, cohabitation, etc, seems very strongly to support and reinforce the importance of this idea, but also from the direction of the substance of the law itself, not only that of adjudications on the basis of it. In their *Cohabitation Handbook*, the members of the Rights of Women group insist very firmly indeed (a) that personal relationships entailing reciprocal responsibilities could not escape public concern, and (b) that therefore any cohabitation arrangement should take the form of a written contract drawn up with wording as meticulously clear as that in the solemnization of marriage. In exploring all the possible forms which such contracts might take, they proposed the development of a full system of Domestic Law, going beyond 'conventional marriage' (though clearly it would have to include this) to provide for any other kind of mutually binding relationship and domestic arrangement which people wished to establish, and also making provision for all those connected issues which still carried unresolved distinctions of status – such as the wife's automatic assumption of the husband's surname, of having to live in his domicile, etc. We need not here go over these specific items, but it is worthwhile to note that in its specialized field of legal activities, the Council of Europe has already given much detailed consideration to these matters (and the positions on them in the law of different European countries) and many of their deliberations are now on record and publicly available (see Note 5, p. 274.) For our purposes it is enough to see that *two* propositions arise which do seem to deserve serious consideration.

First, it would seem entirely to the good – in view of the complex changes in the whole field of domestic relationships and the increasingly detailed analysis, consideration, and unresolved nature of them – if there existed not only a single Family Court in the context of which all such matters could be clearly and efficiently dealt with, but also, as the basis for this, one full body of Domestic Law which could be clear, comprehensive, and readily available, a kind of 'Bill of Rights' for all matters domestic. Clearly the full formulation of this would be difficult, because specific elements of law range, in their roots and implications, in all directions. Even so – along the lines of Roman Law – the drawing up of some such 'Digest of Domestic Law' would not seem to lie beyond the wit and capacity of the legal profession. Indeed, if governments are so concerned about the nature and qualities of the life of domestic groups in society, a Royal Commission to study the possibilities of – and perhaps even prepare an indicative outline of – both a Family Court and a Domestic Law combined would seem to be an excellent idea. Or perhaps, at once, this could be a task for the Council of Europe.

Second – with such a clear Domestic Law, covering all the kinds of relationship and detailed contingencies raised in present controversy (it might, for example, provide in the law, for some institution of marriage like that of the Roman *usus* – bringing some clarity into what is now only cloudily seen as a very vague and misunderstood area of the Common Law of England) – it might then be all to the good to require that any and all domestic commitments entered into should comply with this law; should be publicly entered into, before witnesses, before the Registrar (and that no relationship whose parties did *not* so comply could claim the rights and treatment from society which such law established). This, at least, might rid society of those altogether casual and irresponsible approaches to relationships of cohabitation which seem chiefly to be responsible for the instability of families in society, and bring most harm to children who – in successive liaisons – become unwanted, and are left uncared for.

250

This, at any rate, is one clear direction of effort which – even in the immediate future – could be enormously constructive

Beyond the law itself, however, one other approach to the future of the family has become increasingly clear as we have moved from first to last in our entire argument. This is the recognition of the need for forward-looking as against backward-looking social policies in relation to all the problems of the family and society we have reviewed.

A FORWARD-LOOKING APPROACH IN POLICY-MAKING

This, of course, recalls again the implications of our earlier arguments that no good end can possibly be served by falsely conceived and backward-looking judgments and policies. If our conclusion had been that the family had *declined* as a social institution, morally or otherwise, then we should have to advocate a backward-looking approach to some social policies: an attempt to go back on what had been done before; to put right legislative mistakes which had been made. And there seems, at the present time, to be an all too powerful tendency to adopt a backward-looking point of view which is both false and dangerous. Many appear to believe that, in attempted reforms, we have gone 'too far – too fast', and in our efforts to create a Welfare State have given rise to irresponsibility and moral decay. We have seen, however, that any such corollary stemmed from the abuse – perhaps it is not too strong to say the betrayal – of the Welfare State, and the unforeseen consequences of certain aspects and outcomes of it.

If our conclusion is, however – as, indeed, it is – that, as an outcome of many social improvements, we are, as a society, expecting of the family that it should possess a knowledge of, and should utilize responsibly, the wider network of agencies and provisions of which it is a central element, and also that the family should perform many functions of a more fastidious standard of excellence, then our attitude will be one of helping to clarify this situation for the members of society, of helping them to see clearly and act effectively in relation to these extended responsibilities. Similarly, if we decide that the stresses and strains experienced in family relationships are not the outcome of moral decay, but the unforeseen consequences of improved social policies, we shall adopt the forward-looking view of seeking to reconsider and renew our study of the nature of these problems, to understand those apparent entailments of previous policies which we had not fully anticipated, and to formulate further and effective policies to deal with them. We shall recognize that great improvements have been made, that we need to consolidate them, and then make efforts to move beyond them – to resolve the new problems which have arisen, though, none the less, bearing the lesson of experience in mind, that social reforms *never can* solve human problems once for all; they only solve particular problems to some degree, and are always likely to bring into being new problems which were not foreseen. When these new problems arise, we should not think of going back upon the reforms which have been made, but should realistically appraise them in a reliable historical perspective and then deal with them in such a way as to improve the conditions and relationships of human life still further.

The conclusion of our analysis is, clearly, that this latter, forward-looking attitude to social policy is the only one which can be justified. As part of this attitude, too, it should also be recognized that many problems stemming from the apparent inadequacies and shortcomings of some families are the consequence *not* of the fact that reforms have been effected, but of the fact that some *have not yet gone far enough.* Thus, any child neglect resulting from the increased employment of women is in some measure due to the fact that the provisions for child care envisaged in earlier acts – for example, the provision of nursery schools envisaged in the 1944 Education Act – have not in fact been implemented. The provision of any kind of nursery service has thus tended to be regarded as a provision for the unfortunate, rather than a normal and desirable service for the ordinary family. But there are more striking and more important examples.

We have said that housing conditions and general sanitary and urban conditions have been considerably improved, and this is true. But let us remind ourselves over how short and recent a past these reforms have been carried out, and that they have not, even now, been carried out as far as they should be. As short a time ago as 1951 (only thirty-seven years ago), Sir Alexander Carr-Saunders and his colleagues showed that, taking into consideration all households in England and Wales, 6 per cent were without piped water, 2 per cent were without a cooking stove, 6 per cent were without a kitchen sink, 8 per cent were without a water closet, and as many as 37 per cent were without a fixed bath. These were overall figures, and when specific kinds of household were considered, the figures for some categories were even worse. For example, among men aged 75 or over who were living alone, 13 per cent had no piped water, 10 per cent were without a cooking stove, 16 per cent had no kitchen sink, 15 per cent had no water closet, and 67 per cent were without a fixed bath. These facts and figures now seem very dated, but even in the 1980s – and after very great improvements – it remains the case (for example) that 4 per cent of private households in Great Britain lack the sole use of a fixed bath or shower, 5 per cent lacked the sole use of an inside flush toilet, and 2 per cent only had access to a flush toilet outside the building in which they lived. In privately rented unfurnished accommodation 19 per cent of households lacked the sole use of a bath, and 14 per cent lacked any access to a fixed bath or shower. Almost 10 per cent in unfurnished accommodation and almost half in furnished accommodation lacked the sole use of a flush toilet. Mention of these facts is not to deny the great improvements which have taken place, but it still seems to be the case that many areas of our large towns – particularly those with closing pits and declining manufacturing industries and those we now call the 'inner cities' (and complicated, now, by the existence of the new and underprivileged immigrant communities) – are in deplorable 'slum' conditions, some of them resulting from the mistakes of town-planners and architects, and it is in these areas especially that inadequate family conditions and relationships are found. They are termed, by social pathologists, our 'delinquency-producing' areas.[6] It would seem, then, that any substantial reduction in the incidence of delinquency would be most likely to follow *not* from a condemnation of the moral stature of the families in these areas, but from the extended improvement of their home and environmental conditions.

We still tend to speak of deplorable housing and town conditions as though they were things of the past, but, as anyone will know who remembers the conditions of working-class areas in our towns before the Second World War, and who sees the continuance of these conditions in some areas even now, these conditions are *on our doorstep* in time. Indeed, it is worth bearing in mind that *all* the changes we have been considering in terms of the transformation of our society by industrialization have taken place in the last two or three human life-times, an extremely short period of time, and a reading of Masterman's *The Condition of England*, written in 1909, will show how rapid and recent many of the improvements we have mentioned have been. As Professor Titmuss put it not very long ago:

the violent upheavals of the nineteenth century, the poverty, the unemployment, the social indiscipline, the authoritarianism of men and the cruelties to children, are by no means so remote today in their consequences as some economists and historians would have us believe. The reform of housing conditions, to cite one example of a material kind, was both remarkably slow and late in its development.... One inheritance, several generations later, is that social workers spend much of their time coping with the problems of families disabled and deformed by bad housing conditions.[7]

In spite of many improvements, then, our social problems are far from being over, and the improvements that have been made are far from being secure. Our attitude must therefore be forward-looking, basing itself upon a realistic assessment of the new problems which face us, but must also include the realization that, not only have we *not* gone too far, too fast, but that, in many cases, reforms initiated in the past – and recognized in the past as being just and necessary – have not yet gone far enough, and, indeed, are in constant danger of losing even their present degree of efficacy.

(v) A new thrust required: of argument, education and social action

The particular tasks of reform our discussion has thrown up are very clear and need not be repeated in any detail here. We need to embark upon a new constructive task of community-making – a task of building community back into society – trying to overcome the social isolation evidently experienced by many families; making our 'House of Administration' habitable and fit for individuals to live in as co-operatively related persons. We need a parallel programme of detailed qualitative research. The statistical revelation of differing rates of marital breakdown in different occupational groups, for example, makes it clear that we need more knowledge about the different kinds of families in Britain, not simply about the form of the family; about the different types of family which share common collective conditions, situations, and problems. Beyond all such specific tasks, however, our emphasis has come to lie in one broadly based but fundamental direction: the direction of education, and, in particular, of an education which will instil the basic sentiments which are in danger of being undermined and lost. The establishment of important sentiments in the young, of thoroughly appreciated constellations of values, will not happen without our effort, and it will certainly not happen without our frankness and honesty. An effort of education must parallel all our specific policies, and it must be a sensitive continous education, remaining alive to the social complexities that continue to prevail. The young especially are at risk: in marriage, the family, and their many other involvements in the modern world. Much could now be formulated for them in terms of a situational analysis of what they will have to encounter: not in a misguided effort to take decisions or to arrive at judgments for them, but to place before them as clearly as possible the kinds of situations and considerations with which their decisions and judgments will have to deal, and the probable consequences which could follow from this or that set of judgements and decisions about them.

Though the new crop of critics of the family can be set aside with the old, and though the qualities of marriage and the family can still be upheld with confidence and conviction, a new thrust of education is needed. We need to establish a clear perspective of the considerable improvements that have been accomplished in marriage and the family – indeed, in our whole society – over the past century, and to show how contemporary problems are to be interpreted in these terms. We need to show with complete clarity the insufficiency of the 'negative' and backward-looking critics. We need a renewed effort to provide a clear and effective education at the most basic level of social and moral understanding. And all these – research, reforms, and education – are linked.

The truth is that a new initiative and effort is needed throughout our whole political life: to clarify the values throughout the whole fabric of our society – within which marriage and the family remain a basic part. And the need for this is already being clearly seen within Government itself. One piece of evidence is (in 1986) the Government's plan to 'strengthen regard for moral considerations and the value of family life' in sex education in schools. Sex education, the plan argues, should be offered 'within a moral framework', and the Minister of State for Education, defending the plan, also stressed the need in education to 'promote the fundamental political values that sustain our society'. These are encouraging signs. Much of what must go into this task must come from our own thought and our own researches, but it is worthwhile to remind ourselves that much of what we are seeking to achieve has already been clarified and is available for us if we will only study it. It is here, now that we have looked thoroughly at the more mundane facts and trends that are discernible in relation to the future of marriage and the family, that I would like to turn to some of the ideals which some thinkers have held up in the past, and which might serve to guide us. Some of these thinkers, too, I believe, might be quite surprising.

(vi) The greatest miracle

I have dwelt a little on Shakespeare's portrayal of the ideality of love, and his full understanding of the way in which idealities are real in our human experience, rooted in the love we feel but having qualities of their own which lie beyond the immediacy of our experience and even beyond the range of our conscious articulation, and how, as such, they come to exercise an inner sovereignty over us, becoming essentially involved (even if we do not live up to their standards) in the actuality of our relationships, our conduct, and the qualities of our affections and behaviour. We noted, too – what is obvious – that Shakespeare was not alone. Here, I want to note only a few other examples of writers whose testimony – after the treatment of some of the 'radical' critics – is not altogether what might have been expected. It will be of some importance, too, to see that – widely different as people and writers though they are – there is one quite fundamental point on which they are all agreed.

First, it may be interesting to see that Geoffrey Gorer was not the first to point to the abiding satisfactions to be found in a 'Marriage of Good Friends'. In *The Spectator*, over 250 years ago, at the very beginning of the eighteenth century, such a description was very clearly given. On Monday 22 September 1712, Richard Steele wrote this:

> I have very long entertain'd an ambition to make the word *Wife* the most agreeable and delightful name in nature....
>
> Our unhappiness in England has been that a few loose Men of Genius for Pleasure have turn'd it all to the gratification of ungoverned desires, in spite of good sense, form and order; when, in truth, any satisfaction beyond the boundaries of reason is but a step towards madness and folly. But is the sense of joy and accomplishment of desire no way to be indulged or attain'd? And have we appetites given us not to be at all gratified? Yes certainly. Marriage is an Institution calculated for a constant scene of as much delight as our being is capable of. Two persons who have chosen each other out of all the species, with design to be each other's mutual comfort and entertainment, have in that action bound themselves to be good-humoured, afable, discreet, forgiving, patient

and joyful, with respect to each other's frailties and perfections, to the end of their lives. The wiser of the two (and it always happens one of them is such) will for her or his own sake, keep things from outrage with the utmost sanctity. When this union is thus preserved, the most indifferent circumstance administers delight. Their condition is an endless source of new gratifications.... This passion towards each other, when once well fixed, enters into the very constitution, and the kindness flows as easily and silently as the blood in the veins....

I cannot be persuaded but that the passion a bridegroom has for a virtuous young woman will, little by little, grow into friendship, and then it is ascended to a higher pleasure than it was in its first fervour.... When the wife proves capable of filling serious as well as joyous hours, she brings happiness unknown to friendship itself.... Of each kind of love, the highest praise has been attributed to friendship, and indeed there is no disputing that point, but by making that friendship take place between two married persons.

The Spectator was a kind of literature not even mentioned by the writers of the Womens' Liberation Movement, yet it was widely read and enjoyed, filled with advice against the more superficial attitudes to marriage (for one good example of this, see note 8, p. 274), and there is no doubt that on the subject of 'the Marriage of Good Friends', Steele and Geoffrey Gorer, and – if Gorer is right – a majority of the British people, would obviously see eye to eye.

But let us turn to two examples which the Womens' Liberation writers (and some Marxists) have either quite simply misread or misunderstood. The first is Frederick Engels – portrayed as an arch-critic of the nuclear family; as one of those clamouring for its abolition together with the abolition of capitalism. But what did Engels actually say?

Our sexlove is essentially different from the simple sexual craving, the Eros, of the ancients. In the first place it presupposes mutual love. In this respect woman is the equal of man, while in the antique Eros her permission is by no means always asked. In the second place our sexlove has such a degree of intensity and duration that in the eyes of both parties lack of possession and separation appear as a great, if not the greatest, calamity. In order to possess one another they play for high stakes, even to the point of risking their lives, a thing heard of only in adultery during the classical age. And finally a new moral standard is introduced for judging sexual intercourse.

We not only ask: 'Was it legal or illegal?' but also: 'Was it caused by mutual love or not?'

'Since sexlove is exclusive by its very nature ... marriage founded on sexlove must be monogamous....

Remove the economic considerations that now force women to submit to the customary disloyalty of men, and you will place women on an equal footing with men. All experiences prove that this will tend much more strongly to make men truly monogamous, than to make women polyandrous....

The indissolubility of marriage is partly the consequence of economic conditions ... carried to extremes by religion. Today it has been perforated a thousand times. If marriage founded on love is alone moral, then it follows that marriage is moral only as long as love lasts....

The full freedom of marriage can become general only after all minor economic considerations that still exert such a powerful influence on the choice of a mate for life, have been removed ... Then no other motive will remain but mutual fondness.

I quoted Engels earlier (see also *The Abolitionists*, pp. 71–6), but this shows quite conclusively that, far from wanting to see marriage and the family abolished, Engels believed that it should be monogamous, and based, when all other extraneous elements had been removed, upon 'mutual fondness'. As we noted earlier, his position was – remarkably – in agreement with that of Herbert Spencer. But it is the fundamental basis of a true marriage on which he insists which deserves our attention. It is only when the historically accumulated barriers to the full equality of status between men and women are removed that true marriage can take place. True marriage rests, then, on the *free choice* of both parties.

The point which will probably seem most strange of all to readers of the Womens' Liberation literature – who may have formed their own judgment of Engels from that literature – is that this is also exactly the position of Henrik Ibsen. For Ibsen was, himself, decidedly an idealist, only preoccupied with the choking banalities of social and family life and hating them, in so far as they prevented the full self-knowledge of persons and therefore stood in the way of full and free personal choice. His position, too, on the nature – and also the potentially high qualities – of true marriage was actually and luminously made clear in the very plays some writers have claimed to be *opposed* to marriage: *The Doll's House*, for example.

To begin: in *The Lady from the Sea*,[9] Ibsen has Lyngstrand trying, in halting fashion, to express to Boletta his feelings as to what marriage might be.

Lyngstrand: ... I often think about things like that – and marriage in particular. And I've read a great many books on the subject. I think marriage might almost be regarded as a sort of miracle ... the way the woman is gradually transformed till she comes to resemble her husband.

Boletta: You mean she comes to share his interests?

Lyngstrand: Yes, that's right.

Boletta: Ah, but his abilities – his skill and his talents?

Lyngstrand: Ah yes ... perhaps even them, too.

Boletta: Do you believe, then, that everything that a man has read – or thought out for himself – can be passed on to his wife like that?

Lyngstrand: Yes, I think so. Very gradually. Just like a miracle. But I'm sure it could only happen with a true marriage – one that's affectionate and really happy.

This conversation, however, peters out unsatisfyingly, because Lyngstrand seems unable to see that the process of transformation might well be as much on the part of the husband as of the wife. But the *central* issue in the play (of which the above is a minor theme – both symbolic and actual) concerns the relationship between Wangel and his wife Ellida and the curiously tenacious longing for the sea (away from which she had come) and from 'the Stranger' who once tempted her away from marriage, and domesticity, and the securities of social life on the land – out again, towards the vastness of the sea. Despite the closeness of their marriage over a number of years, the deep fascination of this continued two-fold longing has remained something distancing them at the very heart of their relationship, something unresolved, something at the core of their marriage rendering it untrue. The long-standing, long-brooding inner tension is brought up as an actuality into the forefront of their lives, with a mounting intensity, as the Stranger appears again, asserts his influence over Ellida, and is on the point of winning her and taking her off to the large attraction of the sea and the unknown. So real and deeply true an element is this in Ellida's feelings that Wangel releases her from the constraining bond of their marriage and leaves her completely free to choose:

Wangel: (in quiet grief) I realise it, Ellida. Step by step you're

	slipping away from me. Your longing for the boundless and the infinite – for the unattainable – will, in the end, carry your soul out into the darkness.
Ellida:	Yes, yes, I can feel it – like black soundless wings hovering over me.
Wangel:	It shall not come to that. There's no other possible salvation for you – at least, none that I can see.... So – so I cancel our bargain here and now. You are free to choose your own path. Completely free....
Ellida:	(gazing at him for a while as if speechless) Is that true? Is it true what you say? Do you really mean it – in your heart of hearts?
Wangel:	Yes, I mean it – from the bottom of my sorrowing heart.
Ellida:	But *can* you do it? Could you let it happen?
Wangel:	Yes, I could – I could because I love you so much.
Ellida:	(softly, trembling) Have I come to mean so very much to you?
Wangel:	Our years of marriage have accomplished that.
Ellida:	(clasping her hands) And yet I never saw it!
Wangel:	Your thoughts were elsewhere.... But now – now you are completely free from me and mine. Now your own innermost life can take its true path again, because now your choice is free – and the responsibility is yours, Ellida.
Ellida:	(staring at Wangel, with her hands to her head) Free – and with full responsibility! Oh, that changes everything! (The ship's bell rings again.)
Stranger:	You hear that, Ellida? It's the last bell. Come with me.
Ellida:	(turning to him, she looks full in his face and says resolutely) I can never go with you now.
Stranger:	You will not?
Ellida:	(clinging to Wangel) Oh, Wangel, I can never leave you after this.
Wangel:	Ellida – Ellida!
Stranger:	Is it all over, then?
Ellida:	Yes, for ever.
Stranger:	I see that there's something here that is stronger than my will.
Ellida:	Your will hasn't the slightest power over me any more. To me you are a dead man – who has come from the

260

sea, and will return to it. You hold no terror for me
any more – nor any fascination.

Stranger: Goodbye. (He vaults over the fence.) From now on,
you are no more to me than – than a shipwreck that I
have come safely through. (He goes out.)

Wangel: (looking at her for a moment) Ellida, your mind is like
the sea, it ebbs and flows. What made you change?

Ellida: Oh, don't you see? The change came – as it had to
come – when I could choose freely.

Wangel: And the unknown? That has no fascination for you
now?

Ellida: No fascination and no terror. I could have faced it –
become a part of it – if I had only wished to. Now that
I could choose it, I could also reject it.

Wangel: I'm slowly beginning to understand you. You think and
reason in pictures – in visual images. This longing of
yours – this yearning for the sea, and the fascination
that *he* – this stranger – had for you, were really only
the expression of a new and growing urge in you for
freedom.... That's all.... But now, Ellida – you *will*
come back to me?

Ellida: Oh, my dear, faithful husband. Now I will come back
to you. *Now* I can, because I come to you freely – of
my own free will – on my own responsibility.

Wangel: (looking at her tenderly) Ellida – Ellida.... Oh, to
think that now we can live entirely for each other –

Ellida: – with all our aims in common – yours as well as mine.

Wangel: Yes, that's true, my dear.

The 'sort of miracle' Lyngstrand was fumbling his way towards
could be an actuality – when its ideality had been completely
recognized and known, and fully, freely, and responsibly accepted.
With all the marvellously interwoven symbolism at his command,
Ibsen brings the whole play to a close with a conversation about the
picture of a *dying mermaid* with which it began, between Ellida,
Wangel and Ballested – the artist who was about to paint it:

Ellida: ... once you have become a land animal, there's no
going back to the sea again – nor to the life of the
sea.

Ballested: Why, that's just like my mermaid.

Ellida: Yes, it is rather.

Ballested: Except that the *mermaid* – dies. Human beings, on

	the other hand, can acclimatize themselves.
Ellida:	Yes, they can if they're free, Mr Ballested.
Wangel:	And have full responsibility, Ellida, dear.
Ellida:	(quickly, giving him her hand) Yes, *that's* the secret.

Ibsen's position, though differently approached, is exactly the same as that of Engels. Marriage *has* been, and *can* be, an institutionalized and constraining strait-jacket bound on with unyielding cords of circumstance and inequalities, and as such it has been, and can be, a relationship productive of the deepest misery. When all such obstacles are removed, however – when a relationship of such total closeness and commitment is entered into on the basis of full, free and responsible personal choice – then this is *true* marriage, as it should properly be conceived. Strangely, too – this is exactly Ibsen's message in *The Doll's House* – a play which some of the Womens' Liberation writers seem completely to have misunderstood. It is true that the play portrays the misery and total spiritual frustration in marriage for a wife subjected to traditional inequalities and facing a total lack of understanding of her position, but – at the very end of the play – the crucial point of its ending is that out of the wreck and breaking-up of the conventional marriage, the vision of the *ideal* marriage is born – like a sudden glimpse of light in the gathered darkness which has hitherto been unseen. When Nora is about to leave him, refusing all his offers of help, Helmer asks in his utter distress:

Helmer:	Nora – can't I ever be anything more than a stranger to you?
Nora:	(picking up her bag): Oh, Torvald – there would have to be the greatest miracle of all...
Helmer:	What would that be – the greatest miracle of all?
Nora:	Both of us would have to be so changed that – Oh, Torvald, I don't believe in miracles any longer.
Helmer:	But I'll believe. Tell me: 'so changed that...'?
Nora:	That our life together could be a real marriage. Good-bye. (She goes out through the hall.)
Helmer:	(sinking down on a chair by the door and burying his face in his hands): Nora! Nora! (He rises and looks round.) Empty! She's not here any more! (With a glimmer of hope) 'The greatest miracle of all...'?

The play ends with a question, but its implication is plain. Chosen freely by two individuals confronting each other as complete and equal persons – a *real* marriage would be a *true* marriage and could be '*the greatest miracle of all*'. This was the vision of Ibsen.

In England, too, as long ago as 1869, one of the greatest of Victorians – John Stuart Mill – wrote this:

> What marriage may be in the case of two persons of cultivated faculties ... between whom there exists that best kind of equality, similarity of powers and capacities with reciprocal superiority in them – so that each can enjoy the luxury of looking up to the other and can have alternately the pleasure of leading and of being led in the path of development – I will not attempt to describe. To those who can conceive it, there is no need; to those who cannot, it would appear the dream of an enthusiast. But I maintain, with the profoundest conviction, that this, and this only, is the ideal of marriage and that all opinions, customs and institutions which favour any other notion of it ... are relics of primitive barbarism. The moral regeneration of mankind will only really commence, when the most fundamental of the social relations is placed under the rule of equal justice, and when human beings learn to cultivate their strongest sympathy with an equal in rights and in cultivation.[10]

Just over a hundred years of painstaking reform after that statement was made, we are much nearer, now – for *all* people in our society – to the humane ideal it upholds. 'The Marriage of Good Friends' – on which Richard Steele, Engels, Ibsen, John Stuart Mill, Geoffrey Gorer and ourselves can all be agreed ... *this* is what marriage today is becoming, and tomorrow should be, and is surely enough to guide us.

To end on a rather enigmatic note, there is nothing in this setting out of ideals to contradict all that Robert Louis Stevenson (who also believed in the nature and possibility of true marriage) had to say in the two opening essays of his *Virginibus Puerisque* – which were given no titles – and which ended with the statement that marriage 'is a field of battle, and not a bed of roses'. True – but it is one on which two people of the right metal can win much, and in his essay 'El Dorado', Stevenson also wrote this:

> when you have married your wife, you would think you were got upon a hilltop, and might begin to go downward by an easy slope. But you have only ended courtship to begin marriage. Falling in love and winning love are often difficult tasks to overbearing and rebellious spirits; but to keep in love is also a

business of some importance, to which both man and wife must bring kindness and goodwill. The true love story commences at the altar, when there lies before the married pair a most beautiful contest of wisdom and generosity, and a life-long struggle towards an unattainable ideal. Unattainable? Ay, surely unattainable, from the very fact that they are two instead of one.

Ideals are unattainable – but they enter into the actuality of our experience and behaviour, and, whether we manage to approximate to their standards or, being too little and fallible, fall far short of them, are guides which we cannot escape or deny in our character and conduct. We cannot escape the fact that we are moral beings.

(vii) Family, wider society, world: some final considerations

A few final thoughts come to the forefront of my mind in bringing to a close this whole argument, which has proved, essentially, a defence of monogamous marriage and the form of the family it entails – in and for both modern Britain and the modern world.

The first is that the conjunction between the considerable improvement in the conditions of both the family and society which have been achieved, the ongoing transformation of the world in this same direction, *and* the condition of *crisis* is very real, and it may well be that I have under-estimated and under-emphasized the dimension of crisis in it. As I write, a survey of the beliefs and attitudes of young people in Britain reports that 4 out of every 10 young people below the age of 25 (40 per cent – almost *half* – of our total population of young people) say that 'life holds no meaning for them'. Is not this the kind of danger our analysis envisaged? One writer (in the *Sunday Telegraph*) using exactly the kind of language we have used, refers to this as a 'chilling statistic', claiming that it points to 'a national crisis of alienation not merely from family or society, but from *self*'. 'What lies behind teenage consumerism,' he asks, 'that we desperately need to know?' Well ... our own analysis has been given. But if this 'statistic' is true, if for so many life is devoid of satisfying meaning and purpose, of what concern can matters of character and conduct be? The creation – in our consumer society, with the destruction of the natural-social sequence and the crisis of communications we have mentioned – of a *vacuum*, an emptiness, a void, where there was once the sense of a human *soul*; the loss of '*self*' in society; the sense of *spiritual nonentity* about which we speculated earlier ... seem to have gone very far. The crisis seems undoubtedly to be real. I leave readers to think and judge for themselves, but everything points to the fact that the task of education which faces us is very great.

A second danger is that in this task – in our concern to remedy unhappiness – we may be in danger of focusing our attention *too narrowly* upon the family. Both in terms of personal life and in terms of social reform and administration, we may be in danger of expecting that too much can be done by concentrating upon the family alone. In all the diagnoses of the ills of society, in all the suggestions for improvement, the family tends to be considered far too much in isolation. It is true that the family is a group of basic importance in society; that the primary group sentiments and values established there are of primary importance; but it is also true that there is much more besides – both for ourselves as individuals and in society – and I would like to comment on a few aspects of this point.

First, we have seen that the family is all too frequently *blamed* for too much; indeed, for every ill of society which we do not understand – crime, delinquency, and the like – and this is all much too one-sided. If a young boy is promiscuous, for example, there are those who think immediately that it must be due to his family background and some disturbance he suffered during the early years of life. But during the scandal of some years ago which centred upon the figure of Mr Profumo, Dr A. J. P. Taylor in a light-hearted article mentioned a string of sparkling names of people in high places in the past who had committed similar actions,[11] and – to take some names from this list – does anyone ever ask what it was that the Duke of Wellington, Earl Grey, Lord Melbourne, Palmerston, Disraeli, Dilke, Lloyd George, or Edward VII saw in the shed at the bottom of the garden when they were three years old, and whether their family background was such as to give rise to insecure personality development? And the people who continue to manufacture and advertise cigarettes, knowing that they are maintaining and furthering a high rate of deaths from lung cancer (now numbering some 100,000 a year); or those advertising firms who, without a qualm, will sell chewing gum, fruit-juice, tobacco, the Conservative Party, ladies' underwear, the Labour Party, even the Church of England, if they are given a paying contract for the job; have all these people suffered from poor family backgrounds? Maybe. It is a possibility. But the significant thing is that we never ask. The family has become a scapegoat on which we lay the blame for all those anti-social acts which we happen not to like, and for which we have no other explanation. The truth, surely, is that our human nature is so notoriously ready to set self-control aside for indulgence in appetite so notoriously prone to evil – whether petty or large, great or small – as to require no explanation in terms of some fault or flaw in the family.

Second, it sometimes seems to be thought that if we put the family right, if we live happily within our family groups, concentrating upon being healthy and stable personalities within the home, then the state will no longer totter, the problems of society will be remedied and its delinquencies overcome. And in order to secure this firm family life we hear much about the ethics of sex education and education for family life.

There are the dangers we have touched upon, too, that the family may be in danger of becoming too enclosed a group. There may be a tendency in the more comfortable conditions of our society for people to become content with the garden, the warm living-room, the do-it-yourself kits, and, of course, the television screen. I think it was Mr Jimmy Edwards who once said that we were fast becoming a race of troglodytes. And – with not such a cosy atmosphere – many families in dense urban areas are driven inwards upon themselves in their small high-rise flats not through choice, but simply because they have no social contacts in the hard brick-and-concrete neighbourhood. Whether by compulsion or choice, the family may be becoming very inward-looking; too much, perhaps, immersed in itself.

Now, no one with any sense will criticize the enjoyment of the comforts, pleasures, and privacy of home life, and no one can deny that if family life is secure and happy we shall have the best prospects for an adult population of good citizens. But there is one central point which it does seem to be of the very greatest importance to realize.

The family is not self-contained. Though a group within which our deepest satisfactions are found, the family is also, for the child, an introduction to life in the wider society, and, for the adult, a basis for life in the wider society. If this is forgotten, the relationships and personalities within the family may be both impoverished and spoiled, and may well suffer from the kind of intractable and self-consuming intensity which critics like Leach have attacked. What I mean is that people, if they are impoverished in other and wider aspects of human life, impoverished in certain dimensions of their nature, may look intensely for some kind of satisfaction in marital and family relationships which is simply not there to be found at all. They may come to expect too much. Family relationships may positively suffer from too inward-looking, too self-contained, too enclosed an attitude to the family, and in this context there may well be a positive danger in emphasizing sex, love, and romanticism in general, to the exclusion of

266

other qualities and activities. And there is another aspect of this which is important.

If we examine the matter fully, it becomes clear that there is no such thing as the 'ethics of sex' or 'family ethics' – separate from ethics in general. The ethical principles in the light of which we should regulate our sexual and family relationships are the same as those on which we should base *all* our conduct in *all* human relationships. They are – to glean only a few examples from the moral philosophers – that we should always:

1 try to increase happiness and diminish pain;
2 treat other individuals as persons, as ends in themselves, and never only as a means to some end of our own;
3 behave towards others as we think it right that they should behave towards us;
4 seek to attain the highest level of excellence of which we are capable in any task to which we commit ourselves; and
5 seek to secure, in society, those human rights which these principles entail, and which *require* to be secured for their operation and fulfilment.[12]

It is this mention of *society* which matters. If we are concerned to improve the family and marriage, we cannot do this by concentrating on the family alone, but only by concerning ourselves with the attainment of social justice and the improvement of human relationships throughout the whole of our society; in factories, schools, government, and all other institutions. Consequently, it is not education in the ethics of sexual and family relationships alone which we want; it is education in the widest sense for responsible citizenship, within which sexual and family relationships will have their proper, but not an all-embracing place.

One other point I have made much of, but which, I believe, deserves the greatest emphasis is this: *how new this type of society, and how new this type of family is* – for *all* the members of society – *in the whole history of humanity*. Never before have men, women, and children both within and beyond the family enjoyed such personal freedom, equality of status, and mutuality of consideration within the context of the helpful provisions of sympathetic government. In our own society, this is little more than fifty years old. Only in 1928 did women become political citizens, equal to men. Only since the Second World War has educational opportunity been extended to all our children, and, of course, *much* more has still to be done in this direction. But all this is so new that even our own parents did not enjoy it, and even we ourselves are not acclimatized to it. *This is a new situation in the entire history of mankind.*

And this leads to my final consideration. Earlier, I have argued, and tried to show, that the family in modern Britain was shaped in coming to terms with the characteristics of an industrial society, and as a result of securing, within the whole structure of society, the wider principles of social justice. It requires little imagination to see that what has happened in Britain is now rapidly spreading throughout the world. Industrialization is spreading everywhere. Everywhere, people are clamouring for the rights of man to be institutionally secured in their own independent societies. We have mentioned the example of the new Marriage Law of Communist China[13] which embodies so many principles in common with our own. This is a good example of how similar moral improvements can be brought about by widely differing political régimes. The improvement in the status of women, for example, embodied in this new Chinese Law is a tremendous achievement. 'They were not Negroes or Jews or refugees,' as Marghanita Laski once put it, 'they were simply women – the other part of the human race.'[14] Everywhere, in modern conditions, women are both desiring and beginning to achieve this improved status.

This is the note on which I would most like to end this book.

Throughout the world in the twentieth century, the new type of family we know in Britain – with all the problems this is encountering – is becoming universal. It is becoming the universal family of mankind. And this rests everywhere upon the spread of industrialization, improvements in material and moral welfare, and the securing in every society of human rights and the principles of social justice. Nations are being drawn ever more closely together to resolve common problems and to pursue common purposes. In short, in a difficult, extremely painstaking way, through the United Nations Organization and through many other channels of negotiation, a new family of man is coming into being. After millenia of separating differences and widely different levels of social development, the unity of mankind is within our grasp; is within sight of achievement. The ideals of mankind are now – with our effort, patience, and understanding – within the bounds of realization.

In this situation, can we seriously entertain the idea of looking back, of going back? Can we seriously waste breath and time in speaking of moral decline? Can we really say that – whether in Britain or in the wider contemporary world – we suffer a lack of purpose? Can we seriously speak only negatively of decline and fall? Surely our task and the directions in which the solutions of our many dilemmas most probably lie are perfectly clear?

The stature of an individual, a family, a nation, is made great not by a process of inward-looking and self-examination alone, but also by a devotion to purposes which lie beyond, and are greater than, themselves. We shall not find stable, fulfilled, satisfying family lives sitting round our television sets, inwardly preoccupied with our own appetites or our own personalities. But if, in this critical juncture of our time, we devote ourselves, in co-operation with others, to the achievement of the new family of man whose ethical outlines – despite all the problems – are now so clear before us, then as nations we might be invigorated, as individuals our lives can certainly have clear and worthwhile purpose and meaning, and we need then have less fear for the stability, health, happiness, and character of the families we ourselves rear – for these foundations, among all foundations, are surely those most likely to be firm.

Notes

Introduction

1 Penguin Books, 3rd edn, 1973.
2 Routlege, 1988.
3 SPCK, 1958.

Preparatory Considerations

1 THE SIGNIFICANCE OF THE 1960S

1 *The Family and the Future* (CIBA Symposium), ed. Kathleen Elliot, Churchill, 1970, p.87.
2 See, for example, R. Chester and J. Streather, 'Taking Stock of Divorce', *New Society*, 22 July 1971.
3 See Colin Gibson, 'A Note on Family Breakdown in England and Wales', *British Journal of Sociology*, vol. XXII, no. 3, September 1971, p. 322.

3 THE FAMILY AS THE BASIC DOMESTIC GROUP IN SOCIETY

1 *Human Nature and the Social Order*, Schocken Books, 19th, p.xxviii.
2 *On Social Psychology*, University of Chicago Press, Phoenix Books, 1965, pp. 242–3.
3 *Human Nature and the Social Order*, pp. 32–3.
4 *Social Organization*, pp. 29–30, 32–5. For a full discussion of Cooley's position, see my *The Making of Sociology*, vol. 2, '*Developments*', pp. 482–511.

5 *The History of Human Marriage*, p. 72.
6 *The Future of Marriage in Western Civilization*, p. 170.

4 FAMILY? OR WIDER SOCIAL CAUSATION?

1 *Penguin New Writing*.
2 Thomas Hardy, 'We Are Getting to the End', *Collected Poems*, Macmillan, 1932, p. 886.

Part I The Family in Britain

1 *Hansard*, 9 February 1968, p. 812.
2 This graph was taken from 'Separation, Divorce and Re-Marriage – The Experience of Children', by Dr M. P. M. Richards, in *Relating to Marriage*, National Marriage Guidance Council, 1984, p. 162.
The particular sources are given in all of the other diagrams and tables in this chapter, though almost all of them have been taken from the successive numbers (annual editions) of *Social Trends*, and from the General Household Survey.
3 *Population Studies*, vol. XI, no. 3, March 1958, p. 232.
4 *Social Trends*, no. 15, 1985, Central Statistical Office, p. 39.
5 *Social Trends*, no. 16, 1986, p. 37.
6 *Ibid.*, p. 43.
7 *Registrar General's Statistical Review of England and Wales for 1967*, Part III Commentary, p. 14.
8 *Relating to Marriage*, National Marriage Guidance Council, 1984, p. 164.
9 *Social Trends*, no. 16, 1986, p. 35.
10 *Sex and Marriage in England Today*, Nelson, 1971, p. 65.
11 See *Social Trends*, no. 4, p. 35 and additional note in *Social Trends*, no. 6, 1975, p. 48.
12 *Dual Career Families*, Penguin Books, 1971, p. 308.
13 *The Affluent Worker: Industrial Attitudes and Behaviour*, Cambridge University Press, 1968.
14 *Ibid.*, p. 176.
15 *Ibid.*, p. 180.
16 Bedford Square Press, 1984.
17 HMSO, 1979.

Part II A World in Transformation

1 INTRODUCTION

1 Isaiah 24. 18–21; 51.6.
2 Paul Tillich, *The Shaking of the Foundations*, Penguin Books, 1949.

2 ACCEPTED AREAS OF CAUSATION AND EXPLANATION

1 *The Condition of England*. These quotations are taken from the 1911 edition.
2 Griselda Rowntree and Norman H. Carrier, 'The Resort to Divorce in England and Wales', *Population Studies*, vol. Xl, no. 3, March, 1958, p. 90.
3 *Ibid.*
4 *Collected Poems*, Macmillan, 1932, p. 15, 'The Serjeant's Song'.
5 Lady Drusilla Scott, 'Changes in the Family', *The Times*, 1 November 1985.

3 LARGER ISSUES. CRISIS: THE SHAKING OF THE FOUNDATIONS

1 W. B. Yeats, 'The Second Coming', *Collected Poems*, Macmillan, 1950, p. 210.
2 C. H. Cooley. These quotations are taken from 'Social Organization'. For details and a full discussion of Cooley, see: R. Fletcher, *The Making of Sociology*, vol. 2, 'Developments', Ch. 2, Section 3: 'The Psychological Aspects of Society'.
3 *The History of Human Marriage*, p. 72.
4 *The Future of Marriage in Western Civilization*, Macmillan, 1936, p. 170.
5 *Ibid.*, p. 265.
6 Axel Munthe, *The Story of San Michele*, John Murray, 1936 Edition, p. 142.
7 Macmillan, 1903.
8 See diagram 39.
9 Choruses from *The Rock* (I), 1934.
10 'Whispers of Immortality', *Poems*, 1920.
11 From an interview in *US News and World Report*, reported in the British press 17 January 1981. The book referred to was *The Disappearance of Childhood*.
12 J. and E. Newson, Penguin Books, 1970.
13 *The Republic*, Everyman's Edition. Book II for comments on 'The Simple Society' (pp. 51–2), Book IX on 'The Inflamed Society'.
14 *Ibid.*, p. 270.
15 A. N. Whitehead, *Symbolism: Its Meaning and Effect*, Cambridge University Press, 1928, p. 104.

4 THE FUTURE OF THE FAMILY

1 Quoted in Norman Angell, *The Unseen Assassins*, Hamish Hamilton, 1932.

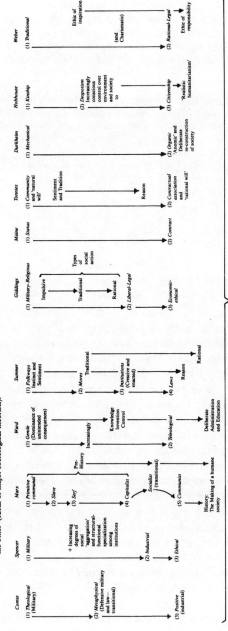

Agreement about the distinguishing features of traditional agrarian societies and contractual commercial and industrial societies and the modern transition from one to the other[8] (Ideas of major sociological theorists).

All agreed upon:

(1) The 'net' pattern of social evolution resulting in the contemporary human situation.

(2) The central significance of the transition from a predominantly 'traditional' to a pre-dominantly 'contractual and rational' social order.

(3) The rapid and radical nature of this modern transformation: its promise and threat.

(4) The necessity for a deliberate reconstitution of institution (social reconstruction); the increasing dominance of rational, ethical purpose in the changing nature of institutions.

(5) Human responsibility for the making of society. The necessity for scientific knowledge of man and society and an 'ethics of responsibility'.

2 Ernest Crawley, *The Mystic Rose*, Spring Books, 1965, pp. 259–61.
3 *The Cohabitation Handbook*, Pluto Press, 1981, pp. 1–2.
4 The discussion of points of law throughout this section draws on my study (chiefly) of: (i) Stephens Commentaries on the Laws of England, (ii) R. W. League, *Roman Private Law*, Macmillan, 1967, and (iii) T. H. Green, *Lectures on the Principles of Political Obligation*, Longmans Green, 1901 (Chapter on 'The Rights of the State in Relation to the Family').
5 See the 'Reports by the Secretary General' and the 'Conclusions and Resolutions' of (at least) the 13th, 14th and 15th Conferences of the European Ministers of Justice (between 1982 and 1986). Also *Legal Co-operation in Europe*, Strasbourg, 1983, chapters II and III on the Law of Persons and Family Law.
6 See, for example, John Barron Mays, *On the Threshold of Delinquency*, Liverpool University Press, 1959.
7 *Essays on the Welfare State*, p. 108.
8 Henry Morley (ed.), *The Spectator*, Routledge. The following is a 'Letter of Queries' – with his answers to each question from the 'Love Casuist' 'confirmed and ratified' by the editor, and published on Friday 26 November 1714:

Sir,

I was Thirteen the Ninth of November last, and must now begin to think of settling myself in the World, and so I would humbly beg your Advice, what I must do with Mr. *Fondle* who makes his Adresses to me. He is a very pretty man, and hath the blackest eyes and whitest teeth you ever saw. Though he is but a younger brother, he dresses like a Man of Quality and nobody comes into a Room like him. I know he hath refused great Offers, and if he cannot Marry me he will never have anybody else. But my Father hath forbid him the House because he sent me a copy of verses, for he is one of the greatest Wits in Town. My eldest Sister, who, with her goodwill, would call me *Miss* as long as I live, must be married before me, they say. She tells them that Mr. *Fondle* makes a Fool of me, and will spoil the Child, as she calls me, like a confident thing as she is. In short, I am resolved to marry Mr. *Fondle*, if it be but to spite her. But because I would do nothing that is imprudent, I beg of you to give me your Answers to some Question I will write down, and desire you to get them printed in The SPECTATOR, and I do not doubt but you will give such Advice, as I am sure I shall follow:-
When Mr. *Fondle* looks upon me for half an Hour together, and calls me *Angel*, is he not in 'Love'?
Answer: *No.*
May not I be certain he will be a kind husband, that has

promised me half my Portion in Pin-Money, and to keep me a coach and six in the Bargain?

No.

Whether I, who have been acquainted with him this whole Year almost, am not a better judge of his Merit than my Father and Mother, who never heard him talk but at Table?

No.

Whether I am not old enough to chuse for my 'self'?

No.

Whether it would not have been rude in me to refuse a Lock of his Hair?

No.

Should I not be a very barbarous creature if I did not pity a Man that is always Sighing for my Sake?

No.

Whether you would not advise me to run away with the poor Man?

No.

Whether you do not think that if I won't have him, he won't drown himself?

No.

What shall I say to him the next time he asks me if I will marry him?

No.

9 These quotations from Ibsen are taken from the Penguin edition of three plays, 1965.
10 From *The Subjection of Women*, Longmans Green Popular Edition, 1911, p. 123.
11 A. J. P. Taylor, 'Are We So Bad?', *TV Times*, 13 September 1963.
12 See Ronald Fletcher, 'A Humanist's Decalogue', *New Society*, October 1963, and reprinted in pamphlet form by the Pioneer Press and in *Youth in New Society*, Rupert Hart-Davis, 1966.
13 *The Marriage Law of the People's Republic of China*, Peking, 1950, pp. 1–6.
14 Marghanita Laski, 'It was a bitter fight for the vote', *News Chronicle*, 1 April 1957.

Suggestions for further reading

Abel-Smith, B. and Pinker, R., *Changes in the Use of Institutions in England and Wales between 1911 and 1951*, Paper to the Manchester Statistical Society, 10 February 1960.

Abrams, M., *Teenage Consumer Spending in 1959* (Part II), London Press Exchange Ltd, 1961.

Abrams, M., 'The Home-centred Society', *Listener*, 26 November 1959.

Abrams, M., 'Subjective Social Indicators', *Social Trends*, No. 4, 1973 (pp. 35–49) and Note in *Social Trends*, No. 6, 1975 (p. 48).

Allen, A., *The Story of Your Home*, Faber & Faber, 1949.

Anderson, J. N. D. (ed.), *Family Law in Asia and Africa*, Allen & Unwin, 1968.

Anderson, M. (ed.), *Sociology of the Family*, Penguin Books, 1971.

Anderson, M., 'What is New About the Modern Family: an Historical Perspective', *In the Family*, Occasional Paper 31, Office of Population Census and Survey, 1983, pp. 1–15.

Andry, R. G., *et al., Deprivation of Maternal Care: A Reassessment of its Effects*, World Health Organization, 1962.

Anshen, R. N., *The Family: Its Functions and Destiny*, Harper Bros., 1949.

Banks, J. A., *Prosperity and Parenthood*, Routledge & Kegan Paul, 1954.

Bell, Colin, *Middle Class Families*, Routledge & Kegan Paul, 1969.

Binder, Pearl, *Russian Families*, Adam & Charles Black, London, 1942.

Bird, R., *Marriage and the Law*, National Marriage Guidance Council, 1981.

Bosanquet, H., *The Family*, Macmillan, 1906.

Bott, E., *Family and Social Network: Roles, Norms, and External Relationships in Ordinary Urban Families*, Tavistock Publications, 2nd edn, 1971.

Breed, C. G. and Van Vliet, A. H., *Marriage and Canon Law* (A concise and complete account), Burns Oates, 1964.

British National Conference on Social Work, *The Family*, National Council of Social Service, 1954.

Bromley, P. M., *Family Law*, Butterworth, 1957.

Bruce, N. and Spencer, J., *Face to Face with Families: A Report on the Children's Panels in Scotland*, MacDonald, 1976.

276

Caird, Mona, *The Morality of Marriage and other essays on the Status and Destiny of Woman*, Redway, London, 1897.

Carr-Saunders, A. M., Caradog Jones, D. and Moser, C. A., *A Survey of Social Conditions in England and Wales*, Oxford, 1958.

Central Office of Information, *Women in Britain* (Pamphlet 67), HMSO, 1964.

Chester, R. and Streather, Jane, 'Taking Stock of Divorce', *New Society*, 22 July 1971.

Church of England Moral Welfare Council, *The Family in Contemporary Society*, SPCK, 1958.

Group appointed by the Archbishop of Canterbury, *Putting Asunder: A Divorce Law for Contemporary Society*, SPCK, 1966.

Cockburn, A. and Blackburn, R., *Student Power*, Penguin Books, 1969.

Cooper, David, *The Death of the Family*, Allen Lane, the Penguin Press, 1971.

Cooper, David and Laing, R. D., *Reason and Violence*, Tavistock Publications, 1964.

Crawley, E., *The Mystic Rose*, many editions; that used here: Spring Books, 1965.

Dicks, H. V., *Marital Tensions*, Routledge & Kegan Paul, 1967.

Douglas, J. W. B., *The Home and the School*, MacGibbon & Kee, 1964.

Dutton, Ralph, *The Victorian Home*, Bracken Books, London, 1984.

Elliott, Katherine, *The Family and its Future*, CIBA Foundation Conference, Churchill, 1970.

Ellis, Havelock, *Little Essays of Love and Virtue*, Black, 1922.

Ellis, Havelock, *Man and Woman*, A. & C. Black, London, 1930.

Ellis, Havelock, *More Essays of Love and Virtue*, Constable, 1931.

Ellis, Havelock, *Sex and Marriage*, Williams & Norgate, London, 1958.

Engels, F., *The Origin of the Family, Private Property and the State*, Charles H. Kerr, Chicago, 1902.

Eppel, E. M., 'Adolescent Values', *New Society*, 28 March 1963.

Eppel, E. M. and M., 'Teenage Values', *New Society*, 14 November 1963.

Eppel, E. M. and M., 'Teenage Idols', *New Society*, 21 November 1963.

Esterson, A., *The Leaves of Spring*, Penguin Books, 1972.

Esterson, A. and Laing, R. D., *Sanity, Madness and the Family*, Penguin Books, 1970.

Farmer, Mary, *The Family*, Longmans, 1970.

Firth, Raymond, 'Family and Kinship in Industrial Society' in *The Development of Industrial Society (Sociological Review*, Monograph No. 8, October 1964).

Firth, Raymond, *Two Studies of Kinship in London*, Athlone Press, 1966.

Firth, Raymond *et al.*, *Families and their Relatives*, Routledge & Kegan Paul, 1970.

Fletcher, Ronald, 'The Making of the Modern Family', *The Family and its Future*, Churchill, 1970.

Fletcher, Ronald, *The Making of Sociology,* vol. 1, *Beginnings*, vol. 2, *Developments*, Michael Joseph/Nelson, 1971 (For the views of Marx, Spencer, Mill, Cooley, Westermarck, and other social theorists.)

Fletcher, Ronald, 'The Marriage of Good Friends', *Marriage Guidance*, 1972.

Fletcher, Ronald, 'The Family and Marriage Today: The Shaking of the Foundations', *Marriage and The Family*, Lutterworth Press, 1985.

Foss, H., *Come Home with Me*, (An anthology of essays), Blandford Press, 1944.

Fox, R., *Kinship and Marriage*, Penguin Books, 1967.

Friedmann, W., *Law in a Changing Society* (Chap. 7), Stevens, 1959.

Garbett, C. F., *In the Heart of South London*, Longmans Green, 1931.

Geddes, D., *An Analysis of the Kinsey Reports*, Muller, London, 1954.

George, D., *England in Transition*, Penguin Books, 1953.

George, V. and Wilding, P., *Motherless Families*, Routledge & Kegan Paul, 1972.

Glass, D. V. and Grebenik, E., *The Trend and Pattern of Fertility in Great Britain*, Papers of the Royal Commission on Population, vol. vi, 1954.

Goldthorpe, J. H. *et al.*, *The Affluent Worker: Industrial Attitudes and Behaviour*, Cambridge University Press, 1968.

Goode, W. J., *World Revolution and Family Patterns*, Free Press, 1963.

Goode, W. J., *The Family*, Prentice-Hall Inc. (Foundations of Modern Sociology Series), 1964.

Goode, W. J., *Readings on the Family and Society*, Prentice Hall, 1964.

Gorer, G., *Exploring English Character*, Cresset Press, 1955.

Gorer, G., *Sex and Marriage in England Today*, Thomas Nelson, 1970.

Gorer, G., Maclure, Stuart, and others, *Teenage Morals*, Councils and Education Press, 1961.

Graveson, R. H. and Crane, F. R. (eds), *A Century of Family Law, 1857–1957*, Sweet & Maxwell, 1957.

Greer, Germaine, *The Female Eunuch*, Paladin Books, 1971.

Greer, Germaine, *Sex and Destiny, the Politics of Human Fertility*, Picador, Pan Books, 1985.

Griffiths, E. F., *Modern Marriage*, Methuen, revised edition, 1963.

Hadas, M., *Imperial Rome*, Time-Life International, 1968 (Ch. 4. 'The Ritual of Daily Life', pp. 79–88) see also Plutarch.

Hall, M. P., *The Social Services of Modern England*, Routledge & Kegan Paul, 1960.

Harris, C. C., *The Family*, Allen & Unwin, 1969.

Haskey, J., 'Children of Divorcing Couples', *Population Trends*, 31, 1983.

Haskey, J., 'Social Class and Socio-Economic Differentials in Divorce in England and Wales', *Population Studies*, 38, 1984.

Haskey, J., 'Marital Status before Marriage and Age at Marriage: their influence on the Chance of Divorce', *Population Trends*, 32, 1983.

Hedgepeth, W. and Stock, D., *The Alternative: Communal Life in New America*, Macmillan, 1970.

Hemming, J., *Problems of Adolescent Girls*, Heinemann, 1960.

Home Office, Working Party, *Marriage Matters*, HMSS, 1979.

Hubback, J., *Wives who went to College*, Heinemann, 1957.

Ibsen, H., *A Doll's House* and *A Lady from the Sea* (any edition of the plays, but that used here: Penguin Books, 1978 reprint).

Itzin, C., *Splitting Up: Single-Parent Family Liberation*, Virago, 1980.

Jenner, H., *Marriages are made on Earth*, David & Charles, 1979. (Interesting insights into the workings of a modern Marriage Bureau.)

Jephcott, P., Seear, N. and Smith, J., *Married Women Working*, Allen & Unwin, 1962.

Kerr, M., *The People of Ship Street*, Routledge & Kegan Paul, 1958.

Kiernan, K. E., 'The Structure of Families Today: Continuity or Change?' *In the Family*, occasional paper 31, Office of Population Censuses and Survey, 1983.

King-Hall, Magdalen, *The Story of the Nursery*, Routledge & Kegan Paul, 1958.

Klein, Josephine, *Samples from English Cultures*, Routledge & Kegan Paul, 1965.

Klein, V., *Working Wives*, Institute of Personnel Management, 1960.

Klein, V., *Employing Married Women* (Occasional Papers No. 17), Institute of Personnel Management, 1961.

Laing, R. D., *The Politics of the Family*, Penguin Books, 1976.

Laing, R. D., *The Divided Self*, Penguin Books, 1965.

See also under Cooper, and Esterson.

Laslett, P., *The World We Have Lost*, Methuen, 1965.

Laslett, P., *Household and Family in Past Time*, Cambridge University Press, 1972.

League, R. W., *Roman Private Law*, Macmillan, 1967 (Part Two, Ch.III, 'Familia').

Leete, R., 'Changing Patterns of Family Formation and Dissolution in England and Wales, 1964–76', *Studies on Medical and Population Subjects*, 39, HMSO, 1979.

Leijon, Anna-Greta, *Swedish Women – Swedish Men*, The Swedish Institute, 1968.

Leissner, A., *Family Advice Services*, Longmans, 1967.

Leslie, G. R., *The Family in Social Context*, Oxford University Press, 1967.

Letourneau, Ch., *The Evolution of Marriage and the Family*, Walter Scott, London, 1891.

Lewis-Faning, E., *Family Limitation and its Influence on Human Fertility during the past Fifty Years*, Papers on the Royal Commission on Population, vol. I, 1949.

Lindsey, B. and Evans, W., *The Companionate Marriage*, Brentano's Library, 1928.

Linner, B., *Sex and Society in Sweden*, Pantheon Books, Random House, 1967.

Linton, R., *The Study of Man* (Chap. 10–11), Appleton Century Co., New York, 1936.

Litwak, E., 'Geographic Mobility and Extended Family Cohesion', *American Sociological Review*, vol. 25, 1960, pp. 385–94.

Litwak, E., 'Occupational Mobility and Extended Family Cohesion', *American Sociological Review*, vol. 25, 1960, pp. 9–21.

Litwak, E. and Szelenyi, I., 'Primary Group Structures and their Functions: Kin, Neighbours and Friends', *American Sociological Review*, vol. 34, 1969, pp. 465–81.

Lofthouse, W. F., *Ethics and the Family*, Hodder & Stoughton, 1912.

Lofthouse, W. F., *The Family and the State*, Epworth Press, London, 1944.

Longfield, Jeanette, *Ask the Family*, Bedford Square Press, 1984.

MacIver, R. M. and Page, C. N., *Society* (ch.11), Macmillan, 1957.

Maidment, S., *Child Custody and Divorce*, Croom Helm, 1984.

Mair, Lucy, *Marriage*, Penguin Books, 1971.

Marris, P., *Widows and their Families*, Routledge & Kegan Paul, 1958.

Masterman, C. F. G., *The Condition of England*, Methuen, 1911.

McGregor, O. R., 'The Social Position of Women in England, 1850–1914', *British Journal of Sociology*, vol, vi, no. 1, March 1955.

McGregor, O. R., *Divorce in England*, Heinemann, 1957.

McGregor, O. R., 'The Stability of the Family in the Welfare State', *Political Quarterly*, vol. 31, no. 2, April–June 1960.

McGregor, O.R., 'Some Research Possibilities and Historical Materials for Family and Kinship Study', *British Journal of Sociology*, vol. xii, no. 4, December 1960.

McGregor, O. R., 'Maintenance, Separation and Divorce', *Twentieth Century*, vol. 172, no. 1020, Winter 1963/4. The whole of this issue of *Twentieth Century* is worth reading.

McGregor, O. R., Louis Blom-Cooper and Colin Gibson, *Separated Spouses* (Legal Research Unit, Bedford College, University of London), 1971.

Mill, J. S., *The Subjection of Women*, 1869.

Millett, Kate, *Sexual Politics*, Abacus, Sphere Books, 1972.

Mitchell, G. D., *Sociology* (Chap. 10), University Tutorial Press Ltd, 1959.

Mitchell, Juliet, *Woman's Estate*, Penguin Books, 1971.

Mitchison, Naomi, *The Home*, John Lane, The Bodley Head, 1934.

Mogey, J. M., *Family and Neighbourhood*, Oxford, 1956.

Morgan, D. H. J., *Social Theory and the Family*, Routledge & Kegan Paul, 1975.

Morgan, Elaine, *The Aquatic Ape*, Souvenir Press, 1982.

Morgan, Elaine, *The Descent of Woman*, Souvenir Press, revised edition, 1985.

Morley, Henry, Edition of *The Spectator* (reproducing original text as corrected by Steele and Addison), Routledge.

Müller-Lyer, F., *The Family*, Allen & Unwin, 1931 (German edition published in 1912).

Myrdal, A. *Nation and Family*, Kegan Paul, Trench & Trubner, 1945.

Myrdal, A., and Klein, V., *Women's Two Roles: Home and Work*, Routledge & Kegan Paul, 1956.

National Marriage Guidance Council, *Relating to Marriage*, 1985.

Newson, J. and Newson, E., *Patterns of Infant Care in an Urban Community*, Allen & Unwin, 1963; Penguin Books, 1965.

Newson, J. and Newson, E., *Four Years Old in an Urban Community*, Allen & Unwin, 1968; Penguin Books, 1970.

Noble, Trevor, *Family Breakdown and Social Networks*, *British Journal of Sociology*, vol. xxi; no. 2, June 1971, pp. 135–50.

Office of Population Censuses and Surveys, Social Survey Division, *General Household Survey, 1981*, OHMS, 1983.

Paterson, Dorothy, *The Family Woman and the Feminist*, Heinemann, 1945.

Peel, J., 'The Hull Family Survey: II Family Planning in the First 5 Years of Marriage', *Journal of Biosocial Science*, vol. 4, no. 3., July, 1972, pp. 333–46.

Peters, R. S., *Authority, Responsibility and Education*, Allen & Unwin, 1959.

Philips, M. and Tomkinson, W. S., *English Women in Life and Letters* (Chap. 10), Oxford, 1927.

Pierce, Rachel M., 'Marriage in the Fifties', *Sociological Review*, 11, 2, July 1963.

Pinchbeck, I., *Women Workers and the Industrial Revolution, 1750–1850*, Routledge, 1930.

Pinchbeck, I. and Hewitt, M., *Children in English Society*, Routledge &

Kegan Paul, 1969.

Plant, M., *The Domestic Life of Scotland in the Eighteenth Century*, Edinburgh University Press, 1952.

Plato, *The Republic*, Everyman's Edition, Book II, p. 52 onwards on the 'Simple' and 'Inflamed' societies, Book IX on the 'Inflamed Society' and the 'tyrannical man'.

Plumb, J. H., *England in the Eighteenth Century* (Part II, Ch. 2, and Part III, Ch. 1), Penguin Books, 1950.

Plumb, J. H., *In the Light of History*, Allen Lane, the Penguin Press, 1972 (especially Part Two, Chs 3, 4 and 5).

Plutarch, *On Love, The Family, and the Good Life, Selected Essays*, translated by M. Hadas, Mentor Books, 1957.

Prickett, John (ed.), *Marriage and the Family*, Lutterworth Press, 1985. (Standing Conference on Inter-Faith Publication.)

Puxon, Margand, *The Family and the Law*, Penguin Books, 1963.

Rapoport, R. and Rapoport, R., 'Work and Family in Contemporary Society', *American Sociological Review*, vol. 30, 1965, pp. 381–94.

Rapoport, R. and Rapoport, R., *Dual Career Families*, Penguin Books, 1971.

Registrar General (Review) *Marriage and Divorce Statistics, 1981*. Series FM2 No. 8, HMSO, 1984.

Rights of Women guide to the law, *The Cohabitation Handbook*, (2nd edn) Pluto Press, 1984.

Robertson Smith, W., *Kinship and Marriage in Early Arabia*, Adam & Charles Black, London, 1907.

Rosser, C. and Harris, C. C., *The Family and Social Change*, Routledge & Kegan Paul, 1965.

Rowntree, G., 'New Facts on Teenage Marriage', *New Society*, 4 October 1962.

Rowntree, G. and Carrier, N., 'The Resort to Divorce in England and Wales, 1858–1957', *Population Studies*, vol. xi, no. 3, March 1958.

Rowntree, G. and McGregor, O. R., 'The Family', *Society – Problems and Methods of Study*, (edited by A. T. Welford and others), Routledge & Kegan Paul, 1962.

Rowntree, G. and Pierce, R. M., 'Birth Control in Britain', *Population Studies*, vol. xv, nos 1 and 2, July and November 1961.

Royal Commission on Population, *Report* (Cmd 7695), 1949.

Royal Commission on Marriage and Divorce *Report* (Cmd 9678), 1956.

Russell, B., *Marriage and Morals*, Allen & Unwin, 1932.

Schapera, I., *Married Life in an African Tribe*, Penguin Books, 1971.

Schoen, R. and Baj, J., 'Twentieth-Century Cohort Marriage and Divorce in England and Wales', *Population Studies*, 38, 1984, pp. 439–49.

Smelser, N. J., *Social Change in the Industrial Revolution: an Application of Theory to the Lancashire Cotton Industry, 1770–1840* (Chs. 9–11), Routledge & Kegan Paul, 1959.

Snowden, R. and Mitchell, D. G., *The Artificial Family*, Unwin Paperbacks, 1983.

Social Science Dept of the London School of Economics, *Woman, Wife and Worker* (DSIR, *Problems of Progress in Industry*, 10), HMSO, 1960.

Social Trends, all numbers up to No. 17, 1987, HMSO.

Spring Rice, M., *Working Class Wives: Their Health and Condition*, Penguin Books, 1939.

Stacey, M., *Tradition and Change: A Study of Banbury*, Oxford, 1960.

Stone, Hannah and Abraham, *A Marriage Manual*, Gollancz, 1936.

Stone, Olive, 'The Family and the Law in 1970', in *The Family and its Future*, Churchill, 1970.

Study Commission on the Family, *Families in the Future*, Final Report, 1983.

Swedish Institute, Stockholm, *Sweden Today: The Status of Women in Sweden* (on Family Law, etc). Report to the United Nations, 1968.

Taylor, Debbie, (ed.), *Women: A World Report*, Methuen, 1985.

Taylor, Jeremy, *Ductor Dubstantium (The Rule of Conscience),* Third Book, Ch. V. 'Of Laws Domestic' (Vol X of 1852 Longmans Edition).

Titmuss, R. M., *Essays on the Welfare State*, Allen & Unwin, 1958.

Titmuss, R. M., *The Irresponsible Society*, Fabian Tract 323, 1960.

Townsend, P., *The Family Life of Old People*, Routledge & Kegan Paul, 1958.

University of New South Wales, *The Australian Family* (many issues of Research Bulletin), Family Research Unit.

Van de Velde, Th.H., *Ideal Marriage*, Heinemann, 1944.

Westermarck, E., *The History of Human Marriage*, Macmillan, 1921.

Westermarck, E., *The Future of Marriage in Western Civilization*, Macmillan, 1936.

Wootton, B., 'Holiness or Happiness', *The Twentieth Century*, November 1955.

Wynn, Margaret, *Fatherless Families*, Michael Joseph, 1964.

Young, M. and Willmott, P., *Family and Kinship in East London*, Routledge & Kegan Paul, 1957; Penguin Books, 1962.

Young, M. and Willmott, P., *Family and Class in a London Suburb*, Routledge & Kegan Paul, 1960.

Zimmerman, C. C., *Family and Civilization*, Harper, New York and London, 1947.

Index

283